MANAGEMENT STRATEGIES AND INNOVATION

MANAGEMENT STRATEGIES AND INNOVATION

Editors

DR. GAJENDRA SINGH
Associate Professor
Department of Business Management
Chauras Campus, HNB Garhwal University
Srinagar, Garhwal (Uttarakhand)

ATUL BAMRARA
Assistant Professor
Department of Business Management
Chauras Campus, HNB Garhwal University
Srinagar, Garhwal (Uttarakhand)

DEEP & DEEP PUBLICATIONS PVT. LTD.
F-159, Rajouri Garden, New Delhi - 110 027

MANAGEMENT STRATEGIES AND INNOVATION

ISBN 978-81-8450-344-9

Typeset by RAHUL COMPOSERS
358, Pocket-B, Phase-2, Sector-16B, Dwarka, New Delhi - 110 075

Printed in India at MAYUR ENTERPRISES
WZ Plot No. 3, Gujjar Market, Tihar Village, New Delhi - 110 018

Published by DEEP & DEEP PUBLICATIONS PVT. LTD.
F-159, Rajouri Garden, New Delhi - 110 027 • Phone : 25435369, 25440916
E-mail : ddpubs@gmail.com • ddpbooks@yahoo.co.in
Showroom :
2/13, Ansari Road, Daryaganj, New Delhi - 110 002 • Telefax : 23245122

Contents

Preface

Management strategies play a pivotal role in effective decision-making for sound operations of business. The continuous growth of business depends on the strength of Research and Development team to innovate the product line time to time. Innovators have become the need of hour due to cut throat competition in every sphere of life as well as varying nature of customers day-by-day.

In the present volume we are attempting to cover some of the latest techniques involved in this rapid growing digital era. This volume is primarily meant for the faculties as well as PG and Research students of various allied areas of Business, viz., Management, Commerce, Economics, Psychology, Sociology, Information Technology, etc.

We thank all the people who have contributed their valuable suggestions right from the project idea is conceived. Our organization, HNB Garhwal University, Srinagar, Garhwal, our publishers, the review team for providing their precious time and valuable feedback and needless to say we are deeply indebted to Dr. R. Ramesh and Dr. Rahul Chamoli for their continuous support and enthusiasm. The acknowledgement will fall short of completion if we fail to mention our sincere thanks to Prof. G.S. Batra of Punjabi University, Patiala and our head of the department Prof. S.P. Kala for their blessings and never-ending motivation to make this project a success.

DR. GAJENDRA SINGH
ATUL BAMRARA

List of Contributors

Mrs. Anli Suresh, Faculty of Commerce, Madras Christian College, Tambaram, Chennai (T.N.).

Mrs. Sagyan Sagarika Mohanty, Lecturer in Marketing and Startegic Management, DRIEMS B-School, Cuttack (Orssa).

Dr. J.M. Arul Kamaraj, Department of Social Work, Loyola College, Chennai (T.N.).

J. Arul Suresh, Department of Social Work, Loyola College, Chennai (T.N.).

Dr. E. Sulaiman, School of Management and Business Studies, Mahatma Gandhi University, Priyadarshini Hills P.O., Kottayam (Kerala).

Dr. Sarbani Mitra, Sr. Lecturer and Coordinator, Department of Master of Public Systems Management (Environment Management), Indian Institute of Social Welfare and Business Management, Management House, College Square West, Kolkata (W.B.).

Dr. K.M. Agrawal, Sr. Lecturer and Coordinator, Department of Master of Public Systems Management (Environment Management), Indian Institute of Social Welfare and Business Management, Management House, College Square West, Kolkata (W.B.).

N. Anitha, Assistant Professor, Department of Management Studies, Velammal College of Management and Computer Studies, Ambattur Red Hills Road, Chennai (T.N.).

C. Selvaraj, Department of Management Studies, Velammal College of Management and Computer Studies, Ambattur Red Hills Road, Chennai (T.N.).

B. Neeraja, Research Scholar, Dr. MGR University.

Arti Chandani, Research Scholar, Dr. MGR University.

M. Deepa, Lecturer, Department of Business Administration, Kuamararani Meena Muthiah College of Arts and Science, Gandhi Nagar, Adyar, Chennai (T.N.).

Mrs. R. Priya, Faculty Department of Management Studies, Velammal College of Management and Computer Studies, Chennai (T.N.).

Md. Abu Taher, Professor, Department of Management Studies, University of Chittagong, Chittagong (Bangladesh).

Balasundaram Nimalathasan, Ph.D., Research Scholar (SAARC), Department of Management Studies, University of Chittagong, Chittagong (Bangladesh).

Arumugam Subramaniam, Senior Lecturer, Department of Management Studies, Faculty of Management Studies and Commerce, University of Jaffna, Sri Lanka.

Prof. A. Suryanarayana, Former Chairperson, Board of Studies, Department of Business Management, Osmania University, Hyderabad (A.P.).

M. Manohar, Associate Professor and Head, Department of Business Management, Matrusri Institute of PG Studies, Osmania University, Hyderabad (A.P.).

Ms. Sira Sivaraj, Chinmaya Institute of Technology, Kannur (Kerala).

A. Ananda Kumar, Doctoral Scholar (Bharathiar University), Department of Management Studies, Christ College of Engineering and Technology, Pondicherry (A.P.).

Dr. K. Jawahar Rani, Professor, St. Joseph Engineering College, Chennai (T.N.).

Mrs. J. Srilekha, Lecturer, Velammal College of Management and Computer Studies.

Jiri Strouhal, University of Economics, Prague, Department of Financial Accounting and Auditing, W. Churchill Square 4, 13067, Prague 3, Czech Republic.

Adela Deaconu, Babes-Bolyai University Cluj Napoca, Department of Accounting, Cluj Napoca, Romania.

Tarun Dhar Diwan, Sri Shankaracharya College of Engineering Technology, Bhilai, Chhattisgarh.

Sridhar Diwan, Programmer, Ministry of IT, Chhattisgarh Government, Chhattisgarh.

Nilmani Verma, Head of the Department, Computer Science Department, MATS University, Raipur, Chhattisgarh.

Bhoopendra Dhar, Assistant Professor, MATS University, Raipur, Chhattisgarh.

Dr. P.T. Vijayshree, Principal and Head, BBA, Kumararani Meena Muthiah College of Arts and Science, Adyar, Chennai (T.N.).

K.A.A. Atthiya Beevi, Lecturer, BBA Department, Kumararani Meena Muthiah College of Arts and Science, Adyar, Chennai (T.N.).

M. Ganesan, Lecturer, Department of Management Studies, Velammal College of Management and Computer Studies, Chennai (T.N.).

Mrs. R. Priya, Lecturer, Velammal College of Management and Computer Studies, Chennai (T.N.).

Dr. K. Shyamasundar, Principal, Mohamed Satak College, Chennai (T.N.).

Dr. Ila Chaturvedi, Reader, Jaipuria Institute of Management, Ghaziabad (U.P.).

1

A Conceptual Review on the Usefulness of Financial Innovations

Mrs. Anli Suresh

1. INTRODUCTION

Innovation is normally defined as the introduction of a new product to a market or the production of an existing one in a new manner. Financial innovations occur because market participants are constantly searching for new ways to make greater profits. The process of "financial innovation" includes changes in financial instrument, institutions, practices and markets.

Financial innovations lower the transaction cost of transferring funds from lower yielding money balances to higher yielding alternatives. Therefore, with financial innovations market participants attempt to minimize risk and to maximize return. Economic and financial history is full of innovations that have, at least initially, caused instability and stress. But policy makers have also recognized that financial innovations have an important role to play in promoting efficiency in the financial intermediation process and thereby support overall economic growth.

Economic and financial history is full of innovations that have, at least initially, caused instability and stress. But policy-makers have also recognized that financial innovations have an important role to play'in promoting efficiency in the financial intermediation process and thereby support overall economic growth. The challenge, as ever, is to make such rules as would protect and promote financial stability without stifling productive financial innovation. It is quite likely that sub-prime mortgages and mortgage securitization, important financial concepts as they are but lately become notorious.

This paper discusses on:

- What is financial innovation?
- Why do financial innovations arise and What function do they serve?
- A Case of Financial Innovation in the western scenario.
- Innovations in Financial Products—In the Indian scenario.
- Advantages and disadvantages of financial innovations.
- Suggestions that characterize innovative approaches.

2. REVIEW OF LITERATURE

In this review piece, I summarize the existing research on financial innovation and highlight the many areas where our knowledge is still very incomplete. A number of comprehensive books on the subject have been written, including Allen and Gale's (1994) comprehensive overview, and entire issues of journals have been devoted to the topic [(e.g., *Journal of Economic Theory* (1995, Volume 65).] The topic of financial innovation has been addressed by a number of AFA presidents, including Merton, Miller, Ross and Van Horne, some in their Presidential Addresses. My goals in this short overview are to cover the breadth of the existing literature briefly, rather than treat one sub-area in detail, and to highlight open issues that researchers may find suitable for future work.

3. WHAT IS FINANCIAL INNOVATION?

Much of the theoretical and empirical work in financial economics considers a highly stylized world in which there are few types of securities (debt and equity, perhaps) and maybe a handful of simple financial institutions (banks or exchanges.) However, in reality there is a vast range of different financial products, many different types of financial institutions and a variety of processes that these institutions employ to do business. The literature on financial innovation attempts to catalog some of this variety, describe the reasons why we observe an ever-increasing diversity of practice, and assess the private and social implications of this activity. "Innovate" is defined in *Webster's Collegiate Dictionary* as "to introduce as or *as if* new," with the root of the word deriving from the Latin word "novus" or new. Economists use the word "innovation" in an expansive fashion to describe shocks to the economy (e.g., "monetary policy innovations") as well as the responses to these shocks (e.g., Euro deposits). Broadly speaking, financial innovation is the act of creating and then popularizing new financial instruments as well as new financial technologies, institutions and markets.

The "innovations" are divided into the following types:

- *Product innovation*: Introduction of a good or service that is new or significantly improved with respect to its characteristics or intended uses. This includes significant improvements in technical specifications, components and materials, incorporated software, user friendliness or other functional characteristics.
- *Process innovation*: Implementation of a new or significantly improved production or delivery method. This includes significant changes in techniques, equipment and/or software.
- *Marketing innovation*: Implementation of a new marketing method involving significant changes in

product design or packaging, product placement, product promotion or pricing.

- *Organizational innovation*: Implementation of a new organizational method in the firm's business practices, workplace organization or external relations.

4. EVOLUTION

1. Why do Financial Innovations Arise?

Dramatic changes have occurred in capital markets in recent years. Globalization and innovation are two of the most significant forces driving that evolution. The pace of financial innovation has gathered momentum in recent years as information technology and financial engineering have significantly changed the global capital market environment. The influence of these catalysts is evidenced by the increased diversity of investment instruments such as structured credit, investment vehicles such as exchange traded funds and by the array of innovative investment strategies.

2. The Driving Forces behind Financial Innovations

- *Deregulation*: Foremost among these driving forces has been deregulation. Deregulation has sometimes been a conscious choice by the authorities and sometimes recognition that financial innovation has made existing regulations ineffective. Some of the restrictions that have been removed have been domestic in character, such as those that limited banks' freedom to offer market clearing interest rates on deposits or loans, or prevented different kinds of intermediary from competing in each other's traditional fields of business. Other restrictions have been external, such as exchange controls designed to limit international flows of capital. Whatever the nature of the initial restrictions, however, deregulation has enabled financial institutions to compete more freely with each other and to broaden the range of services they offer to customers, both domestic and international.

- *Uncertainty*: Another important influence on financial market developments has been uncertainty—the growing awareness that interest rates and exchange rates can move in unexpected ways that increase the risks associated with economic activity. The 1970s saw the break-down of the Bretton Woods exchange rate system and the beginning of a period of floating exchange rates among the major industrial countries. The 1970s also saw the beginning of a period of fiscal indiscipline and high inflation during which domestic interest rates became much more difficult to predict. As a result, asset values became more volatile than they had been in the 1950s and 1960s. Individuals and commercial firms sought to protect themselves against the consequence of volatile asset prices, and this spurred financial institutions to develop products to meet the new demand to hedge risk.
- *Computer Revolution*: Financial innovation was also greatly assisted by the enormous increase in data-processing power resulting from the computer revolution. This has had two effects. Firstly, it has reduced the costs of financial transactions and made possible a large increase in financial intermediation relative to final output. Secondly, it has spawned the growth of products, especially derivative products, whose value would be impossible to calculate on a continuous basis without advanced mathematical techniques and the computing power to apply them.
- *Search for Innovation*: A change in the economic environment will stimulate a search for innovations that are likely to be profitable. Individuals and financial institutions operating in financial markets were confronted with drastic changes in economic environment, inflation and interest rates climbed sharply. In order to survive; they search new financial products that might be profitable. Volatility of interest rates was increased. This interest-risk also

led financial innovation. The development of variable-rate debt instruments such as certificates of deposits, mortgages, the creation of the futures market for financial instruments and creation of an options market for debt instruments.

3. What function do they serve?

Merton's (1992), Finnerty (1992) identifies the following functions delivered by financial systems:

(1) moving funds across time and space;
(2) the pooling of funds;
(3) managing risk;
(4) extracting information to support decision-making;
(5) addressing moral hazard and asymmetric information problems;
(6) facilitating the sale of purchase of goods and services through a payment system; and
(7) reallocating risk and reducing agency costs and increasing liquidity

4. Critical Review of the Functions

(1) Innovation exists to complete inherently incomplete markets

In an incomplete market, not all states of nature can be spanned, and as a result, parties are not able to move funds freely across time and space, or to manage risk.

(2) Innovation persists to address inherent agency concerns and information asymmetries

Much of contracting theory (or the security design literature) explores how contracts can be written to better align the interests of different parties or to force the revelation of private information by managers.

(3) Innovation exists so parties can minimize transaction, search or marketing costs

Merton (1989) discusses how the presence of transaction costs provides a critical role for financial intermediaries.

Financial intermediaries permit households facing transaction costs to achieve their optimal consumption-investment program. Merton uses this argument to explain how equity swaps can be an efficient way to deliver returns to multinational investors.

(4) *Innovation is a response to taxes and regulation*

While many authors have pointed out the link between taxes and innovation, Miller (1986) is often cited on this point: "The major impulses to successful innovations over the past twenty years have come, I am saddened to have to say, from regulation and taxes." The list of tax and regulatory induced products would include zero coupon bonds, Eurodollar Eurobonds, various equity-linked structures used to monetize asset holdings without triggering immediate capital gains taxes, and trust preferred structures.

(5) *Increasing globalization and risk motivate innovation*

Most essays on financial innovation identify globalization and increasing volatility as drivers of innovation. With greater globalization, firms, investors and governments are exposed to new risks (exchange rates or political risks), and innovations help them manage these risks.

(6) *Technological shocks stimulate innovation*

Shocks to technology are thought to provide a "supply-side" explanation for the timing of some innovations. Advances in information technology support sophisticated pooling schemes that we observe in securitization. IT and improvements in telecommunications (and more recently the Internet) has facilitated a number of innovations (not all successful), including new methods of underwriting securities (e.g., Open IPO), new methods of assembling portfolios of stocks (folio FN), new markets for securities and new means of executing security transactions.

(7) *Reallocating risk and reducing agency costs and increasing liquidity*

The BIS (1986) has a slightly different scheme to identify the functions performed by innovation, focusing on the transfer of risks (both price and credit), the enhancement of liquidity, and the generation of funds to support enterprises (through credit and equity.)

5. A CASE OF FINANCIAL INNOVATION IN THE WESTERN SCENARIO

One example of innovation as it relates to financial instruments is the development of structured credit products. At their inception, the buyers of products such as credit derivatives were banks, who purchased protection from traditional insurers to manage their exposures to the corporate loans they retained on their balance sheets. Spurred largely by the 1988 Basel Accord, demand for credit derivatives grew as banks realized that they could transfer the credit risk of borrowers to entities not subject to bank capital requirements while at the same time retain the ownership of and revenue from such loans.

The market evolved from primarily a bank/insurer market to one with a much broader range of non-bank participants, including asset managers, hedge funds, pension funds, and securities firms. There are many additional positive externalities associated with this development. For example, market makers of corporate issuances can reduce their exposure to single name credits but at the same time increase their role as liquidity providers to particular issuances without taking on too much concentration risk in a single entity. As a result, users and providers of capital gain more efficient pricing. Moreover, through credit derivatives investors (or protection sellers) can isolate their investment solely to an entity's credit risk as opposed to risks associated with investing in a single debenture, such as liquidity risk.

The range of products also evolved from more traditional-type credit protection to single-name credit default swaps (CDS), to multi-name CDS, and more recently, to more complex securitized asset-backed instruments such as credit derivative indices (including those backed by commercial mortgages, subprime residential mortgages, and leveraged loans), collateralized debt obligations (CDOs), and collateralized loan obligations (CLOs). Whereas credit derivatives initially were hedging instruments whose prices were derived directly from the price of a single, less complex underlying asset (a corporate loan and its implied credit risk/ default probability), credit derivatives now increasingly include more complex instruments whose prices are derived from a basket of underlying assets, securitized assets, or tranched assets.

1A. Case Study—Notional amount of Derivatives and US Gross Fixed Capital Formation, 2000-08

Like most innovations, the theory behind the most-recent financial developments made sense. Innovative financial products such as credit default swaps and collateralized debt obligations were supposed to promote an efficient allocation of risk and hence allow those market participants to bear the risk of an asset who could do so best. Freed from the burden of such risk, non-financial companies would be able to engage in more-productive capital formation, generating growth for the entire economy. Furthermore, financial companies would be more stable because they would be able to get illiquid assets off balance sheets and not be tied to collateral. This mantra of Wall Street investors and financial economists alike implied that expansion in the use of newer derivatives and the like would lead to an expansion in the country's capital stock, and that these financial products would be useful to non-financial companies, not just to banks.

The growth of derivatives and real-sector investment in the United States tell a different story (Figure 1). Between 2003 and 2008, US gross fixed capital increased by about 25 percent, a reasonable number during an economic expansion, but hardly a boom. During the same five-year period, the global amount of over-the-counter (OTC) derivatives increased by 300 percent, while derivatives held by the 25 largest US commercial banks rose by 170 percent. Clearly, growth in new financial products has outpaced fixed capital formation both globally and in the United States by a large margin. This has been especially true since 2006, when investment stagnated, but derivatives continued to grow at a rapid rate. There only seems to be a weak link, if any, between the growth of the

Fig. 1
Notional amount of Derivatives and US Gross Fixed Capital Formation, 2000-08

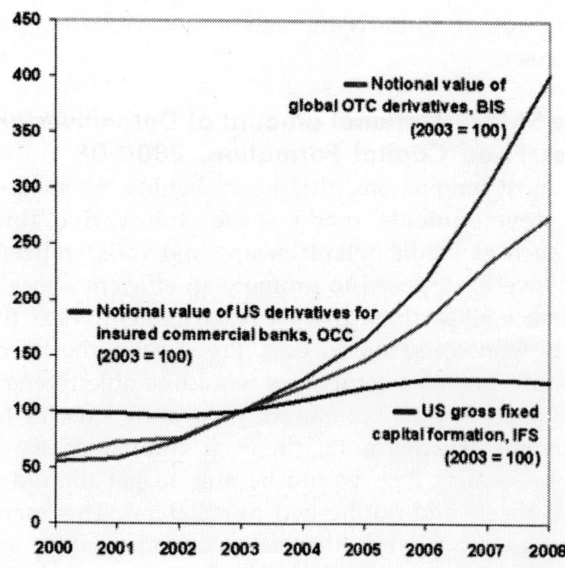

Source : Bank for International Settlements (BIS), International Financial Statistics, via Datastream (IFS), Office of the Comptroller of the Currency (OCC).

newest complex—and now proven dangerous if not toxic—financial products and real corporate investment.

Another way to assess the presumptive benefits for the real economy of these products is to analyze who made use of derivative instruments. Figure 2 shows the share of OTC derivatives by counterparty as of June 2008 (78 percent of all global derivatives for which such a level of detail is available are included). Reporting dealers, mainly banks and investment banks, accounted for 41 percent of all counterparties (double-counting is eliminated). Other financial institutions acted as counterparties in almost half of all cases. Only 11 percent of all counterparties were non-financial costumers. Hence, almost 90

FIG. 2
OTC Derivatives by Counterparty as of June 2008 (BIS)

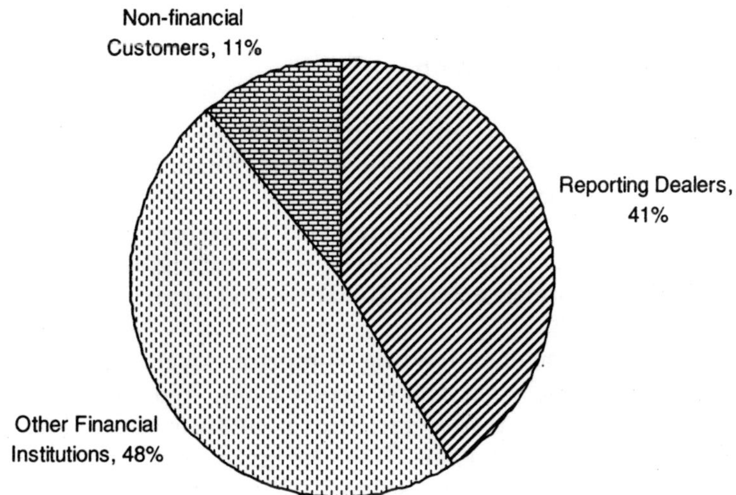

Source : Bank for International Settlements (BIS).

percent of all derivative contracts took place between financial institutions. Had their usage by financial institutions generated either a boom in productive lending or a more resilient financial system, then, even if unused by non-financial companies directly, these new products could still have been productive. Since we have clearly seen the opposite over this time period, it is a revealing indicator that the non-financial companies for whom these products were prescribed did not themselves use them.

6. INNOVATIONS IN FINANCIAL PRODUCTS

Starting from simple pre-deducted interest loans, hundies and gold receipts, the 20th century witnessed major developments in the financial products front.

The new instruments changed the age-old classical economists' belief that capital is not mobile, thus shaking the very edifice of classical theories. Needless to say, innovations in financial products were hastened by rapid developments in accounting and the emergence of newer techniques alongside. Though financial products are multifarious, yet people feel that they are not user-friendly.

1. Broad Classification

(1) Payment products include retail, corporate and trade-related products, and financial/securities products.
(2) Trade finance includes bills of exchange, collection bills, letters of credit, factoring, forfeiting, performance/bank guarantee, and export and import bills.
(3) Commercial lending comprises overdrafts, cash-credits, open loans, goods loans, hypothecation of stock-in-trade facilities, medium-term loans, syndicated loans, financial guarantees, acceptance instruments, and so on.
(4) Structured finance includes commercial and real-estate finance, project and start-up finance (or equity loans), buy-outs of management or leveraged buy-outs, subordinated debts, and so on.
(5) Equipment finance consists of project loans or long-term acceptance bills, leasing and hire purchases (leasing could be financial or operational or a combination of both) and sellers-participated loans. There could even be long-term quarterly/half-yearly equated bills acceptance arrangement.
(6) Money market products are certificate of deposits, commercial paper, treasury receipts/bills and repurchase agreements (also, money market mutual fund units).
(7) Capital market products are bonds and debentures, government bonds/gilt-edged securities (bonds include option linked, coupon linked and secured bonds, and convertible/non-convertible bonds), equities of all types, including preference and ordinary.

(8) Derivative products include foreign exchange forward covers, rate agreements, financial futures, swap and options. As these cover the risks in the exchange markets, they are also known as risk-management products.

(9) Consumer products are personal loans, housing loans, white goods, car loans, hire-purchase and lease arrangements, and mutual and pension-related funds. Plastic money credit/debit cards are other products which fall under this category.

(10) Indigenous products include both local and ethnic financial products such as chit funds and benefit funds, which offer credit off-takes through local and indigenous arrangements.

(11) Postal products in the Indian context are similar to pension and provident fund arrangements. They include National Saving schemes, where one can have both loan and withdrawal facility and also enjoy tax benefits.

(12) Other than these, there are the Islamic products which do not have an interest component, as charging interest goes against Islamic principles. The products, however, cover the whole spectrum of financial instruments but the interest component is camouflaged aged as service charges, 'pre-estimated profit share' or actual profit-sharing, as the case may be.

However, most of the instruments operate on the principle of interest and opportunity cost of the fund and try to manage risk by spreading the investments' range and charging sufficiently enough to cover the statistical loss. Among all the financial instruments, the outstanding ones are credit cards for consumers, forfeiting and derivatives in the context of foreign exchange, hire purchase and leasing for equipment, mutual funds and insurance-linked products for individuals, and, among the indigenous products, chit funds.

2. Generic Classification

The products can also be generically classified as interest

and non-interest (or commission-based), secured and unsecured, liquid and tradable and non-tradable, and based on guarantee (LC and BG, for instance), risk (like derivatives), equity, foreign exchange, and so on.

(1) Plastic money

This form of money was slow to enter India mainly because of the sentimental value for hard cash, inadequate banking habits, the prevalence of small-value transactions and the credit-shy culture. Even after its arrival, it took almost a decade for even giant banking institutions such as State Bank of India to begin dealing with it. Transactions using plastic money involve the payment of a small fee to the issuing bank and the collection of a percentage-based commission from the shops/establishments which submit the bills. The risk dispersal is based on statistical calculations. In fact, plastic money has almost wiped out hard currency in the US and the country's central bank spends far less now on printing cash, making it difficult for one to get new notes. Some of the cards even have international usage.

(2) Factoring and forfeiting

Like credit cards, these are also not yet popular in India, mainly because of the smallness of the amounts involved per transaction. For factoring to be successful, public sector companies will need to be disciplined—they often delay payments to supplies made by small units. Some modifications to the existing commercial law would help make factoring workable. Factoring gets the nomenclature forfeiting when done in the context of foreign bills. Though forfeiting has good scope and is a convenient product, banks and other financial institutions have not yet explored this avenue well enough.

(3) Derivatives

(a) An option is a right to buy (or sell) a currency at a predetermined rate on a future date and does not mean an obligation, as the holder of an option can even exercise the option of 'not buying the currency.

(b) Swap is an agreement to exchange one currency for another at a predetermined rate on a future date. These are financial or foreign exchange derivatives and are useful for covering risks in the foreign exchange market.

The good thing about option is there is no compulsion to put through the transaction on the day stipulated. If the option is not exercised, the holder of the option only loses the option premium paid by him. But the outstanding feature of the instrument is that it is tradable and has a market. The price of an option is determined by the risk and the opportunity cost involved.

3. Comparison of Financial Innovation between West and East

In the West, forward cover for foreign exchange has virtually been replaced by option instruments. Options are accounted for and even depicted in the balance-sheets of banks and MNCs as assets, disclosed in accordance with the accounting standards prescribed by the respective professional institutions. Hire purchase and leasing: While hire leasing is popular abroad, in India it is hire purchase. In most of the cases, interest is charged at a flat rate and not on diminishing-balance basis. In India, this is a popular mode of financing vehicles meant for public transportation such as, taxis, autos, pickup vans, and so on. Operational lease reverts the equipment to the leasing company, and, in the case of financial lease, the lessee owns the equipment.

Any company going in for capital equipment must analyse the buy/lease option to avoid locking up funds, and this has given rise to a number of formulae/mathematical models in the realm of financial management. Indigenous chit funds: Though chit funds in India have become the proverbial 'cheat' funds, there is no denying the fact that they are excellent indigenous products. Here, a limited group of people can reap the benefits of collective saving and finance the one in need. The opportunity cost needs to be borne by the priority bidder, and the other participators in the chit share the higher bid price among themselves as 'discounts' in the monthly remittance. The fund is administered by a manager, who gets a percentage of the fund managed as fees.

Chit funds are being run successfully in isolated pockets of Tamil Nadu (where private limited companies are also involved) and Pune (where private players voluntarily do it for very high rates).

7. INNOVATIONS IN FINANCIAL PRODUCTS—IN THE INDIAN SCENARIO

At the outset, it is easy to tell why new financial products come about: they come about because people in the economy find them useful. If we look at a stream of new products like index funds, index futures, index options, etc., we see a common thread where these products are extremely successful internationally because they fulfil basic economic objectives of people in the economy.

A closely related issue is that of transactions costs. Financial products do not exist in a vacuum; they are created by financial intermediaries who would typically need to hedge away most of the risk generated by having sold the product. For example, few finance companies would be comfortable with selling options on TISCO naked: they would prefer to be hedged by some mechanism (such as owning shares of TISCO, or some dynamic trading strategy). When ICICI sells index warrants, they are exposed to risk unless they hedge that risk away (either by using index futures or by directly investing in all the index stocks). Someone who sells futures on Nifty Junior would find it very useful to hedge himself by buying futures on Nifty, since the two indexes are closely correlated.

All this hedging involves trading, and brings up the problem of liquidity. Suppose the hedging that is required for the creation of product A involves trading on the market for B. It is desirable that the market for B is highly liquid. If the market for B is illiquid (i.e. the hedging involves large transactions costs) then product A will become expensive and less attractive. Here we see the peculiar nature of financial innovation:

1. As long as the market for B is illiquid, it will be hard

for A to come about. The market for B will have to have a minimum level of liquidity, otherwise A will become too expensive and will not succeed.

2. Once A succeeds, it fuels liquidity of B, because users of A implicitly generate trading in B.
3. Once A succeeds, other new products can be conjured, on the assumption that A is available.

The economist Robert C. Merton has coined an evocative phrase "the spiral of innovation" to describe the dynamic tension of this process:

> "As products such as futures, options, swaps and securitized loans become standardized—and move from intermediaries to markets, the proliferation of new trading markets in those instruments makes feasible the creation of new custom—designed financial products that improve "market completeness"; to hedge their exposures on those products, their producers, financial intermediaries, trade in these new markets and volume expands; increased volume reduces the marginal transaction costs and thereby makes possible further implementation of more new products and trading strategies by intermediaries, which in turn leads to still more volume. Success of these trading markets and custom products encourages investment in creating additional markets and products, and so on it goes, spiraling towards the theoretically limiting case of zero marginal transaction costs and dynamically—complete markets."

In India, the best example of these linkages is seen in the relationship between the underlying spot market, index funds, index futures and index options:

1. The prerequisites for an index fund are : (a) program trading facilities, and (b) an index where all components are liquid and convenient to trade. These conditions are now fulfilled, and index funds have now come to exist in India.

2. Once index funds come to exist, they make it possible for people to sell options on the index while being covered (i.e., they would own units of the index fund before selling somebody the right to buy the index). This could happen on exchanges which trade index options or over the counter.
3. Index futures make the implementation of index funds easier.
4. Index funds generate an order flow for index futures markets, and help make them more liquid.
5. Index futures markets enable index options markets.
6. Access to index futures and index options makes index funds more attractive, since users can couple their investments in index funds with risk management using the futures and options.
7. Index options make possible innovative new products like "guaranteed return funds" (i.e. an index fund bundled with a put option protecting against some level of downside loss) or "index linked bonds" (i.e., an instrument which is 95% debenture and 5% invested in call options on the index).
8. These new products in turn generate order flow for index futures and index options markets.
9. In all this, a steady stream of arbitrage keeps the spot, futures and options prices in line with each other. As volumes grow, the sophistication of arbitrageur's increases, and prepares them to similarly function on the next phase of development of the market.

This set of products is a perfect illustration of the process that was outlined early in this article. The key ingredients here are *new products which are useful to economic agents,* a building—block approach towards *obtaining low*—cost implementation of new products, and a spiral of innovation in which the innovations all reinforce each other.

This perspective, of innovations driving what is traded and influencing the order flow coming to markets, has a significant impact upon the growth of the securities industry. So far, the major driver of change in the securities industry in India has been the pressing problem of reorganizing market mechanisms so as to bring down the enormous trading costs which were present. In this, the complexity of instruments, and product development, was just not an issue. Transactions involved onerous costs even if they were as simple as buying 100 shares of TISCO (the costs were brokerage, *gala*, impact cost, counterparty risk, back office cost and bad paper risk). These costs were so high that the first problem which stared in the face of the securities industry was to find ways to reduce them; in addition, these high transactions costs also served to make more complex instruments and trading strategies infeasible.

Today in India, the enormous transformation of markets has given us new market practices in trading, clearing, and settlement. This collapse of transaction costs is a very significant achievement. We are now close to having an Indian securities industry where normal market practice in trading, clearing and settlement are equal to the best practices in the world, and superior to those found in many OECD countries.

As we approach the end of this phase of development in the securities industry, the question arises about what lies next. If our objectives in trading were limited to trading TISCO, then there is no frontier that lies beyond a world with electronic trading, Clearing Corporation and depository.

In order to understand the energy and dynamism of the worldwide securities industry, we have to take a bigger view of trading. Here the universe of financial instruments and trading strategies is not static. Instead, financial instruments are crafted to solve problems for real people while being constrained to be implementing able in the light of existing levels of transactions costs. In such an approach, we would have a steady stream of innovations which make up a spiral of innovation. In this spiral, each step is implementing able, each step strengthens liquidity in other instruments in the economy, and each step paves the way for further innovations that follow it.

8. ADVANTAGES OF FINANCIAL INNOVATIONS

(1) Tax Advantage
(2) Reduce Transaction Cost
(3) Reduces Agency Cost
(4) Risk Reallocation
(5) Increased Liquidity
(6) Regulatory or Legislative Factors
(7) Level and Volatility of Interest Rates
(8) Level and Volatility of Prices
(9) Academic Work
(10) Accounting Benefits
(11) Technological Development and Other Factors

9. DISADVANTAGES OF FINANCIAL INNOVATIONS

Interest rate influences the price of almost all products of the economy and of course interest rate in turn is influenced by several factors.

- Volatility in interest rates creates problem for several players in the market but there are people who like volatility of interest rates and hence want to assume additional risk.
- Financial Innovation can help these two parties to swap their risk appetite on their rate volatility. Derivatives increase risk not only for their users but also for the whole system. The fears of micro and macro-financial crises have ballooned with the growth of derivatives. They cause wild fluctuations in assets prices by disrupting the market for those assets.
- The expansion of derivatives market may reduce the volume of business on the new issue market. The growth of derivatives increases the regulatory (supervisory) burden, regulatory concerns and regulatory cost in the economy. They weaken the regulatory framework.
- The importance of Preference shares as a medium of

investment for individuals has declined and now they are mostly held by institutional investors.

- The working of stock markets in India is characterized by unethical practices of diverse forms on the part of existing companies, new companies and entrepreneurs, brokers and other operators on the market.
- In Indian stock market there is excessive speculation and there is a structural and organizational imbalance in the growth of stock markets.
- There is no positive relation between price movements and the volume of new issue. The trading on Indian stock markets is extremely thin and restricted.
- These factors are seriously hampering. Financial innovation in Indian markets. Indian stock exchanges are mostly oligopolistic in nature and weak clients often become the victims to pay *badla* charge which violates the trading norms. The authorities have issued a number of guidelines to Stock Exchanges, Bank, financial institutions, companies, brokers, sub-brokers, jobbers, etc. to improve the working of stock exchanges.
- Still equity culture and sound functioning of Indian stock markets are very weak in practice and which in turn is seriously hampering the financial innovation process and its related advantages.

10. SUGGESTIONS THAT CHARACTERIZE INNOVATIVE APPROACHES

- *Involvement of the civil society*: Availability of credit and finance for low-income families affects all people in a cross-Sectored manner and should be improved through institutional interfacing between government, the private sector, non-governmental organizations, community-based organizations, trade unions, the scientific-academic community, and others.

- *Institutional development*: The development of a technical and legal/enforcement framework for implementing sound credit management practices is made possible through proper institutions for planning, developing, implementing, monitoring and evaluating activities. Capacity building is a fundamental component of institutional development.
- *Participatory approaches*: Participatory approaches, when balanced with representation structures, are key elements in improving the decision-making process toward effective credit management. The issue is not to adopt either a bottom-up or top-down methodology, but to keep both of these in mind depending on the scale if activities.
- *Finding entry points*: All elements of the community resource base and interventions are interconnected. Effective credit management practices should find entry points that are acceptable to people and their representatives. To ensure complimentarily, entry points should be identified using a holistic view.
- *Appropriate Technology Choice*: Affordability, user-friendliness, a balance between internal and external options, ease of operations and maintenance, demand-driven approaches, and capacity building opportunities are some of the elements that should be considered when designing credit policies and programs.

11. CONCLUSION

The 20th century saw a variety of financial products based on interest, commission and opportunity cost. But risk-based products, such as derivatives and cards, had only begun to emerge this was when everyone thought that the range of financial products had stagnated. The new risk-based financial instruments are proving to be user-friendly and popular. This millennium could well see more such instruments. With interest spread between deposits and advances slowly narrowing banks will have to gear themselves to the use of credit-scoring models based on statistical risk-sharing, rather than employing elaborate lending and recovery machinery which involves huge costs.

The financial innovations brought a lot of unknown-unknowns, together with the fast trend of globalization. It means that structural changes through financial innovations occurred. The best illustration for this is the so-called "originate-to-distribute" model, i.e. extending credits and claims distribution to chained financial intermediates and end-users, which replaced the so-called "originate-to-hold" banking model, i.e. issuance of credits and holding to their maturity. It really opened new possibilities for the financial system to broaden and manage risks and maturity mismatches. Some of the banks developed this model into a complete integrated business strategy and primary source of financing of their activities. They securitized the loans, transferred the risk to others in a short period of time, in order to borrow capital over and over again, in order to sell the claim again, and to benefit promptly, but it definitely lowered the lending standards despite inadequate supervision and regulation, the financial innovation process that started in the final quarter of the 20th century probably improves overall economic performance during normal times. It does, however, increase the likelihood of abnormal times—panics, manias and crashes—occurring, and exacerbates the scope and severity of financial crises."

References

ICRA (2005) Basel II and India, ICRA rating feature, March 2005.

Journal of Financial and Quantitative Analysis, December 1986.

M.H. Miller, Financial Innovation: The Last 20 Years and the next.

M.Y. Khan, Indian Financial System, 2006.

Press room, U.S. Department of The Treasury, 26th September 2007.

www.crisistimeline.com

www.financial policy .org

www.industrial economist.com

www.rbi.org.in

www.thehindubusinessline.com

2

Surrogate Advertisement : Is it Ethical?

MRS. SAGYAN SAGARIKA MOHANTY

INTRODUCTION

Advertising is a well-known and most widely used method for promoting a product, service or an idea. The process of delivering a message about ideas, goods and services, through the media, paid by an identifiable sponsor is called as advertising. Advertisements have a strong influence in our life and day-to-day purchase activity. We like advertisement because they not only create awareness but provide useful information help us for taking final decision. In the present arena of globalization when competition became cutthroat, marketers reshuffle their strategies and modify their marketing mix to survive and win over the competition. Similarly, advertisement has undergone radical changes during these periods and came out with the concept of good advertisement.

WHAT IS GOOD ADVERTISEMENT

An ad whose public is not only strongly sold by it but both the public and advertising world can remember it as an admirable piece of work called as good advertisement.

HOW DO ADVERTISERS CREATE GOOD ADVERTISEMENT

David Ogilvy in his book *Ogilvy on Advertising* has given this statement: "I do not regard advertising as entertainment or an art form, but as a medium of information". Ogilvy first examines how to produce advertising that sells. He states that the wrong advertising can actually reduce the sales of a product. All advertisements do not increase sales to some degree. So advertisers or ad agencies always create advertisement that has the potentiality to sell in the market. Three key factors needed to be considered for creating successful and good advertisement.

1. Creativity resulting from teamwork
2. Communication
3. Effectiveness.

People say it is easier to create a memorable advertisement than to create an advertisement that makes the product memorable. A number of tests have proved that people often remember a commercial, but not a product. This problem is called vampire creativity. It occurs primarily with advertisements that are too entertaining, too original, too involving, or too provocative. Here are four unbreakable rules of creativity:

1. Make it relevant to the customer
2. It should be promising to the customer
3. Don't let it stand alone
4. Always put the product in the center of the commercial

Among the three factors, 'communication' could be a

measurer of the others, and most important factor from the consumers' point of view. For advertising to be useful, communication between the company that originates the advertisement and the potential customer must take place. Communication can be defined as an unique tool used by marketer in an attempt to persuade consumers to act in a desired manner. An effective communication must include both transference and understanding of meaning.

The real communication is a two-way process requiring active participation by both the sender and the receiver of the message to facilitate the transfer of meaning. When the real communication occurs, the other two factors, creativity and effectiveness, could be worth it. Otherwise, no matter how great the creativity or effectiveness is it won't be useful at least in advertising business

WHY DO ADVERTISERS ADVERTISE?

The simple yet highly complex reality is that advertising works in different ways and to different effects depending on many intrinsic and extrinsic values.

Today's market is very dynamic and highly competitive and customers are believed to be the life and blood of any business. In a market over crowded with brands, models and multiple options the major task of marketer is to create and retain customers by maximizing customer satisfaction. Today advertising plays an important role in building brands by persuading human minds, through a whole range of communication media. The hub of advertising today is to go beyond mere selling. Advertisement has to create positive image that linger in customer's mind and lead to brand building and optimum customer satisfaction. Different types of advertisement supplements brand in different stages of product life cycle and in different environment.

As a form of mass communication, advertising delivers relevant messages to target audiences and by changing mental states, it can perform a number of functions. Advertising moves consumers from being unaware of a product or service to finally purchasing it. An ad is considered effective if it propels the consumer a step further in this process. The different functions of advertising are viewed as follows:

1. *Stimulates Demand*—By informing consumers about the availability of a product in the market, advertising stimulates latent needs, and reinforces the aroused needs. By motivating customers with colorful background, music, jingles it increases aggregate market demand
2. *Strengthens other Promotion mix Elements*—Advertisement makes customer aware regarding the existence of product, price level and the place of availability. Advertisement prepares the stage in which the sales people act with all stage fit. Advertising reaches a relatively large audience and makes them favorably predisposed. Ads carry the sales, promotional messages and often produce quick sales response.
3. *Develops Brand Preference*—Consistent and persuasive advertising often induces brand trial or purchase. When the product delivers the promised quality, service and value, it creates satisfied customers who become instrumental in spreading a favorable word-of-mouth. Satisfied customers also develop brand preference, which gets reinforced by repeated ads.
4. *Cuts Costs*—Advertising may be instrumental in cutting down production and selling costs. Increasing unit sales decrease unit costs. Advertisement can create awareness and attract customers at a comparatively less cost.
5. *Lowers Prices*—In any market-based and competitive economy, when unit cost of a product goes down, there are external and internal pressures which compel companies to lower prices to the advantage of consumers. This often leads to deeper market penetration.
6. *Competitive Weapon*—Advertising by itself and coupled with other promotion-mix elements, may prove to be an extremely potent weapon to counter-competitive moves. Advertising has an established

role in creating brand personality and image and escalating non-price competition.

ADVERTISING : FOR GOOD OR EVIL?

How fair is the game of business? Business and commerce take place in a frame, an arena defined by unwritten rules. Within the business arena, *normal* ethics is required. Business should achieve its goal and objectives with fairness and honesty. Without these universal rules, these values, the game could not be played. While discussing the controversial aspect of marketing, like unfair competition, unreasonable trade practices, false promises, doing injustice to the customers, many times it is found that the chief culprit is advertising. Here are three charges leveled against advertisers:

They sell us dreams; allure us into confusing dreams with reality.

They pander to our desires for things that are bad for us.

They manipulate us into wanting things we don't really need.

All this can be summed up in the popular sentiment that advertisers mockingly use a world of fantasy and illusion in an attempt to control us. Advertising is principally a tool of brand competition and brand reputation puts all possible endeavors to influence and stimulate target groups. Sometimes advertisement through its colorful background, appealing stories and beguiling jingles spreading wrong signals to the youth and children who tend to imitate the same in their own lives. According to a recent NIMHANS study, kids as young as 19 are today taking alcohol. The age just a few years back was 27. The study warns that in the next few years, children aged 15 years will take up drinking."

Surrogate Advertising

Khub jamega Rang jab Mil Bethenge tin Yar, Hum, Aap or Mera Bagpiper". The advertisement of Bagpiper club Soda comes with the same music, same background and punch line as the one for the popular liquor brand telecast before the ban on liquor advertisements. This phenomenon, known as "surrogate advertising" (duplicating the brand image of one product extensively to promote another product of the same brand), has become commonplace. Surrogate advertising... a trend which is fast catching up and has suddenly attracted a lot of innovative and creative brains around the country. The rule says, "Advertisements which lead to sale, consumption and promotion of ban products should not be allowed." So, in Surrogate Marketing, a product which is different from the main product is advertised, and has the same brand name as the main product. The product is called as "surrogate" and advertising through different Medias called "Surrogate advertising"!

HOW SURROGATE ADVERTISING ORIGINATES?

In India, the trend of surrogate advertisement gathered momentum with the Cable TV Network Regulation Act, which prohibits tobacco and liquor advertisements on TV channels. On one hand, the government cannot allow public advertising of liquor, cigarette and tobacco companies which creates health as well as social hazards. But ironically, liquor and cigarette sales are the biggest revenue generators in terms of taxes and duties on these items. This has led to one of the biggest ironies of the country—Sales of these items are not banned, yet advertising on the same are strictly prohibited. Because of the double-faced attitude of the government Liquor and Tobacco companies try to find innovative ways to build their brand to maximize sale of their product. They started launching new products under the same umbrella brand name is known as brand extension, which can be carried out for related products (e.g.: Tata Salt and Tata Tea) or unrelated products (e.g.: Tata Tea and Tata Indica). Brand extension has its own merits and advantages for the strong and popular brands. It helps the new product and in some cases banned product to get heavy customer acceptance. Brand extension across products should be permitted, except when the purpose clearly is to encourage consumption of a product whose promotions are prohibited by law. Because heavy advertisement in these cases wont let the customer to forget their liquor and tobacco brands available in the market. Surrogate advertisement provides handful opportunities for these companies to compensate the losses arising out of the ban on advertisements of products like tobacco and liquor. It is acted as a new weapon of Proxy War against the government regulation for prohibiting promotion of banned products.

With an objective of enhancing brand recall, of banned product companies relying on "Surrogate advertisement" not only in different medias but followed by some very innovative practices like:

1. Sponsoring events and launching their own awards for bravery and lifetime achievement.
2. Creating beautiful catchy jingles to carve a strong position in the mind of the audience.
3. Taking advantage of innovative packaging to create differentiation and to attract customers.
4. Internet advertising has become a lucrative area to enhance the publicity for these products and companies.

SURROGATE ADVERTISEMENT BY TOBACCO AND LIQUOR INDUSTRY

Examples from tobacco industry—Red & White bravery awards, Wills lifestyle, Four Square white water rafting, etc. Examples from liquor industry—Bagpiper soda and cassettes and CDs, Hayward's soda, Royal Challenge golf accessories and mineral water, Kingfisher mineral water, White Mischief holidays, Smirnoff cassettes and CDs, Imperial Blue cassettes and CDs, Teacher's achievement awards, etc. Catchy jingles of Kingfisher (oola la la) a popular one.

ETHICS AND SURROGATE ADVERTISING

As in the modern business arena Ethics has given paramount importance and value, it should definitely practice in every aspect and field of management. Business ethics can be defined as the study and evaluation of decision-making by businesses according to moral concepts and judgments. Ethics are principles and values that govern the advertising process. Ethics would involve things like not cheating on the consumer by giving wrong information of the product and its features. Ethics would mean sticking to the laws and regulations that govern advertising in a given country. Ethics would mean giving all information on the product and its usage which is mandatory and essential for the knowledge of people buying it.

But how fair is the advertising game, really? Do they consider ethics while creating one advertisement? How the society is affected by this business practices? Instead of other charges against advertisement the most unethical part is that it panders to our desires for things that are bad for us and for our society.

COLLISION OF PRACTICING SURROGATE ADVERTISEMENT

A market survey in 2001 revealed that advertising has a direct influence on the consumption habits of 431 million people in India and an indirect impact on 275 million 'aspirants' from the lower income group. As the rule says, "Advertisements which lead to sale, consumption and promotion of banned product (like Cigarette, Tobacco and Liquor) should not be allowed. Considering this and realizing that the liquor industry found innovative ways around the ban: Surrogate advertisements for cocktail mixers, fruit juices and soda water using the brand names of the popular liquors. The very purpose of banning liquor advertisements is defeated by surrogate advertising.

Nearly 50 per cent of the television owners have access to cable channels, there is no doubt that the hidden call for alcohol consumption behind the surrogate advertisements is not escaping the eyes of viewers in the world's fourth highest liquor-consuming country. Sociological studies have shown that, in India, a significant share of income of a large section of the population is spent on liquor, potentially leading to financial misery and health hazards. The relaxation allowed by government and the inclination of Indian masses towards liquor and Tobacco products has motivated some companies to such an extent that they started advertise the product that are not even produced and sold in the market. For example: Jagatjit Industries, (the maker of Aristocrat Whisky) advertised a product called 'Aristocrat Apple Juice'. The company reportedly confirmed availability of the fruit juice in Delhi, Haryana, Punjab and Rajasthan, yet, no reputed shop in Delhi had ever seen it, or sells it.

In the absence of any formalized policy of the government both domestic as well as multinational companies try to explore Indian market by the help of surrogate advertisement. These gimmicks, in turn, help the consumers build a strong equity for the parent brand. In this evil practice Indian society particularly younger generation are highly influenced and worst affected.

As far as social responsibility and ethics is concerned business should earn profit without posing any harm to the society and people. Surrogate advertisements are not only ambiguous, but also false and fraudulent in many cases. With surrogate advertising so widespread, this is required to tackle the problem head-on, otherwise it may drag our society and younger generation into miseries

GOVERNMENT REGULATION REGARDING SURROGATE ADVERTISEMENT

The government of India has allowed the tobacco, alcohol and cigarette producers to advertise their co-products on television. The advertisement of any products bearing the name of the prohibited product was earlier banned. However, due to the genuine demand of the advertising industry was finally considered. The Information and Broadcasting Ministry has allowed the surrogate advertising of cigarette, tobacco, alcohol, and other intoxicants but has banned the display of "prohibited products" during the commercial. Besides, the advertisement should not contain any nuances or phrases promoting prohibited products and also the commercial must not use situations typical for promotion of prohibited products when advertising other products. The above mentioned rules were issued through a Gazette notification by the Ministry on

February 27 this year, and were included in the existing provisions of the Cable Television Network Rules, 1994, titled as Cable Television Network (Amendment) Rules, 2009. (ANI)

Understanding the gravity of the situation, the government has come up with following rules to rein in surrogate advertising of liquor and tobacco products:

1. The new rules prohibit companies from making references to their liquor and tobacco brands in the advertisements of non-liquor or non-tobacco products.
2. The companies will also have to ensure sufficient availability of such products in the market on which there is no ad ban.
3. While the health ministry has been pitching for a blanket ban on surrogate advertisements of liquor and tobacco products, the I & B ministry has amended the Act, making it mandatory for such advertisements to be passed by the Censor Board.
4. Moreover, the money spent on their advertisements should not be disproportionate to the actual sales turnover of the products. This has been done to check the practice of liquor and tobacco companies of floating brands of non-prohibited items just to be able to make surrogate advertisements.
5. According to this new rule no direct or indirect reference to the banned products can be made. The use of same colours, presentations, layout or phrases as in the original ads has been prohibited. Even the story board or visuals should not resemble.
6. To make sure these rules are followed in the right spirit, the government has made it mandatory for the ads to be cleared by the Censor Board.

MEASURES TAKEN BY ASCI

Advertising Standards Council of India is a self-regulatory voluntary organization of the advertising industry. The Role and Functioning of the ASCI and its CCC (consumer complain council) in dealing with complaints received from

Consumers and Industry, against Advertisements which are considered as False, Misleading, Indecent, Illegal, leading to Unsafe practices, or Unfair to competition, and consequently in contravention of the ASCI Code for Self-Regulation in Advertising.

The Advertising Standard Council of India (ASCI) has pulled up top liquor companies United Breweries and Diageo India for surrogate advertising during April-June period in the year 2008, compelling them to withdraw their promotional campaigns. United Breweries had to withdraw advertisement for its packaged drinking water Kingfisher with a visual depicting 'a dancing couple' carrying the headline 'where the night rocks'. The Consumer Complaints Council (CCI) of ASCI upheld the complaint made against the advertisement, saying the visual and the headline was not relevant to the product advertised.

Section 6 of the ASCI code states: 'Advertisements for products whose advertising is prohibited or restricted by law or by this code must not evade such restrictions by professing to be advertisements for other products the advertising of which is not prohibited or restricted by law or by this code. In judging whether or not any particular advertisement is an indirect advertisement for product whose advertising is restricted or prohibited, due attention shall be paid to the following:

(a) Visual content of the advertisement must depict only the product being advertised and not the prohibited or restricted product in any form or manner.
(b) The advertisement must not make any direct or indirect reference to the prohibited or restricted products.
(c) The advertisement must not create any nuances or phrases promoting prohibited products.

CONCLUSION

Advertisement is one of the most popular and widely accepted media for creating awareness and providing information to the customers. Ethics are moral principles and values that govern the action and decisions of an individual or groups. Many laws and regulations are put into force that determines what is permissible in advertising. Advertising is highly visible business activity and any lapse in ethical standard can often be risky. Above discussion of every aspect reveals that surrogate advertising is a cynical attempt of promoting product that is not in society's interest. It drags our society and future generation into desolation. If one believes that ethics is the best policy and it should be practiced in every aspect of business then it would be required to stand up strongly against the dishonest practices of surrogate advertising. God has created this world however human being have created the world of money, commodities, trade, and exchange. It's a world, full of gorgeousness and viciousness in equal proportions. It is required to maintain balance so that both business and society can be benefited in a fair means. Ethics can be used as a fundamental weapon to control the advertising world of fantasy and creativity and use this as the betterment of the society and human being. Society has created and flourish business, therefore business should take moral responsibility not to degrade the same society.

References

Advertising Express, ICFAI Publication.

Chunawalla, S.A., Sethia K.C., Foundation of Advertising.Publication of Government of India, Ministry of Information and Broadcasting.

Sen, Shunu (2001), "Using Surrogates to Effect," *Businessline's Catalyst*, August 2.

Subramaniam, Nithya (2002), "Ministry takes a hard look at surrogate ads," *Businessline*, July 3.

Van, Osselaer, Stijn, M.J. and Chris, Janiszewski (2001), "Two Ways of Learning Brand Associations", *Journal of Consumer Research*, 28(2), 202-223.

zhttp://encyclopedia.laborlawtalk.com/Advertisement.

3

Strategic Human Resource Development Practices in Information Technology Industries

J.M. Arul Kamaraj and J. Arul Suresh

INTRODUCTION

The world faces two major development challenges. The first is to ensure that the fruit of development reach the neediest through equitable distribution of the resources, opportunities and benefits. The second is to develop human capabilities and address the changes of development, political, economic and social. The few countries that have been able to meet both these challenges have demonstrated the importance of investing in developing people and improving the qualities of their life through the adoption of Human Resource Development Strategies. The concept of Human Resource

Development assumes immense importance of Human Resource Development plays vital role meeting the changing requirement of highly skilled and competent human resource due to globalization. The abundant physical resource alone cannot benefit the growth of the country without human resource component which transforms physical resource into productive resource in fact the difference in the level of economic development of the country to largely reflection of difference in the quality of their human resources. In this focus the researcher conducted a study the Strategic Human Resource Development Practices in Information Technology Industries at Chennai, Tamil Nadu.

HUMAN RESOURCE DEVELOPMENT

Human Resource Development is a growing and influential discipline, which is increasingly critical to the survival and success of every organization. This is illustrated by the concept of learning organization and the knowledge organization, which demonstrate the essential requirement of all people within organization. Furthermore, with this spirit of information and worldwide communications, competitive advantage mixed on technology many only maintain for short period of time before competitor's catch up. The only source of sustainable competitive advantage is to learn faster and more creatively than the other competing organizations. That will only be achieved through swift and effective human resource development strategies. The unique Human Resource Development Practices make any Human Resource Development very unique and very productive. The simple and focused Human Resource Development Practices contribute more to the quality and quantity-based product and thus the positive impact could be seen on the employee too. In short, the best Human Resource Development Practices are those that create a value-based culturally strong, empowered organization where distances are notional.

Human Resource Development is the framework for helping employees develop their personal and organizational skills, knowledge, and abilities. Human Resource Development includes such opportunities as employee training, employee career development, performance management and development, coaching, succession planning, key employee identification, tuition assistance, and organization development. The focus of all aspects of Human Resource Development is on developing the most superior workforce so that the organization and individual employees can accomplish their work goals in service to customers.

Human Resource Development can be formal such as in classroom training, a college course, or an organizational planned change effort. Or, Human Resource Development can be informal as in employee coaching by a manager. Healthy organizations believe in Human Resource Development and cover all of these bases. Human Resource Development is concerned with the development of human resource in an organization. Development means improving the existing capabilities to the human resource in the organization and helping them to acquire new capabilities required for the achievement of the corporate as well as individual goals.

Human Resource Development believes that individual in an organization have unlimited potential for growth and development and that their potential can be developed and multiplied through appropriate and systematic efforts. Given the opportunities and by providing the right type of climate in the organization, individuals can be helped to given full expression of their potential, contributing to the achievement of goals of the organization and thereby ensuring optimization of human resources.

Human Resource Development is multi-dimensional. It has been defined by economists, social scientists, industrialists, managers and other academicians in different ways and from different angles. In a broad sense Human Resource Development is the process of increasing knowledge will and capacities of all the people in a given society.

CHARACTERISTICS OF HUMAN RESOURCE DEVELOPMENT

It is a system having several interdependent part of sub-system such as procurement, appraisal, development, etc. Change in anyone sub-system leads to the change in other parts. For example, if there is change in the promotion policy where seniority is replaced with merit, the chain reactions on affected keeping the difficulties in framing acceptable guidelines regarding merit in mind. Human Resource Development is a planned and systematic way of developing people. Human Resource Development is an amalgamation of various ideas, concepts, principles and practices drawn from a number of soft sciences such as sociology, psychology, anthropology, economic, etc.

Human Resource Development is a continuous learning process and not merely a set of mechanism or techniques. The techniques such as Training and Development, Performance Appraisal and Career Advancement, etc. are used to intimate and facilitate and promote this process is a continuous way. But these mechanisms have not a universal application. Mechanisms are to be examined, reviewed, reoriented and recast to see whether they are promoted or hindering the process. Human Resource Development is cooperation massive effort in the organization may a major role in the development of employees but the cooperation of other parts of an organization is necessary in such an effort. The following are the four basic agents of development are the employee or individual, the immediate boss of the employee, the human resource development department and the organization.

Human Resource Development is an administrative function. Human Resource Development manager is a line manager and has an important place in the organization chart previously it was treated as a staff functions. But the American society for Training and Development suggested that Human Resource Development should be an entrepreneurial function, to increase the importance of the Human Resource Development observes that Human Resource Development manager should be a problem solver, risk taker, inters dependent rather than remedial teacher, caution taker and dependent. He should create opportunities for the employees in place of minimizing performance gaps.

The components of Human Resource Development have a wide range. Some persons have used human resource development, organizational development as synonyms. But Human Resource Development is the development of an individual through learning process while organizational development is the development of proper environment through organizational behaviour.

Human Resource Development is concerned with the development of people working at all levels e.g., workers, technical staff, employees and executives in an organization, while Management Development is mainly concerned with the development of executives and management in the organization. It is also different from human resource management. Human Resource Development is interlinked proactive, useful and applicable in all functional areas of management and top management's responsibility is for twenty-four hours while human resource management is independent reactive and personnel function having the responsibility up to office hours only. Human Resource Development is a science as well as an art. It is a science because of its mechanisms and principles and it is an art due to its philosophy and skills. But the degree of art is greater than the degree of science as it is related with the skills, values, attitudes and perception of human beings.

Human Resource Development is a positive relationship between Human Resource Development and organizational effectiveness. The constraints of Human Resource Development such as environment, technology, competitions, resources, past practices, history, nature of business, management policies, etc. being the same, an organization that has better Human Resource Development philosophy, climate, sub-system and better people is likely to be more effective than an organization that does not have more competent people, job satisfaction, better development roles, more team work, high productivity and profitability, better images, low cost, less labour turnovers, less absenteeism, minimum overtime and good industrial relations in an organization.

Human Resource Development is a strategy to transform human resource input into outputs. The inputs are the people, the individuals, groups and the total human organization. The transformation processes are the managerial sub-system for acquiring, developing, allocating, conserving, utilizing, and evaluating people. The out-puts are the services provided by the individuals and group to the organization in which they are employed in particular and to the society in general.

PRINCIPLES OF HUMAN RESOURCE DEVELOPMENT

Corporate policy on the human resource; the company must state its human resources policy explicitly. The policy should be communicated through the organization and should be vigorously pursued. The survey conducted by the centre for Human Resource Development at XLRI in 1984 revealed that only 17 out of 53 organizations had a formally stated policy focusing on Human Resource Development.

Commitment of top management; complete faith and support of top management is essential for the success of HRD. Managers at all levels will support Human Resource Development effort only when the chief executive considers his people as the greatest asset. He must have respect for all individuals. Actions speak louder than words. The chief executive may take the following action to promote Human Resource Development. Create an enabling culture where under individuals can grow up to their full potential. Chair the Human Resource Development task force himself. Attend the initial Human Resource Development orientation programmes for line managers. Human Resource Development is to focus on the employee development throughout.

Sound planning is very essential for Human Resource Development. The Human Resource Development needs differ from one organization to another. Therefore, the Human Resource Development need for the organization should be prepared for the proper utilization of new skills. Otherwise skilled employees may get frustrated and may resign to join some other organization. After this an action plan should be prepared to develop the necessary skills. The action plan should focus on developing the diagnostic and problem-solving capabilities of the total organization. Due attention should be given to the internal and external environment to the organization. Proper linkages should be created between the various sub-systems of Human Resource Development.

It is very important to provide conducive climate for Human Resource Development activities. Human Resource

Development effects can be successful only when the climate in the organization is positive and developmental. Openness or freedom to express one's ideas and opinion, trust and mutuality among people, team spirit or collaboration and reasonable freedom for experimentation and risk taking.

EFFECTIVENESS OF HUMAN RESOURCE MANAGEMENT

Effectiveness of various personnel programmes and practices can be measured and evaluated by means of organizational health and human resource accounting.

- *Organizational health*: Organizational health may be studied by looking into employees' contribution to organizational goals and the employee job satisfaction. Employee satisfaction could be understood by labour turnover, absenteeism, commitment and the like. Low rate of absenteeism and high rate of employee commitment indicate employee-satisfaction about the job and the organization. Employee contribution to organizational goals can be measured through employee productivity of different types.
- *Human Resource Accounting, Audit and Research*: Effectiveness of human resource management can also be found out through human resource accounting, audit and research.
- *Human Resource Accounting*: It is a measurement of the cost and values of human resources to the organization. Human resource management is said to be effective if the values and contribution of human resources to the organization is more than the cost of human resources.
- *Human Resource Audit*: Human resource audit refers to an examination and evaluation of policies, procedures and practices to determine the effectiveness of Human Resource Management. Personnel audit measures the effectiveness of

personnel programmes and practices and determines what shoūld or should not be done in future.

- *Human Resource Research*: It is the process of evaluating the effectiveness of human resource policies and practices and developing more appropriate ones.

HUMAN RESOURCE DEVELOPMENT

It is a planned and systematic way to developing people, further, it is undertaken on a continuous basic, learning, as well as knows lifelong process and goes on and on.

HRD INVOLVES DEVELOPMENT OF COMPETENCIES

Basically it tries to develop competencies at four levels. At the individual levels, employees are made to realize the importance of playing their roles in tune with overall goals and expectation of other people (regarding such roles) by enriching and redesigning jobs, the roles of employees are made more meaningful and interesting. At the interpersonal level, more stress is laid on developing relationship based on trust, confidence and help, at the group level, task force, cross functional teams are created to cement inter-group relations. At the organization level, the organization is made to nature a development climate, where every effort is made to harness human potentials while meeting organizational goals.

ROLES OF HUMAN RESOURCE DEVELOPMENT

Arising from the research conducted on behalf of the American Society for Training and Development, Mclegan and Suhadolnik (1989) pointed out the following dimensions carried out by Human Resource Development professions. They are researcher, marketer, organizational change agent, needs analyst, programme designer, instructor, facilitator, individual career development advisor, administrator, and evaluator and human resource development manager.

The role of the Human Resource Development department is influenced and affected by the various forces operating in the external and internal environment. These factors include technology, market and competitive forces, geographical and physical circumstances, political, socio-cultural, legal, demographic and economic factors. At the organization environment levels, a department needs to be aware of its role and forces which affect its operation and success.

STRATEGIC HUMAN RESOURCE DEVELOPMENT

The word strategy forms the Greek word strategic means generalship and is related to the science and art of welfare. Strategy, according to Johnson and Scholes (1993) "is the direction and scope of an organization over the long-term, which makes its resources to the changing environment and in particular its markets, customers or clients so as to meet stakeholder expectations".

Beer and Spector (1989) stated that "Strategic Human Resource Development can be viewed as a proactive system wide intervention, with in linked to strategic planning and cultural change. This contrasts with the traditional view of training and development as consisting of reactive, place meal interventions in response to specific problems. Human Resource Development can only be strategic if it is incorporated into the overall corporate business strategy. It is in this way that Human Resource Development function attains the status it needs to survive and to have a long-term impact on overall business competitive and technological pressures".

Strategic Human Resource Development enables the organization to respond to challenges and opportunities through the identification and delivery of human resource development interventions. It also makes the individuals, supervisors, line managers and top managers to be informed of their roles and participate in Human Resource Development delivery. Management to have operational guidelines which explain the reasons for investment in Human Resource Development. A positive public relations awareness for new and potential employees to know that skills deficiencies will be provided for. Policies which related the Human Resource

Development function to the other operating functions. Information to be disseminated which explain the training, education, development and learning. Training, education, development and learning opportunities to have a coordinated role within a systematic process.

HUMAN RESOURCE DEVELOPMENT IN INDIAN INDUSTRY

Since the early 1970s when the concept of Human Resource Development first began to be recognized by some organizations in India, a large number of organizations in the country have began to display an interest in Human Resource Development. While many organizations appear to have simply re-labeled their personnel department as Human Resource Developments or Human Resource Management departments to keep up with the fashions of the time, there are some which seem to have done considerable work in setting up of a separate Human Resource Development system. On the basis of some studies done on this subject it can be inferred that the main factors behind the setting up of a separate Human Resource Development function in any organization are the philosophy of fits top management and the nature of its top management and the nature of its business. The more diversified the business of an organization and the more the amount of faith and commitment of top management of Human Resource Development, the greater is the tendency to set-up separate Human Resource Development departments. Some important organizations in our country which have introduced Human Resource Development are Bank of Baroda, Larsen and Toubro, Voltas, Crompton and Greaves, Indian Oil Corporation, Steel Authority of India, and Bharat Heavy Electrical

In the end, it may be said that while a lot of progress has been recorded in the field of Human Resource Development in the last 25 years, there is a lot more that needs to be achieved. So far the efforts have largely been limited to large six profit organizations only. Even here the focus of all Human Resource Development has been mostly neglected. Service sector organizations and government departments still treat Human

Resource Development as synonymous with training. Organizations in the small scale sector have not even thought of Human Resource Development.

STATEMENT OF THE PROBLEM

Human Resource Development deals with creating conducting that enable people to get the best out of themselves and their lives. Development is a never-ending process. As people develop themselves in new directions in new problems and issues arise, requiring them to develop new competencies to meet the changing requirement aspirations and problems.

At the individual level these goals may include developing capabilities for ensuring a happy and healthy living. The dimensions of such happiness may vary from individual to individual. They may include a good education or skill base that maybe the key to income based itself, self-respect, security and recognition in the society, good family and a sense of belongingness to a group, society or organization.

At the organizational level the goals of Human Resource Development is normally to have competent and motivated people or employees to ensure higher level of productivity and growth of the organization. Organizations normally direct their Human Resource Development efforts towards the development of competencies, culture and commitment among employee individuals or in groups. Organizations use little even if they have excellent technological and other resources based.

At the national level Human Resource Development aims at ensuring that people in the country live longer, live happier, free of diseased and hungry, have sufficient skill based to earn their own livelihood and well being, have a sense of belongingness and pride through participation in determining their own destinies. The promotion of the well-being of individuals, families and societies provides a human resource agenda for all the countries the world over.

The most important and common objective of Human Resource Development at all levels is competence of capacity building for a healthy and happy living. Competencies help people to bring happiness to their lives. They are the best possible means to achieve a variety of goals. They are also a powerful means for income generation and up-gradation of quality of life in the family organization or country. The only exception where such competency building is not needed is perhaps for those who are born rich and have an access to all comforts and happiness through their economic situation. However, individuals, organizations and countries with good economic base seem to have become even richer through investments on Human Resource Development and continue to spread a considerable part of their other resources on developing new competencies.

The business world every minutes changes and challenges unlike Human Resource Development in most companies. Since the future and success of any organization depends upon its dynamic and skilled personnel, it is thus important know and practice the Human Resource Development Practices.

NEED AND IMPORTANCE OF THE STUDY

Human Resource Development is the most important requirement of any dynamic organization. The concept of Human Resource Development practice is a multi-dynamical. It is about developing the people, place and organization. Real development is that any organization will get generated only if there is proper development of the power or personnel.

Human Resource Development through essentially a micro-concept has micro-implications at the micro-level. Human Resource Development is considered to be mainly organizational in nature and has been vogue in corporate sector, human resource development as function is referred to as a process through which employees are helped in a continuous and planned way of acquire and develop capabilities required to perform various activities associated with their present expected future roles.

Human Resource Development is also essential view of decreased motivational behaviour. Net expectation for the quality governance has pushed to recognize the need for better management of its employees by better development and optimum utilization of the potential of its men and women power.

There can be no organization without Human Resource Development Practices. There are many Human Resource Development Practices are available as like millions of companies exist in the world. Then what is that which makes a company unique and successful? It is not the mere existence of practice but unique Human Resource Development practices which makes the company unique and successful. Thus this research is most important in current scenario.

OBJECTIVE

General Objective

To study and analyze the Strategic Human Resource Development Practices in Information Technology industries at Chennai, Tamil Nadu.

Specific Objectives

- To know the personal data to the respondents.
- To find out the responsibility and applicability of Strategic Human Resource Development Practices.
- To study the assistance of Strategic Human Resource Development Practices for organizational goals.
- To examine the Strategic Human Resource Development Practices' contribution to the organization.
- To understand personal and professional enhance the individual contribution to the organization.

RESEARCH METHODOLOGY

The research design adopted in this study is "Descriptive Research Design". The major goal of the descriptive research is to describe events phenomena and situations. In this research the researcher describes the Strategic Human Resource Development Practices—so Descriptive Research Design is the most suitable Research Design to this study. The researcher selected 15 Information Technology industries at Chennai for this research. Researcher made Pilot study and conducted Pre-test with 20 samples. The Pre-test enabled the researcher to add and delete the most relevant questions from the questionnaire in respect to IT industries. Then the necessary change was done in the questionnaire and was modified accordingly. The management did not allow the researcher to collect the data in the working hours. So the researcher adopted convenience sampling. This is also known an Accidental Sampling. In this sampling the researcher studies that entire persons who are most conveniently available or who accidentally come in his contact during rest time, lunch time and after the working hours. Sample size taken for the purpose of the study is 150. Since the study is about the Strategic Human Resource Development Practices, which plays a key role organizational growth and success, the researcher has decided to develop an appropriate tool and Structured Questionnaire Method. The researcher personally visited in all the selected IT industries and collected the data. In the present study, the researcher mainly made use of the primary data collected from respondents obtained through the administration of questionnaire. The secondary source of data is collected from materials like books, journals, magazines and related websites. The researcher analyzed the data with the help of statistical package for social sciences (SPSS). It enables the researcher for coding and tabulation.

MAJOR FINDINGS

- In this study majority of respondents (68 percent) belong to the age group 26-35 years.
- In this research, majority (78 percent) of respondents are male.
- Majority of the respondents (69 percent) of respondents have completed their under graduation.
- Majority (72 percent) of respondents have 5 years experience.
- More number (44 percent) of respondents' monthly income is ranging from Rs. 10,001-15,000.

- Most (76 percent) of respondents are aware of the Strategic Human Resource Development Practices to some extent only.
- Most (92 percent) of respondents encourage best Human Resource Development Practices.
- In this research more number (46 percent) of respondents said that the existing Human Resource Development practice in the organization is formal.
- Most (96 percent) of respondents said that the Strategic Human Resource Development Practices meet the goals of the organization.
- More number (38 percent) of respondents said that the Strategic Human Resource Development Practices' goals and objectives meet to create positive environment.
- Majority (68 percent) of respondents felt that the identification and implementation of the Strategic Human Resource Development Practices through employee satisfaction survey in the organization.
- In this research more number (48 percent) of respondents felt that the origination of the Strategic Human Resource Development Practices come from first line management.
- In this research half (50 percent) of respondents felt that the potential candidates are identified through placement Consultants.
- Majority (52 percent) of respondents felt that the psychometric test is not conducted.
- Most (98 percent) of respondents absolutely believed that background check is done in the organization.
- Most (86 percent) of respondents said that the expenses for the outstation candidates is met by the organization.
- Most (86 percent) of respondents said that travel expenses are covered after the selection of the candidates.
- Most (80 percent) of respondents said that the probation period is for only three months.
- In this research more number of (42 percent) respondents felt that the type of induction

programme is conducted in the organization is formal.

- More number (42 percent) of respondents said that the induction programme was just less than one week.
- Most (94 percent) of respondents said that the organization used to give gift to new joiner at the time of joining.
- In this research half (50 percent) of respondents felt that the training need is analyzed through employee performance in the organization.
- Majority (54 percent) of respondents felt that training provided to the employees to enhance their technical skills.
- Majority (66 percent) of respondent felt that on-the-job training is adopted to train the employees.
- Majority (58 percent) of respondents considered that the rating scale performance method is used in the organization.
- Most (72 percent) of respondents felt that for the employee evaluation 360 degree feedback is used.
- Most (74 percent) of respondents said that the duration for conducting appraisal is six months.
- In this research majority (54 percent) of respondents are satisfied with the current appraisal system.
- In this study majority (72 percent) of respondents felt greater extent that the present Human Resource Development Practices encourage the employee in their career growth.
- Majority (58 percent) of respondents said that communication pattern in the organization is highly formal.
- Majority (54 percent) of respondents felt that the communication pattern in the organization is good while 46 felt it just satisfactory.
- Most (78 percent) of respondents said that the employee participation in the organization is encouraged only some extent.
- In this study more number (48 percent) of

respondents felt that the type of reward in the organization is monetary.

- Most (80 percent) of respondents stated that only performance brings rewards and recognition.
- Most (72 percent) of respondents said that outing is the recreational activity followed in the organization.
- In this study more number (42 percent) of respondents said that monthly is the duration kept for conducting recreational activities.
- Majority (68 percent) of respondents felt employee satisfaction survey is the retention strategic to retain employees and also to attract prospects.
- Most (98 percent) of respondents agreed that the organization conducts the exit interview very seriously.
- Most (94 percent) of respondents are satisfied with existing Human Resource Development Practices in the organization.

SUGGESTIONS

- Since 76 percent of the respondents are aware of the Strategic Human Resource Development practices to some extent only, so the organizations could carry out some effective and current best Strategic Human Resource Development practices in the organization while generating more awareness of the present human resource development practices.
- In this study 46 percent of respondents said that the existing human resource development practices in the organization is informal. Thereby, the Strategic human resource development practices could be made more professional.
- In this research 42 percent of respondents said that the duration for the induction programme was just less than a week, the duration for induction programme can be increased so as to give any fresher a fully fledged experience for better confidence and higher productivity.

- There are 54 percent of the respondents who satisfied with the current appraisal system, it is recommended that the current appraisal system needs to be reconsidered or improved.
- In this study 72 percent of the respondents felt that the present Strategic human resource development practices encourage the employees in their career growth only some extent. Thus, it is suggested to have some effective human resource development practices that encourage the employees in their career growth may be implemented.
- In this research 54 percent of the respondents felt that the communication pattern in the organization is just satisfactory, thereby, the communication pattern needs improvement in certain areas to be very effective.
- Since 78 percent of the respondents said that the employee participation in the organization is encouraged only some extent the organization could encourage the employee to contribute their ideas and suggestions through various employee participative programmes.

CONCLUSION

The development is the result of human labour, ingenuity, vision and capacity for innovation, cooperation and change. To get the right kind of development it is essential to have the right set of Human Resource Development Practices which bring uniqueness and high profit to the organization.

In this research an attempt has been made to study the Strategic Human Resource Development Practices of Information Technology industries at Chennai, Tamil Nadu which focuses on dimensions like recruitment and selection, induction, training and development, performance appraisal, career progression, communication and decision-making, reward and recognition, employee recreation and employee retention. The study has been undertaken to understand the existing, perception and prominence of organizational Strategic human resource development practices in fulfilling organizational goals.

The Strategic human resource development practices of Information Technology industries at Chennai, Tamil Nadu could be conclusively deserved as one that is proactive, realistic and welcoming towards meeting the needs, values and feeling of its employees. Though there is an urgent need to introduce more effective Strategic human resource development practices the existing practices serve as key practices which bring the desired organizational growth and better results. Thus, it is these best Strategic human resource development practices which constructively work towards the successful attainment of personal and organizational vision and objectives.

This research study will be useful in providing knowledge on hand experiences on the Strategic human resource development practices and how effective they contribute to the growth and development Information Technology industries at Chennai, Tamil Nadu. It is not the mere existence of the existing Strategic human resource development practices which make an organization visible but it is the best Strategic human resource development practices which are practiced constantly will bring greater glory, high employee satisfaction, and good profit.

References

Aswathappa, K., 2006, "Human Resource and Personnel Management: Test and Cases", Tata McGraw Hill Publishing Company Limited, New Delhi.

David Megginson, Paul BenField, Jennifer Joy Matthews, 2005, "Human Resource Development", Kogan Page India Pvt. Ltd., New Delhi.

Goel, S.L., Gautham, P.N., 2005, "Human Resource Development in the 21st Century : Concepts and Case Studuies", Deep & Deep Publication Pvt. Ltd., New Delhi.

Harish Chandra, 2006, "Human Resource Development : Theories and Practices", Akansha Publishing House, New Delhi.

John, P. Wilson, 2005, "Human Resource Development", Kogan Page, London and Sterling, V.A.

Rao, T.V., Verma, K.K., Anil, Khandelwal K., Abraham, S.J., 2002, "Alternative Approaches and Strategics of Human Resource Development", Rawat Publications, Jaipur and New Delhi.

Rao, T.V., 1996, "Human Resource Development Experiences, Interventions, Strategies", Saga Publications India Pvt. Ltd., New Delhi.

Santosh Gupta, Sachin Gupta, 2005, "Human Resource Development Concepts and Practices", Deep & Deep Publications Pvt. Ltd., New Delhi.

Srinivas, R. Kandula, 2002, "Strategic Human Resource Development, Practices", Prentice Hall of India Private Limited, New Delhi.

Udai Pareek, 2005, Training Instruments in HRD and OD", Tata McGraw Hill Publishing Company Limited, New Delhi.

http://humanresources.about.com/od/glossaryh/f/hr_development.htm

http://www.cftri.com/department/hrd.htm

http://www.amazon.com/Strategically-Integrated-HRD-Six-Step-Results-Driven/

4

CRM Practices in Private Sector Banks in India

A Case Study

E. SULAIMAN

ABSTRACT

With globalisation and increasing competition the banks started concentrating on customer satisfaction and customer retention. Modern marketing concept began with customer satisfaction and has now reached the advance stage of customer delight and customer ecstasy. This can be achieved only through strong customer base. In such a situation the concept of Customer Relationship Management becomes inevitable. In India most of the private sector banks have been implementing this strategy. There exists different opinion regarding successful materialisation of CRM concept. In this context, this article mainly emphasis on the analysis of the CRM practices in private sector banks in India.

Key Words : Customer Relationship Management (CRM); Customer Retention; Customer Satisfaction; and Customer Orientation.

1. INTRODUCTION

Millions of banks across the world reaffirm their faith in strengthening relationships with the valuable asset of business—customers, inching every initiative towards their benefit. In India, most of the private sector banks have been implementing this strategy. The present study aims to analyze the CRM practices in private sector banks in India with special reference to *Federel Bank.* This study provides some useful insights for managerial action. Firstly, bank managers can rely on this industry-specific scale in order to measure service quality delivered to their customers. Secondly, from a strategic standpoint, bank managers can determine the relative importance of the four service quality dimensions in predicting customer satisfaction and customer loyalty. Thirdly, multi-branch bank organizations can use the current scale to evaluate service quality delivered to customers in different branches and track the relative performance of various branches over time. Fourthly, bank managers can employ the service quality scale to identify distinct customer clusters or segments with varying perceptions about service quality. Fifthly, the service quality scale can also be administered to frontline employees and their customers simultaneously to compare customer perceptions of service quality with frontline employee perceptions. Finally, from a competitive standpoint, bank managers can use the existing scale to assess their strengths/ weaknesses relative to competitors across service quality dimensions.

2. OBJECTIVES OF THE STUDY

1. To measure the effectiveness of CRM practices on the customer satisfaction related with variables such as interaction quality, service environment, handling complaints and empathy.
2. To analyse the effectiveness of CRM for increasing performance outcomes of the bank.
3. To identify the critical factor contributing to customer satisfaction.

3. HYPOTHESIS

1. There is no significant difference between mechanism of handling complaints adopted by bank and customer satisfaction.
2. There is no significant relation between banking technology adopted by bank and satisfaction level of consumers.
3. There is significant difference between importance given by banks on customers' orientation and satisfaction level of customers.
4. There is no significant relation between importance given by banks on interaction quality and relationship management; and customer satisfaction.
5. There is significant difference between CRM practices adopted by the bank and its effectiveness in providing better satisfaction to customers.
6. CRM system followed by the bank is effective to increase the performance outcomes of the bank and customer satisfaction.

4. METHODOLOGY USED FOR THE STUDY

The present study is both descriptive and empirical in nature. Both primary and secondary data have been used for the study. Primary data has been collected through a structured questionnaire. Separate questionnaire have been developed for the purpose of collecting data from customers and branch managers of the bank. Secondary data have been collected from various sources such as books, journals, dissertations, periodicals, reports, publications and websites related to the subject. All the existing customers of urban branches of *Federal bank* in *Ernakulam* district of Kerala constitute the universe for the study. Two stage sampling has been used for selection of the sample units. Firstly, the entire universe has been divided into 15 urban branches of the bank. Sampling has been done for the selection of 50 customers from the 15 urban branches of the bank by adopting simple random sampling method. Further, data also has been collected from branch managers of 15 urban branches of the bank. The effectiveness of CRM practices has been analysed by using paired comparison test between the importance mean given by the bank on different variables of CRM system and satisfaction mean of the sample customers; and performance outcomes of the bank. Factoring analysis was also used for identifying important factors contributing customer satisfaction in banks.

5. ANALYSIS AND DISCUSSIONS

For analysing the CRM practices and customer satisfaction, paired comparison test were employed under the different variables influencing CRM effectiveness between importance mean given by the branch managers (M1, 2, 3...) on variables taken for the study; and customer satisfaction mean (C1, 2, 3...) and performance outcome of the bank (M1, 2, 3...).

1. Handling Customer Complaints

For analysing the effectiveness of grievance redress mechanism, paired comparison test was conducted among the three pairs of variables.

Pair 1 : The Table 1 shows paired comparison between importance given by the bank on speedy handling of complaints of customers and satisfaction of customers on time taken to sort out the complaint; and the correlation between the variable and its sample test shown in the Tables 1.1 and 1.2.

TABLE 1

Paired Statistics

Between Importance Given by the Bank on Speedy Handling of Complaints of Customers and Satisfaction of Customers on Time taken to sort out the Complaint

Variables		*Mean*	*N*	*Std. Deviation*	*Std. Error Mean*
Pair 1	M20* &	4.4667	15	0.51640	0.13333
	C6.2*	3.2667	15	0.45774	0.11819

*M20. We manage quickly the complaints of our customers.

*C6.2 The time taken to sort out your complaint

Source : Primary data.

TABLE 1.1
Paired Correlation

	Variables	N	Correlation	Significance
Pair 1	M20 and C6.2	15	0.342	0.211

Source : Primary data.

TABLE 1.2
Paired Samples Test

	Variables	Paired Differences			t	df	Sig (2-tailed)
		Mean	SD	Std. Error Mean			
Pair 1	M20 & C6.2	1.2000	0.56061	0.14475	8.290	14	0.000

Source : Primary data.

The 't' value of pair sample test depicts that there is significance difference between the variables at 5% significance level, i.e. speedy grievance resolution of the banks and customer satisfaction in time taken to handle the complaint are significant.

Pair 2: Comparison between the importance given by banks to inform the customers about the complaints resolved and customer satisfaction in the follow up contact received by the customer after making complaints (Tables 2, 2.1 and 2.2).

There is significant difference between the pair values (significance at 5% level), i.e. mean difference between information provided by the banks to the customers about their complaint being sort out and the satisfaction level of follow up contact received by the customer is significant.

Pair 3: The paired comparison between the importance given by the bank in solving the conflicts of the customer and the customer satisfaction in the way of handling complaints; and the correlation between the variable and its sample test depicted in the Tables 3, 3.1 and 3.2.

Bank's importance mean in solving consumer conflicts and customer satisfaction mean in handling complaints has

TABLE 2
Paired Statistics
Between the Importance Given by Banks to Inform the Customers about the Complaints Resolved and Customer Satisfaction in the Follow-up Contact Received by the Customer after Making Complaints

Variables		*Mean*	*N*	*S.D.*	*Std. Error Mean*
Pair 2	M21* &	4.2000	15	0.41404	0.10690
	C6.4*	3.2000	15	0.77460	0.20000

*M21. We inform about all the actions implemented to solve our customer complaints.
*C6.4 The follow-up contact you receive
Source : Primary data.

TABLE 2.1
Paired Correlation

Variables		*N*	*Correlation*	*Significance*
Pair 2	M21 and C6.4	15	0.535	0.040

Source : Primary data.

significant difference at 5% level. Further, there exist moderate positive correlations between rating scale of bank's effort too inform about all the actions implemented to solve our customer complaints and customer satisfaction in handling complaints.

While analysing paired comparison test between different variables influencing effectiveness of grievance redress mechanism and customer satisfaction; all the variables shows significant difference at 5% level. Therefore, the alternate hypothesis put forwarded by the researcher: Ha: 'There is significant difference between grievance redress mechanism adopted by the bank and customer satisfaction', can be accepted. So, it can be inferred that importance given by the bank to solve customer complaints are effective to improve customer satisfaction.

Table 2.2
Paired Samples Test

Variables		Paired Differences					t	df	Sig. (2-tailed)
		Mean	S.D.	Std. Error Mean	95% Confidence Interval of the Difference				
					Lower	Upper			
(1)		(2)	(3)	(4)	(5)	(6)	(7)	(8)	(9)
Pair 2	M21 - C6.4	1.0000	0.65465	0.16903	0.6375	1.3625	5.916	14	0.000

Source : Primary data.

TABLE 3
Paired Statistics
Between the Importance Given by the Bank in Solving the Conflicts of the Customer and the Customer Satisfaction in the Way of Handling Complaints

Variables		*Mean*	*N*	*S.D.*	*Std. Error Mean*
Pair 1	M19* &	4.3333	15	0.48795	0.12599
	C6.1*	3.4667	15	0.91548	0.23637
Pair 2	M20* &	4.4667	15	0.51640	0.13333
	C6.1*	3.4667	15	0.91548	0.23637
Pair 3	M21* &	4.2000	15	0.41404	0.10690
	C6.1*	3.4667	15	0.91548	0.23637
Pair 4	M22* &	4.4000	15	0.50709	0.13093
	C6.1*	3.4667	15	0.91548	0.23637
Pair 5	M23* &	4.1333	15	0.35187	0.09085
	C6.1*	3.4667	15	0.91548	0.23637

* M19. We inform our customers about any mistake or error in their transactions.

* M20. We manage quickly the complaints of our customers.

* M21. We inform about all the actions implemented to solve our customer complaints.

* M22. The bank processes to resolve conflicts are formalized and are carried out strictly.

* M23. The customers use to have good attitude in case of conflict because of the close relationship we have created in the past.

* C 6.1 The way your complaint was handled.

Source : Primary data.

TABLE 3.1
Paired Correlation

Variables		*N*	*Correlation*	*Significance*
Pair 1	M19 and C6.1	15	-0.053	0.850
Pair 2	M20 and C6.1	15	0.413	0.126
Pair 3	M21 and C6.1	15	0.678	0.005
Pair 4	M22 and C6.1	15	-0.277	0.318
Pair 5	M23 and C6.1	15	0.237	0.396

Source : Primary data.

TABLE 3.2

Paired Samples Test

Variables		Paired Differences					*t*	*df*	*Sig.*
		Mean	*S.D.*	*Std. Error Mean*	*95% Confidence Interval of the Difference*				*(2-tailed)*
					Lower	*Upper*			
(1)		(2)	(3)	(4)	(5)	(6)	(7)	(8)	(9)
Pair 1	M19 - 6.1	0.8667	1.06010	0.27372	0.2796	1.4537	3.166	14	0.007
Pair 2	M20 - 6.1	1.0000	0.84515	0.21822	0.5320	1.4680	4.583	14	0.000
Pair 3	M21 - 6.1	0.7333	0.70373	0.18170	0.3436	1.1230	4.036	14	0.001
Pair 4	M22 - 6.1	0.9333	1.16292	0.30026	0.2893	1.5773	3.108	14	0.008
Pair 5	M23 - 6.1	0.6667	0.89974	0.23231	0.1684	1.1649	2.870	14	0.012

Source : Primary data.

2. Technologies used for Banking Services

Relationship between banking technology offered by the bank and customer satisfaction on the benefit of technologies is two factors for comparison have been analysed by comparing three pairs of variables related with benefits of banking technology (Tables 4, 4.1 and 4.2).

TABLE 4
Paired Statistics
Relationship between Banking Technology Offered by the Bank and Customer Satisfaction on the Benefit of Technologies

Variables		*Mean*	*N*	*S.D.*	*Std. Error Mean*
Pair 1	M24* &	4.1333	15	0.35187	0.09085
	C3.2*	3.6000	15	0.50709	0.13093
Pair 2	M24* &	4.1333	15	0.35187	0.09085
	C3.3*	3.0000	15	0.75593	0.19518
Pair 3	M24* &	4.1333	15	0.35187	0.09085
	C3.4*	3.4667	15	0.83381	0.21529

* M24. The bank offers the best technologies as material support to the services.
* C3.2 Adequate number of ATMs.
* C3.3 Convenience of ATMs.
* C3.4 Internet banking services.
Source : Primary data.

TABLE 4.1
Paired Correlation

Variables		*N*	*Correlation*	*Significance*
Pair 1	M24 and C3.2	15	-0.480	0.070
Pair 2	M24 and C3.3	15	-0.537	0.039
Pair 3	M24 and C3.4	15	-0.471	0.07

Source : Primary data.

TABLE 4.2

Paired Samples Test

Variables		Paired Differences					*t*	*df*	*Sig. (2-tailed)*
		Mean	*S.D.*	*Std. Error Mean*	*95% Confidence Interval of the Difference*				
					Lower	*Upper*			
	(1)	*(2)*	*(3)*	*(4)*	*(5)*	*(6)*	*(7)*	*(8)*	*(9)*
Pair 1	M24 -C3.2	0.5333	0.74322	0.19190	0.1217	0.9449	2.779	14	0.015
Pair 2	M24 - 3.3	1.1333	0.99043	0.25573	0.5849	1.6818	4.432	14	0.001
Pair 3	M24 - 3.4	0.6667	1.04654	0.27021	0.0871	1.2462	2.467	14	0.027

Source : Primary date.

It is inferred from the test that the mean difference between banking technologies offered by the bank and the level of satisfaction of the customers in the technology provided is significant at 5% level. Therefore, null hypothesis put forward by the researcher; Ho: 'There is no significant relationship between baking technology adopted by banks and satisfaction level of customers', can be rejected and Ha can be established, 'there is significant relationship between baking technology adopted by banks and satisfaction level of customers'. However, there exists negative paired correlation between variables; it indicates customers are not fully satisfied with adequate number of ATMs, Convenience of ATMs and Internet banking services offered by the bank. A moderate and significant negative correlation has observed in the case of convenience of ATM's.

3. Customer Orientations

Relationship between importance given by banks on customer orientation and customer satisfaction has been analysed with four sets of pairs relating to effectiveness of customer orientation (Tables 5, 5.1 and 5.2).

It is inferred from the test that difference in the mean score of bank's efforts to understand customer needs and customer satisfaction is significant at 5% level. So, the alternate hypothesis put forward by the researcher; Ha: 'There is significant difference between importance given by banks on customer orientation and customer satisfaction', can be accepted. However, there exists negative paired correlation in the case of satisfying customers need better than our competitors; integrate and coordinate all functions of the firm in order to achieve the customer's satisfaction; and marketing research to know current and future consumer needs. It indicates bank's effort in this regard was not fully achieved to get better result on customer orientation. But, a moderate and significant positive correlation has observed in the case employee's effort to collect information about customers.

4. Interaction Qualities

Paired Comparison between the interaction quality of the bank and the customer's satisfaction level in interaction of the

TABLE 5
Paired Statistics
Between Importance Given by Banks on Customer Orientation and Customer Satisfaction

Variables		*Mean*	*N*	*S.D.*	*Std. Error Mean*
Pair 1	M1 &	4.2667	15	0.45774	0.11819
	C4.4	3.8000	15	0.67612	0.17457
Pair 2	M2 &	4.4667	15	0.51640	0.13333
	C4.4	3.8000	15	0.67612	0.17457
Pair 3	M3 &	4.4000	15	0.50709	0.13093
	C4.4	3.8000	15	0.67612	0.17457
Pair 4	M4 &	4.3333	15	0.48795	0.12599
	C4.4	3.8000	15	0.67612	0.17457

* C4.4. Understanding customer needs.
* M1. Our main objective is satisfying customers need better than our competitors.
* M2. Integrate and coordinate all functions of the firm in order to achieve the customer's satisfaction.
* M3. We makes use of marketing research to know current and future consumer needs.
* M4. We encourage our employees to collect information about customers.

Source : Primary data.

TABLE 5.1
Paired Correlation

Variables		*N*	*Correlation*	*Significance*
Pair 1	M1 and C4.4	15	-0.277	0.318
Pair 2	M2 and C4.4	15	-0.123	0.663
Pair 3	M3 and C4.4	15	-0.167	0.553
Pair 4	M4 and C4.4	15	0.650	0.009

Source : Primary data.

employees has been analysed with the help of 12 pair of variables relating to the effectiveness of interaction quality (Tables 6, 6.1 and 6.2).

TABLE 5.2
Paired Samples Test

Variables		Paired Differences					*t*	*df*	*Sig. (2-tailed)*
		Mean	*S.D.*	*Std. Error Mean*	*95% Confidence Interval of the Difference*				
					Lower	*Upper*			
(1)		*(2)*	*(3)*	*(4)*	*(5)*	*(6)*	*(7)*	*(8)*	*(9)*
Pair 1	M1 - C4.4	0.4667	0.91548	0.23637	-0.0403	0.9736	1.974	14	0.048
Pair 2	M2 - C4.4	0.6667	0.89974	0.23231	0.1684	1.1649	2.870	14	0.012
Pair 3	M3 - C4.4	0.6000	0.91026	0.23503	0.0959	1.1041	2.553	14	0.023
Pair 4	M4 - C4.4	0.5333	0.51640	0.13333	0.2474	0.8193	4.000	14	0.001

Source : Primary data.

TABLE 6

Paired Statistics

Between the Interaction Quality of the Bank and the Customer's Satisfaction

Variables		*Mean*	*N*	*S.D.*	*Std. Error Mean*
Pair 1	M11* &	4.1333	15	0.35187	0.09085
	C8.1*	3.6667	15	0.61721	0.15936
Pair 2	M11* &	4.1333	15	0.35187	0.09085
	C8.2*	3.6667	15	0.72375	0.18687
Pair 3	M11* &	4.1333	15	0.35187	0.09085
	C8.3*	3.5333	15	0.63994	0.16523
Pair 4	M12* &	4.4000	15	0.73679	0.19024
	C8.1*	3.6667	15	0.61721	•0.15936
Pair 5	M12* &	4.4000	15	0.73679	0.19024
	C8.2*	3.6667	15	0.72375	0.18687
Pair 6	M12* &	4.4000	15	0.73679	0.19024
	C8.3*	3.5333	15	0.63994	0.16523
Pair 7	M13* &	4.0667	15	0.25820	0.06667
	C8.1*	3.6667	15	0.61721	0.15936
Pair 8	M13* &	4.0667	15	0.25820	0.06667
	C8.2*	3.6667	15	0.72375	0.18687
Pair 9	M13* &	4.0667	15	0.25820	0.06667
	C8.3*	3.5333	15	0.63994	0.16523
Pair 10	M11* &	4.1333	15	0.35187	0.09085
	C10*	2.2667	15	0.59362	0.1532
Pair 11	M12* &	4.4000	15	0.73679	0.19024
	C10*	2.2667	15	0.59362	0.15327
Pair 12	M13* &	4.0667	15	0.25820	0.06667
	C10*	2.2667	15	0.59362	0.15327

* M11. Sends regularly mails to our customers with personalized information, which has interest to them.
* M12. We offer a 24 hrs. telephone to our customers.
* M13. We contact with our customers to check their level of satisfaction.
* C8.1 The time taken by members to answer the telephone.
* C8.2 The way in which staff members answer your call.
* C8.3 The ease of reaching the person; you need to speak with?
* C10. This bank informs customers about its financial operation.

Source : Primary data.

TABLE 6.1
Paired Correlation

Variables		*N*	*Correlation*	*Significance*
Pair 1	M11 and C8.1	15	-0.439	0.102
Pair 2	M11 and C8.2	15	-0.374	0.170
Pair 3	M11 and C8.3	15	-0.338	0.217
Pair 4	M12 and C8.1	15	0.314	0.254
Pair 5	M12 and C8.2	15	0.000	1.000
Pair 6	M12 and C8.3	15	-0.182	0.517
Pair 7	M13 and C8.1	15	-0.299	0.279
Pair 8	Q13 and C8.2	15	-0.255	0.359
Pair 9	M13 and C8.3	15	-0.231	0.408
Pair 10	M11 and C10	15	0.160	0.570
Pair 11	M12 and C10	15	-0.098	0.728
Pair 12	M13 and C10	15	-0.124	0.659

Source : Primary data.

Significance difference can be observed among the different variables between the pair values of the bank's interaction quality and satisfaction level of the customers except among the pair 8 variables. However, negative low intensity correlation can be observed among the variables constituting pairs of 1, 2, 3, 6, 7, 8, 9, 11 and 12. It indicates bank's effort to increase interaction quality with customers was not a remarkable one. There has some weakness on the banker's effort for providing personalised information and toll free call services.

6. Personal Relations and Commitment

Relationship between the bank's degree of commitment and personal relationship with the customers and the customer's satisfaction has been studied by using variables constituting 15 pairs influencing effectiveness of personal relation and commitment (Tables 7, 7.1 and 7.2).

TABLE 6.2
Paired Samples Test

Variables		Paired Differences					t	df	Sig. (2-tailed)
		Mean	S.D.	Std. Error Mean	95% Confidence Interval of the Difference				
					Lower	Upper			
(1)		(2)	(3)	(4)	(5)	(6)	(7)	(8)	(9)
Pair 1	M11- C8.1	0.4667	0.83381	0.21529	0.0049	0.9284	2.168	14	0.038
Pair 2	M11- C8.2	0.4667	0.91548	0.23637	-0.0403	0.9736	1.974	14	0.048
Pair 3	M11- C8.3	0.6000	0.82808	0.21381	0.1414	1.0586	2.806	14	0.014
Pair 4	M12 -C8.1	0.7333	0.79881	0.20625	0.2910	1.1757	3.556	14	0.003
Pair 5	M12 -C8.2	0.7333	1.03280	0.26667	0.1614	1.3053	2.750	14	0.016
Pair 6	M12 -C8.3	0.8667	1.06010	0.27372	0.2796	1.4537	3.166	14	0.007
Pair 7	M13 -C8.1	0.4000	0.73679	0.19024	-0.0080	0.8080	2.103	14	0.04
Pair 8	M13 -C8.2	0.4000	0.82808	0.21381	-0.0586	0.8586	1.871	14	0.082
Pair 9	M13 -C8.3	0.5333	0.74322	0.19190	0.1217	0.9449	2.779	14	0.015
Pair 10	M11-C10	1.8667	0.63994	0.16523	1.5123	2.2211	11.297	14	0.000
Pair 11	M12 - C10	2.1333	0.99043	0.25573	1.5849	2.6818	8.342	14	0.000
Pair 12	M13 - C10	1.8000	0.67612	0.17457	1.4256	2.1744	10.311	14	0.000

Source : Primary data.

TABLE 7
Paired Statistics
Relationship between the Bank's Degree of Commitment and Personal Relationship with the Customers and the Customer's Satisfaction

Variables		*Mean*	*N*	*S.D.*	*Std. Error Mean*
Pair 1	M14* &	4.4667	15	0.51640	0.13333
	C4.1*	3.9333	15	0.70373	0.18170
Pair 2	M15* &	4.4667	15	0.51640	0.13333
	C4.1*	3.9333	15	0.70373	0.18170
Pair 3	M16* &	4.3333	15	0.48795	0.12599
	C4.1*	3.9333	15	0.70373	0.18170
Pair 4	M17* &	4.3333	15	0.48795	0.12599
	C4.1*	3.9333	15	0.70373	0.18170
Pair 5	M18* &	4.4000	15	0.50709	0.13093
	C4.1*	3.9333	15	0.70373	0.18170
Pair 6	M14* &	4.4667	15	0.51640	0.13333
	C4.2*	3.7333	15	0.79881	0.20625
Pair 7	M15* &	4.4667	15	0.51640	0.13333
	C4.2*	3.7333	15	0.79881	0.20625
Pair 8	M16* &	4.3333	15	0.48795	0.12599
	C4.2*	3.7333	15	0.79881	0.20625
Pair 9	M17* &	4.3333	15	0.48795	0.12599
	C4.2*	3.7333	15	0.79881	0.20625
Pair 10	M18* &	4.4000	15	0.50709	0.13093
	C4.2*	3.7333	15	0.79881	0.20625
Pair 11	M14* &	4.4667	15	0.51640	0.13333
	C4.4*	3.8000	15	0.67612	0.17457
Pair 12	M15* &	4.4667	15	0.51640	0.13333
	C4.4*	3.8000	15	0.67612	0.17457
Pair 13	M16* &	4.3333	15	0.48795	0.12599
	C4.4*	3.8000	15	0.67612	0.17457
Pair 14	M17* &	4.3333	15	0.48795	0.12599
	C4.4*	3.8000	15	0.67612	0.17457
Pair 15	M18* &	4.4000	15	0.50709	0.13093
	C4.4*	3.8000	15	0.67612	0.17457

* M14. To invest time and resources to foster the relationship with our customers.
* M15. We try that our relationship with our customers are long lasting.
* M16. We feel committed with our customers.
* M17. Our employees maintain close relationship with our customers.
* M18. We tries to understand the point of view of the customer.
* C4.1. Friendilness and courtesy.
* C4.2. Warm relationship.
* C4.4. Understanding customer needs.

Source : Primary data.

TABLE 7.1
Paired Correlation

Variables		*N*	*Correlation*	*Significance*
Pair 1	M14 and C4.1	15	-0.105	0.710
Pair 2	M15 and C4.1	15	0.288	0.297
Pair 3	M16 and C4.1	15	0.277	0.317
Pair 4	M17 and C4.1	15	-0.139	0.622
Pair 5	M18 and C4.1	15	0.080	0.777
Pair 6	M14 and C4.2	15	-0.196	0.483
Pair 7	M15 and C4.2	15	0.323	0.240
Pair 8	M16 and C4.2	15	0.244	0.380
Pair 9	M17 and C4.2	15	-0.305	0.268
Pair 10	M18 and C4.2	15	0.106	0.707
Pair 11	M14 and C4.4	15	0.082	0.772
Pair 12	M15 and C4.4	15	0.286	0.301
Pair 13	M16 and C4.4	15	0.000	1.000
Pair 14	M17 and C4.4	15	-0.217	0.438
Pair 15	M18 and C4.4	15	0.458	0.086

Source : Primary data.

Significance difference can be observed among the different variables between the pair values of the customer's satisfaction; and personal relationship and commitment on the part of the bank. However, negative low intensity correlation can be observed among the variables constituting pairs of 1, 4, 6, 9 and 14. It indicates bank's effort to increase customer satisfaction and personal relationship was not a remarkable one. There has some weakness on bank's effort to boost personal relationship and commitment.

While analysing the variables constituting interaction quality; and personal relation and commitment on the part of bank and customers' point of view; significant difference can be observed among the variables at 5% level. So, the alternate hypothesis put forward by the researcher; Ha: 'There is significant difference between importance given by banks on

Table 7.2
Paired Samples Test

Variables		Paired Differences							
		Mean	*S.D.*	*Std. Error Mean*	*95% Confidence Interval of the Difference*		*t*	*df*	*Sig. (2-tailed)*
					Lower	*Upper*			
(1)		(2)	(3)	(4)	(5)	(6)	(7)	(8)	(9)
Pair 1	M14 - C4.1	0.5333	0.91548	.23637	0.0264	1.0403	2.256	14	0.041
Pair 2	M15 - C4.1	0.5333	0.74322	.19190	0.1217	0.9449	2.779	14	0.015
Pair 3	M16 - C4.1	0.4000	0.73679	.19024	-0.0080	0.8080	2.103	14	0.05
Pair 4	M17 - C4.1	0.4000	0.91026	.23503	-0.1041	0.9041	1.702	14	0.111
Pair 5	M18 - C4.1	0.4667	0.83381	.21529	0.0049	0.9284	2.168	14	0.048
Pair 6	M14 - C4.2	0.7333	1.03280	.26667	0.1614	1.3053	2.750	14	0.016
Pair 7	M15 - C4.2	0.7333	0.79881	.20625	0.2910	1.1757	3.556	14	0.003
Pair 8	M16 - C4.2	0.6000	0.82808	.21381	0.1414	1.0586	2.806	14	0.014
Pair 9	M17 - C4.2	0.6000	1.05560	.27255	0.0154	1.1846	2.201	14	0.045
Pair 10	M18 - C4.2	0.6667	0.89974	.23231	0.1684	1.1649	2.870	14	0.012
Pair 11	M14 - C4.4	0.6667	0.81650	.21082	0.2145	1.1188	3.162	14	0.007
Pair 12	M15 - C4.4	0.6667	0.72375	.18687	0.2659	1.0675	3.568	14	0.003
Pair 13	M16 - C4.4	0.5333	0.83381	.21529	0.0716	0.9951	2.477	14	0.027
Pair 14	M17 - C4.4	0.5333	0.91548	.23637	0.0264	1.0403	2.256	14	0.041
Pair 15	M18 - C4.4	0.6000	0.63246	.16330	0.2498	0.9502	3.674	14	0.003

Source : Primary data.

interaction quality and relationship management; and customer satisfaction' can be accepted.

6. Satisfactions on the Overall Performance

Paired comparison has been done between CRM practices followed by banks and satisfaction of customers on the overall performance of the bank by considering three pairs of variables relating to the CRM system (Tables 8, 8.1 and 8.2).

TABLE 8
Paired Statistics
Relationship between CRM Practices Followed by Banks and Satisfaction of Customers on the Overall Performance of the Bank

Variables		*Mean*	*N*	*S.D.*	*Std. Error Mean*
Pair 1	*M6 &	4.2667	15	0.45774	0.11819
	*C4.11	3.8667	15	0.51640	0.13333
Pair 2	*M7 &	4.2667	15	0.70373	0.18170
	*C4.11	3.8667	15	0.51640	0.13333
Pair 3	*M8 &	4.4000	15	0.50709	0.13093
	*C4.11	3.8667	15	0.51640	0.13333

* M6. We design CRM systems and solutions to know better every customer.
* M7. We make use of specific technology which allow us to monitoring our customers.
* M8. Created information system in order to make more efficient each contact with the customer.
* C4.11. Overall performance.

Source : Primary data.

TABLE 8.1
Paired Correlation

Variables		*N*	*Correlation*	*Significance*
Pair 1	M6 and C4.11	15	-0.443	0.098
Pair 2	M7 and C4.11	15	0.301	0.275
Pair 3	M8 and C4.11	15	-0.327	0.234

Source : Primary data.

TABLE 8.2
Paired Samples Test

Variables		Paired Differences					*t*	*df*	*Sig.* (2-tailed)
		Mean	*S.D.*	*Std. Error Mean*	*95% Confidence Interval of the Difference*				
					Lower	*Upper*			
	(1)	(2)	(3)	(4)	(5)	(6)	(7)	(8)	(9)
Pair 1	M6 - 4.11	0.4000	0.82808	0.21381	-0.0586	0.8586	2.871	14	0.042
Pair 2	M7 - 4.11	0.4000	0.73679	0.19024	-0.0080	0.8080	3.103	14	0.034
Pair 3	M8 - 4.11	0.5333	0.83381	0.21529	0.0716	0.9951	3.477	14	0.017

Source : Primary data.

There is a significant difference between CRM practices followed by the bank and the customer's satisfaction on the overall performance of the bank (at 5% level). Therefore, alternate hypothesis put forwarded by the researcher Ha: There is significant difference between CRM practices followed by the bank and customer's satisfaction can be accepted. However, negative low intensity correlation can be observed among the variables constituting pairs of 1 and 3. It indicates that there has some weakness in the CRM system followed by the bank and it was not much effective to enhance the customer satisfaction level.

7. Outcome of CRM System

Performance outcomes of CRM System and customer's overall satisfaction about the services of the bank has been presented with the help of paired comparison of nine pairs of variables relating to outcomes of the CRM system (Tables 9, 9.1 and 9.2).

TABLE 9
Paired Statistics
Performance Outcomes of CRM System and Customer's Overall Satisfaction

Variables		*Mean*	*N*	*S.D.*	*Std. Error Mean*
(1)		*(2)*	*(3)*	*(4)*	*(5)*
Pair 1	*M27 &	4.2000	15	0.41404	0.10690
	*C14	2.0000	15	0.37796	0.09759
Pair 2	*M28 &	4.6000	15	0.50709	0.13093
	*C14	2.0000	15	0.37796	0.09759
Pair 3	*M29 &	4.2667	15	0.45774	0.11819
	*C14	2.0000	15	0.37796	0.09759
Pair 4	*M29 &	4.2667	15	0.45774	0.11819
	*C14	2.0000	15	0.37796	0.09759
Pair 5	*M30 &	4.2000	15	0.41404	0.10690
	*C14	2.0000	15	0.37796	0.09759

(*Contd.*)

TABLE 9 (Contd.)

(1)		(2)	(3)	(4)	(5)
Pair 6	*M27 &	4.2000	15	0.41404	0.10690
	*C15	1.6000	15	0.63246	0.16330
Pair 7	*M28 &	4.6000	15	0.50709	0.13093
	*C15	1.6000	15	0.63246	0.16330
Pair 8	*M29 &	4.2667	15	0.45774	0.11819
	*C15	1.6000	15	0.63246	0.16330
Pair 9	*M30 &	4.2000	15	0.41404	0.10690
	*C15	1.6000	15	0.63246	0.16330

* M27. The bank has increased its market shares on last years.
* M28. We have reduced the number of complaints and conflicts.
* M29. Increased the percentage of retained customers.
* M30. Competitive advantage over the competitors based on relationship with the customers.
* C14. Overall, how satisfied are you with the service you receive?
* C15. Over the last year, has our service.

Source : Primary data.

TABLE 9.1
Paired Correlation

Variables		*N*	*Correlation*	*Significance*
Pair 1	M27 and C14	15	.000	1.000
Pair 2	M28 and C14	15	.373	.171
Pair 3	M29 and C14	15	.000	1.000
Pair 4	M29 and C14	15	.000	1.000
Pair 5	M30 and C14	15	.000	1.000
Pair 6	M27 and C15	15	-.218	.435
Pair 7	M28 and C15	15	.579	.024
Pair 8	M29 and C15	15	.148	.599
Pair 9	M30 and C15	15	.055	.847

Source : Primary data.

TABLE 9.2
Paired Samples Test

Variables		Paired Differences						df	Sig. (2-tailed)
		Mean	S.D.	Std. Error Mean	95% Confidence Interval of the Difference				
					Lower	Upper			
(1)		(2)	(3)	(4)	(5)	(6)	(7)	(8)	(9)
Pair 1	M27 - C14	2.2000	0.56061	0.14475	1.8895	2.5105	15.199	14	0.000
Pair 2	M28 - C14	2.6000	0.50709	0.13093	2.3192	2.8808	19.858	14	0.000
Pair 3	M29 - C14	2.2667	0.59362	0.15327	1.9379	2.5954	14.789	14	0.000
Pair 4	M29 - C14	2.2667	0.59362	0.15327	1.9379	2.5954	14.789	14	0.000
Pair 5	M30 - C14	2.2000	0.56061	0.14475	1.8895	2.5105	15.199	14	0.000
Pair 6	M27 - C15	2.6000	0.82808	0.21381	2.1414	3.0586	12.160	14	0.000
Pair 7	M28 - C15	3.0000	0.53452	0.13801	2.7040	3.2960	21.737	14	0.000
Pair 8	M29 - C15	2.6667	0.72375	0.18687	2.2659	3.0675	14.270	14	0.000
Pair 9	M30 - C15	2.6000	0.73679	0.19024	2.1920	3.0080	13.667	14	0.000

Source : Primary data.

It is observed that the difference between bank's performance outcome and the overall customer's satisfaction of the banks performance is significant at 5% level. So, the alternate hypothesis put forwarded by the researcher, Ha: 'CRM system followed by the bank is effective to increase the performance outcomes of the bank and customer satisfaction', can be accepted. There is moderate positive correlation can observed in the performance outcomes such as reducing number of complaints and low positive correlation exist in terms of increased percentage of retained customers. But, in the case of outcomes such as increase market share and competitive advantage; the banks cannot able to achieve better result.

The variables relating to the customer's satisfaction and loyalty and relationship closeness can be analyzed with the help of correlation coefficient (Table 10).

TABLE 10
Association between Satisfaction and Loyalty and Relationship Closeness

Sl. No.	*Variables*	*Correlation co-efficient*
1	C12.1 and C14	0.687*
2	C12.2 and C14	0.436*
3	C12.3 and C1 4	0.642*

* Significant at 5% level.

* C12.1. Recommend this bank to a friend or relative?

* C12.2. Remain a customer of this bank?

* C12.3. Buy another product or service from this bank?

* C14. Overall, how satisfied are you with the service you receive?

Source : primary Data.

It is observed that (Table 10) all the three variables have moderate degree of correlation. So, it is inferred that satisfied customers of the bank are willing to recommend the bank to another customer; remain as a customer of the bank; and buy another product or service from the bank.

8. Major Factors Contributing to Customer Satisfaction

For the identification of major factors contributing customer satisfaction, 'SERVQUAL' scale has been employed and analyzed the variables by using the technique of Factor analysis. This exercise led to the identification and labeling of the following dimensions of service quality: service environment, interaction quality, reliability, empathy, and technology. Service environment refers to the appearance of the service providers and appearance of the interior and exterior of the bank facilities. Interaction quality encompasses attitudes and behaviors of the service providers and their interaction style with customers. Empathy is defined as individualized attention given to customers and willingness of the bank personnel to help customers and resolve their problems in a timely manner. Reliability refers to dependability of service and accuracy of records and information. Finally, technology dimension was defined as the quality of ATMs and the proper functioning of computerized systems. The communalities show (Table 11) the major factors contribute to the customer's satisfaction on the basis of scores.

TABLE 11
Communalities

Variables	*Initial*	*Extraction*
(1)	*(2)*	*(3)*
C3.1	1.000	.208
C3.2	1.000	.727
C3.3	1.000	.799
C3.4	1.000	.759
C5.1	1.000	.708
C5.3	1.000	.806
C6.4	1.000	.647
C4.1	1.000	.806
C4.2	1.000	.817
C4.9	1.000	.543

(Contd.)

TABLE 11 (*Contd.*)

(1)	*(2)*	*(3)*
C4.10	1.000	.835
C4.4	1.000	.775
C4.5	1.000	.629

Source : Primary Data.

1. Service Environment (C3.1, and C4.10).
   Exterior and Interior environment of the bank (C3.1) and Professional appearance (C4.10).
2. Service Technology (C3.2, C3.3, and C3.4).
   Internet banking services (C3.2); Convenience of ATMs (C3.3); and Adequate number of ATMs (C3.4).
3. Interaction Quality (C4.1, C4.2, C4.4, and C4.5).
   Friendliness and courtesy (C4.1); Warm relationship (C4.2); Understanding customer needs (C4.4); and Speedy services (C4.5).
4. Grievance Resolution (C5.1, C5.3, and C6.4).
   A mistake on your account (C5.1); A mistake with a standing order or direct debit (C5.3); and The follow-up contact you received (C6.4).
5. Empathy (C4.9): Willingness to listen and respond (C4.9).

From the Component Score Coefficient Matrix (Table 11.1), the following three factors can be identified as major factors on the basis of maximum scores; C4.10 (Professional Appearance); C4.2 (Warm relationship) and C3.4 (Availability of ATMs). As a whole, from the Factor Analysis, it has been identified that among the five factors in SERVEQ Analysis (Service Environment, Interaction Quality, Technology, Reliability, and Empathy); there are three major contributing factors to customer satisfaction such as: Service Environment (C4.10); Service Technology (C3.4); and Interaction Quality (C4.2).

TABLE 11.1

Component Score Coefficient Matrix

Variables	*Components*			
C3.1	.059	.048	.056	.096
C3.2	-.140	.459	.111	-.009
C3.3	-.139	.452	-.041	.009
C3.4	-.013	.094	-.187	.286
C5.1	-.026	.114	.455	-.036
C5.3	.095	-.058	.500	.150
C6.4	.235	-.041	-.181	-.137
C4.1	.352	-.209	.032	-.027
C4.2	.181	-.077	-.020	.211
C4.9	.159	.093	.076	-.026
C4.10	-.176	.002	.086	.696
C4.4	.389	-.062	.130	-.354
C4.5	.027	.252	-.024	.012

C4.10. Professional appearance is a major factor, which contribute to the factor of Service Environment.

C3.4. Availability of ATMs is a major factor, which contribute to the factor of Service Technology.

C4.2. Warm relationship is a major factor, which contribute to the factor of Interaction Quality.

Source : Primary Data.

6. CONCLUSION

The study reveals that the importance given by the bank to solve customer complaints is effective to improve customer satisfaction. There is significant relationship between baking technology adopted by banks and satisfaction level of customers. However, customers are not fully satisfied with adequate number of ATMs, Convenience of ATMs and Internet banking services offered by the bank. There is significant difference between importance given by banks on customer orientation and customer satisfaction. However, the study indicates that the bank's effort in this regard was not fully achieved to get better result on customer orientation.

There is significant difference between importance given by banks on interaction quality and relationship management; and customer satisfaction. It indicates bank's effort to increase customer satisfaction and personal relationship was not a remarkable one. There has some weakness on bank's effort to boost personal relationship and commitment; personalised information; and toll-free call services. CRM system followed by the bank is effective to increase the performance outcomes of the bank and customer satisfaction; while the study also indicates that there has some weakness in the CRM system followed by the bank and it was not much effective to enhance the customer satisfaction level. In the case of outcomes such as increase market share and competitive advantage; the banks cannot able to achieve better result. Satisfied customers of the bank are willing to recommend the bank to another customer; remain as a customer of the bank; and buy another product or service from the bank.

From the Factor Analysis, it has been identified that among the five factors in SERVEQ Analysis (Service Environment, Interaction Quality, Technology, Reliability, and Empathy); there are three major contributing factors to customer satisfaction such as Service Environment, Service Technology, and Interaction Quality. Professional appearance is a major factor, which contributes to the factor of Service Environment; Availability of ATMs is a major factor, which contributes to the factor of Service Technology; and Warm relationship is a major factor, which contribute to the factor of Interaction Quality.

References

Bayon, T., Gutsche, J., and Bauer, H. (2002), 'Customer Equity Marketing: Touching the Intangible', *European Management Journal*, 20, 213–22.

Bligh, Philip and Douglas Turk (2004), CRM unplugged-releasing CRM's Strategic Value. Hoboken: John Wiley & Sons, ISBN 0-471-48304-4.

Karimi, J., Somers, T.M., and Gupta, Y.P. (2001), 'Impact of Information Technology Management Practices on Customer Service', *Journal of Management Information Systems*, 17, 125–58.

Mihelis, G., Grigoroudis, E., Siskos, Y., Politis, Y. and Malandrakis, Y. (2001) 'Customer Satisfaction Measurement in the Private Bank Sector', *European Journal of Operational Research*, 130, 347-60.

Morgan, N.A., Clark, B.H., and Gooner, R. (2002), 'Marketing Productivity, Marketing Audits, and Systems for Marketing Performance Assessment: Integrating Multiple Perspectives', *Journal of Business Research*, 55, 363-75.

Mulhern, F.J. (1999), 'Customer Profitability Analysis: Measurement, Concentration, and Research Directions', *Journal of Interactive Marketing*, 13 (Winter), 25-40.

Parasuraman, A., Zeithaml, V.A., and Berry, L. (1998), 'SERVQUAL: A Multiple Item Scale for Measuring Customer Perceptions of Service Quality', *Journal of Retailing*, 64, 12-37.

Rigby, Darrell K. and Frederick F. Reichheld, Phil Schefter. (2002), 'Avoid the four perils of CRM', *Harvard Business Review* 80(2): 101–109. doi:10.1225/8946.

Ryals, L., and Knox, S. (2001), 'Cross-functional Issues in the Implementation of Relationship Marketing through Customer Relationship Management', *European Management Journal*, 19, 534-42.

Stamoulis, D., Kanellis, P., and Martakos, D. (2002), 'An Approach and Model for Assessing the Business Value of E-Banking Distribution Channels: Evaluation as Communication', *International Journal of Information Management*, 22, 247-61.

Winer, R.S. (2001), 'A Framework for Customer Relationship Management', *California Management Review*, 43, 89-105.

5

A Business Strategy for Marketing the Products and Services of T&CG/SHGs

An Analytical Case Study on Baluchari Sarees of Bishnupur

SARBANI MITRA AND K.M. AGRAWAL

ABSTRACT

In India, small-scale industries account for about 40% of the total industrial output and are only second to the agricultural sector in providing employment. West Bengal, which is a leading State in propagation of Cottage and Small Scale Industry, with around 3,50,000 units, provides employment to about 2.2 million people. Various districts and regions of West Bengal are famous for its Cottage and Small Scale Enterprises especially Bankura for its handloom and crafts, Birbhum for its dokra artifacts, Dhanekhali for the handloom and textiles, etc. Bankura produces a wonderful piece of art in the form of

Baluchari Saree. With the liberalization of market economy, Baluchari Saree of Bishnupur, Bankura is lagging behind with the modern market system in terms of quality of product and skill, access to market, marketing plan, distribution channel, packaging, production process, etc. It is the fact that the manufacturers of this art and craft need infrastructure development, creation of industrial estates, marketing and raw material support, skill upgradation, advanced production process, smooth distribution channel, good access to market, skill of packaging, etc.

To bridge these gaps, a market survey was conducted at Bankura to understand the local economic circumstances and demand for particular skills and product—Baluchari Saree in the local and wider markets in both product and service sectors and also to formulate a sustainable business strategy for marketing the product and services.

The prime objectives of the study were to scan the production process of Baluchari Saree; to explore existing status of its production; to conduct market survey for Baluchari Saree and skills promoted or have scope of promotion to understand market demand, training need, existing gaps (in terms of production technology and equipment, product service and delivery, packaging, marketing and promotion, financial issues, etc.) and market access of skills at present and future context; to monitor external and internal marketing environment of Baluchari Saree and to identify the existing problems in its production. The study aims to develop a sustainable business strategy for marketing the Baluchari Saree to access the wide scope of modern market economy by the Thrift and Credit Group (T&CG)/Self-Help Group (SHG). Detailed interviews through a structured questionnaire were conducted with the various entrepreneurs in Bishnupur to assess their viewpoints with respect to the market potential and gaps. The study also projects brief insights of market assessment of Baluchari Saree for T&CG/SHG members of Bishnupur Municipality.

From the survey it was revealed that there is deficiency of fund. Weavers also face obstacles in getting proper market. There is also deficiency of skill. Manufacturers suffer from poor production process. Furthermore, there is deficiency of procurement of raw materials. It was also revealed that they don't have any arrangement of availing of quality control laboratory facility. In majority of cases, no promotional campaign like trade fair, exhibition, etc. has been organized. In most of the cases weavers are not using any special type of packaging for their products. On the basis of the situation, the study evaluates strengths, weaknesses, opportunities and threats of manufacturing of Baluchari Saree in Bishnupur. It further identifies various problems that the Baluchari weavers are now facing. Based on this, the study has attempted to explore a sustainable marketing strategy for promoting and developing the Baluchari industry.

Key words: Cottage and Small Scale Industry, Business strategy; Artifact of Bankura; Baluchari Saree of Bishnupur; Weavers of Bankura, Segmentation, targeting and positioning.

INTRODUCTION

In India, small-scale industries account for about 40% of the total industrial output and are only second to the agricultural sector in providing employment. West Bengal, which is a leading State in propagation of Cottage and Small Scale Industry, with around 3,50,000 units, provides employment to about 2.2 million people. West Bengal has a well-defined plan for advancement of this sector through the active support of West Bengal Small Industries Development Corporation and other agencies under the Department of Cottage and Small Scale Industries. Various districts and regions of West Bengal are famous for its Cottage and Small Scale Enterprises especially Bankura for its handloom and crafts, Birbhum for its dokra artifacts, Dhanekhali for the handloom and textiles, etc.

Though the number of units in West Bengal is high, the incidence of sickness, poor management and the paucity of finances are causes for concern. The prevalence of middlemen has also resulted in the impoverishment of the artisans. The most affected Cottage and Small Scale Industries of West Bengal are textiles; embroideries like kantha; boutique; jute artifacts; thermocol or sholapith; terracotta artifacts, etc.

The district of Bankura boasts of a variety of arts and crafts. For example—the terracotta horses which are a trademark of West Bengal's art. Bankura also specializes in terracotta ornaments, which have made quite a fashion statement in the metropolitan cities. Last but not the least, Bankura produces a wonderful piece of art in the form of Baluchari Saree, which are not only expensive, but also a possession of pride. With the liberalization of market economy, Baluchari Saree of Bishnupur, Bankura is lagging behind with the modern market system in terms of quality of product and skill, access to market, marketing plan, distribution channel, packaging, production process, etc. It is the fact that the manufacturers of this art and craft need infrastructure development, creation of industrial estates, marketing and raw material support, skill upgradation, advanced production process, smooth distribution channel, good access to market, skill of packaging, etc. With Tantusree, Tantuja and Manjusha purchasing 'good stock' till 1997, weavers did not have too many problems. But with these outlets facing severe financial crisis, they have failed to take sizeable orders in the recent years. From purchasing raw material to selling the products, weavers of Bishnupur are facing problems.

To bridge these gaps, a market survey was conducted at Bankura to understand the local economic circumstances and demand for particular skills and product - Baluchari Saree in the local and wider markets in both product and service sectors and also to formulate a sustainable business strategy for marketing the product and services.

The prime objectives of the study were as follows:

- To scan the production process of Baluchari Saree and its specialty and to explore existing status of its production.
- To conduct market survey for Baluchari Saree and skills promoted or have scope of promotion to understand market demand, training need, existing gaps (in terms of production technology and equipment, product service and delivery, packaging, marketing and promotion, financial issues, etc.) and market access of skills at present and future context.
- To monitor external and internal marketing environment of Baluchari Saree and to identify the existing problems in its production.
- To develop a sustainable business strategy for marketing the Baluchari Saree to access the wide scope of modern market economy by the T&CG/SHG.

METHODOLOGYB

The study has been conducted on the basis of both qualitative and quantitative techniques. The prime source of information was from desk reviews of necessary documents/ reports, field visits, key informant interviews, observations, focus group discussions and consultations with key stakeholders. For the purpose, structured questionnaires had been developed for various stakeholders of Bishnupur.

STATUS OF HANDLOOM INDUSTRY

One of the earliest to come into existence in India, textile industry accounts for 14% of the total industrial production, contributes to nearly 30% of the total exports and is the second largest employment generator after agriculture. The handloom sector plays a very important role in the country's economy. It is one of the largest economic activities providing direct employment to over 65 lakh persons engaged in weaving and allied activities. As a result of effective Government intervention through financial assistance and implementation of various developmental and welfare schemes, this sector has been able to withstand competition from the power loom and mill sectors. This sector contributes nearly 19% of the total cloth produced in the country and also adds substantially to export earnings. Handloom is unparalleled in its flexibility and versatility, permitting experimentation and encouraging innovations. The strength of Handloom lies in the introducing innovative designs, which cannot be replicated by the Power loom sector. Thus, Handloom forms a part of the heritage of India and exemplifies the richness and diversity of our country and the artistry of the weavers.

There are total 14,473 handlooms in Bankura District. About 36,183 persons are engaged in weaving activities. There are total 132 registered handloom weavers cooperative societies in Bankura under which 11,185 number of looms are present and 13,307 weavers are working. Table 1 presents the status of handloom production in Bankura in 2004-05. More than 1,000 number of looms are operational in Bishnupur Municipality, from which total handloom including Baluchari

Saree is produced of the total worth of approx. Rs. 81.6 lakhs, which is more than 50% of the cost of production of total handloom in Bishnupur Municipality.

TABLE 1
Status of Handloom Production in Bankura in 2004-05

Name of block/ municipality	*No. of looms*	*Total handloom production (in Rs.)*	*Cost of production (in Rs.)*	*Wages paid (in Rs.)*
Bankura I	762	67,00,000	35,00,000	22,00,000
Bankura II	686	54,30,000	28,00,000	18,00,000
Bankura Municipality	2,126	77,00,000	39,27,000	26,18,000
Bishnupur Block (Silk)	154	14,00,000	6,80,000	4,00,000
Bishnupur Municipality	1,220	1,60,00,000	81,60,000	54,40,000
Sonamukhi Block (Silk)	79	8,00,000	4,08,000	2,72,000
Sonamukhi Municipality	527	1,34,00,000	96,00,000	58,00,000
Total	14,473	12,18,40,000	6,58,69,000	4,29,12,000

Source : www.bankura.org (accessed on August, 2009) and Handloom Development Officer, Bankura.

ARTIFACTS OF BANKURA

The artifacts of Bankura showcase the rich history of the State. The textile of Bankura is famous over the world. This district is renowned for production of its versatile production of Silk, Baluchari Saree. Other traditional products are bed-sheet, bed-cover, door and window screen, towel (Gamcha), cotton saree, silk saree, silk shirting, tassar shirting, etc. The Baluchari Saree of Bankura is a specialty, as it is not only expensive, but exclusive as well. Each saree tells a story of mythology. Table 2 presents status of major non-farm sector activities in Bankura. It reveals that maximum number (more than 30,000, i.e. 14.02% of total workers) of people are getting involved in weaving Baluchari Saree compared to other major rural non-farm activities in Bankura. The region is not only famous for its history of artifacts, but also for tourism.

TABLE 2
Status of Major Rural Non-farm Sector Activities in Bankura

Activity	*No. of People Employed*	*Percentage of Workers*
Baluchari Saree making	33,000	14.02
Conch shell products	2,500	1.06
Terracotta	2,300	1.00
Dokra	300	0.13
Stone carving	200	0.85

Source : http://www.thaindian.com/newsportal/india-news/famous-bankura-horse-of-west-bengal-may-become-history_10046858.html (accessed on August, 2009).

In the history of textile in Bengal, Baluchari came much after Maslin. Two hundred years ago Baluchari was used to be practised in a small village called Baluchar in Murshidabad district, from where it got the name Baluchari. In the 18th century, Murshidkuli Khan, Nawab of Bengal patronized its rich weaving tradition and Baluchari flourished from that time onwards. But this flourishing trend later declined, specially during British rule, due to political and financial reasons it became a dying craft as most of the weavers were compelled to give up the profession.

Later in the first half of 20th century, Subho Thakur, a famous artist, felt the need of recultivating the rich tradition of Baluchari craft. Though Bishnupur was always famous for its silk, he invited Akshay Kumar Das, a master weaver of Bishnupur to his center to learn the technique of jacquard weaving. Sri Das then went back to Bishnupur and worked hard to weave Baluchari on their looms.

Once Bishnupur was the capital of Malla dynasty and different kinds of crafts flourished during their period under the patronage of Malla kings. Temples made of terracotta bricks were one achievement of these rulers. A major influence of these temples can be seen in Baluchari Saree. The endpiece/anchal has the main decoration depicting narrative motifs. Mythological stories taken from the walls of temples and woven on Baluchari Saree, is a common feature in Bishnupur. Thus the intricately carved terracotta temples of Bishnupur provide ample inspiration for the weavers who reproduce whole epics on the pallu of the sari. The border of baluchari sarees contains repeating pictorial themes. The field of the saree is covered with small butis and a beautiful floral design runs across the edges.

Silk weaving of Baluchar continues to be an important landmark of Bengal's handloom tradition. Table 3 explores that in West Bengal cocoon production cost is 10.64% of cocoon production cost of the country, whereas in Bankura cocoon production cost is 46.03% of cocoon production cost of the State. On the other hand, in West Bengal quantum of raw silk production is 9.07% of raw silk production of the country, whereas in Bankura quantum of raw silk production is 39.25% of raw silk production of the State.

TABLE 3
Comparative Analysis of Production Status of Silk

Country/State/ District	*Production of cocoons (In Lakhs)*	*Percentage of Contributions*	*Raw Silk (In Metres)*	*Percentage of Contributions*
India	2368	—	452	—
West Bengal	252	10.64 (with respect to India)	41	9.07
Bankura	116	46.03 (with respect to West Bengal)	15.7	39.25

(as on 31.3.2008).

Source : http://www.thaindian.com/newsportal/india-news/famous-bankura-horse-of-west-bengal-may-become-history_10046858.html (accessed on August, 2009)

PROCESS OF PRODUCTION OF BALUCHARI SAREE

The Baluchari sarees are inspired from Jamdanis of Dhaka. Baluchari is woven with two varieties of silk threads one from Bangalore and the other from West Bengal. One of the silk types is set vertically and the other is set horizontally in the special looms. Weaving of Baluchar sari is a very arduous job. Two types of silk are selected as base material- one for warf (*tana or shana*) and another for weft (*or verna*). Quality of silk yarn for warf is superior to that for the weft for carrying weights of the material. The designs are so complicated that sometimes a dozen weavers are employed to work on a single piece of sari. Generally two designs are used for the Anchals, two for the sari borders and two for the buti motifs. Before fixing the threads on the loom, the silk threads are washed in boiling water. On the next day, it is coloured by dipping in hot colours. Then the threads are rolled on the spinning wheels. After toiling for nearly five to six months we get those beautiful exquisite Baluchari sarees. The specialty of Baluchari Saree rests on the fabric, weaving technique and the traditional designs. The importance of the process is that these sarees can stand any amount of washing. The production process of Baluchari Saree is depicted in Figure 1.

FIG. 1

Flow Diagram for Producing Baluchari Saree

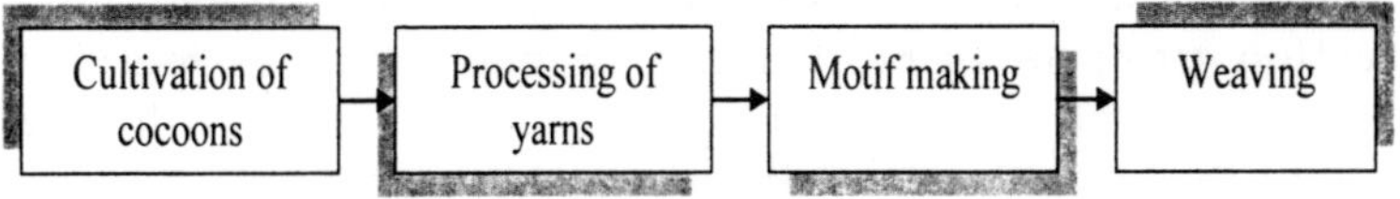

Cultivation of cocoons: As the fiber or filament composing the cocoon of the silkworm is constructed into a beautiful and durable fabric, silkworms are bred for the sole purpose of producing raw silk.

Processing of yarns: To make the yarn soft, it is boiled in a solution of soda and soap and then dyed in acid colour, according to the requirement of the saree. The yarn is stretched from both the sides in opposite directions putting some force with both palms. This process is needed to make the yarn crisper.

Motif making: Making of the motifs for 'pallavs' and other part of Baluchari is in itself an intricate process. The design is drawn on a graph paper, it is coloured and punching is done using cards. After punching, these cards are sewed in order and fixed in the jacquard machine.

Weaving: After jacquard loom has been introduced, weaving of a Baluchari Saree takes five to six days to get completed. Two weavers work on it on shifting basis.

Baluchari thus prepared becomes the sign of aristocracy, the attire of status. Maintenance of quality of Baluchari Saree is taken care of precisely. The quality is checked from the stage of dyeing of the yarn to the packaging of the saree.

STATUS OF WEAVERS OF BALUCHARI SAREE

Number of People involved, looms and revenue have been declined after 2006 by 30%-40%. General condition of the Baluchari weavers is bad (approx. monthly family income is Rs. 4000) and normal family size is 8. Therefore, next generation is not interested to join the profession as it is not that remunerative and other professions are more lucrative compared to weaving. Even migration takes place from traditional locations to other towns and cities. Detailed interviews through a structured questionnaire were conducted with the various entrepreneurs in Bishnupur to assess their viewpoints with respect to the market potential and gaps. This section projects brief insights of market assessment of Baluchari Saree for Thrift and Credit Group (T&CG)/Self-Help Group (SHG) members of Bishnupur Municipality.

Raw-materials, Production Process and Products: From the survey it was explored that T&CG/SHG members in Bishnupur, being involved in Baluchari Saree weaving, etc., purchase raw materials from local market. On an average, it was found from the survey that they prepare 4-5 pieces of Baluchari Saree monthly. The quantity of raw materials purchased from local market for a specific case (4-5 pieces of Baluchari Saree) with the present rate of each material in market is presented in Table 4. It was explored that the daily total costs of production of 4-5 pieces of Baluchari Saree is Rs. 550. After selling in local market, they are getting Rs. 1,400-2,000. So profit becomes Rs. 850-1,450. An original baluchari saree costs Rs 2,000 upwards, but copies are available at Rs. 1000. It was also explored that they collect the raw material all the year round. As per requirement they stock the materials in their own premises.

TABLE 4
Details of Raw-materials for Weaving of Baluchari Saree

Sl. No.	*Raw material*	*Quantity per month*	*Cost per unit*
1.	Colour	100 gm	Rs. 350/-
2.	Wood	50 kg	Rs. 150/-
3.	Soap	4 pieces	Rs. 50/-
4.	Soda	1 kg	

Product Service and Delivery: It was also revealed from the survey that 54.55% of T&CG/SHG members in Bishnupur, who are involved in Baluchari Saree weaving, sell their product to the wholesalers/middlemen. Hardly, customers come to purchase product to the weavers' houses. In 54.55% cases, products are used locally and in remaining cases, it remains outside West Bengal, but remains within country.

Financial Issues: Majority of the T&CG/SHG members in Bishnupur, who are involved in Baluchari Saree weaving, has their own manufacturing unit. In majority (63.64%) of the cases, the weavers themselves invest their own money for starting their unit, whereas in a very few cases, they have taken loan from mahajan and sometimes from bank. During last one year, average turnover from the manufacturing unit ranges between Rs. 600-24,000 mostly sale basis. In all of the cases, turnover is by cash.

Market Prospect: It was revealed from the survey that there is steady internal market as well as good export prospects in case of Baluchari Saree.

GAP ANALYSIS

This section projects brief insight of gap analysis of manufacturing of Baluchari Saree taken up by T&CG/SHG of Bishnupur Municipality.

45.45% of the surveyed T&CG/SHG members, who are involved in Baluchari Saree weaving, confess that one of the major problems in manufacturing the product is lack of enough fund, though 18.18% lament that lack of improved technology is also another problem, some others also mentioned about lack of government support, lack of availability of superior quality raw material and lack of adequate space.

Production Technology and Equipment: More detailed analysis on the gaps existing in weaving Baluchari Saree revealed that there is deficiency of fund. Weavers also face obstacles in getting proper market. There is also deficiency of skill. Manufacturers suffer from poor production process. Furthermore, there is deficiency of procurement of raw materials. It was revealed from the survey that they don't have any arrangement of availing of quality control laboratory facility. To overcome these obstacles, easy availability of fund could be suggested. Even, easy access to market is highly appreciated and some skill upgradation training could be suggested. Moreover, updated process and smooth procurement channel could be suggested. It was also revealed that in Bishnupur, T&CG/SHG members, who are involved in Baluchari Saree weaving, are not facing any problem due to the lack of skilled manpower. It was further revealed that T&CG/SHG members are not facing any problem due to the lack of knowledge regarding improved product design. It may also be due to their ignorance of knowledge about the product re-positioning strategies that may have multiplier effect in acceptance of even low and middle-income group of customers.

Product Service and Delivery: In majority (63.64%) of cases, no promotional campaign like trade fair, exhibition, etc. has been organized. Yet, most of them felt that such kind of campaign would encourage them to manufacture more innovative products and as well as boost up their sale.

Packaging: In most of the cases weavers are not using any special type of packaging for their products. It may be due to the fact due to being totally ignorant that how attractive packaging material can promote the product in market and provoke the customer to be accepted.

Marketing and Promotion: It was also explored from the survey that in Bishnupur T&CG/SHG members, who are involved in Baluchari Saree weaving, have not taken any step to promote their product in market. Even they don't have any linkage/tie-up for marketing their product. Even, 36.36% of the surveyed Baluchari Saree manufacturers feel that they are not getting proper channel to promote their product; 36.36% feel that they are not meeting their profit target as expected. A few feel that they are also facing problems due to distributional issues as well as poor logistic facilities.

Increase in Market Demand and Potential: All of the T&CG/ SHG members in Bishnupur, who are involved in Baluchari Saree weaving, need to concentrate more on government support for the purpose of increasing current internal demand. Further, they feel that some upgradation is very much needed for their manufacturing unit. According to the opinion of most of the manufacturers, if they could get sufficient fund, they will be able to upgrade their unit. 18.18% desire to concentrate on having necessary guidance. 45.45% want to get necessary government support. 36.36% wants to avail technical training. A few (45.45%) want to avail superior quality raw-material. Some desire to have improved technology/process, marketing/skill upgradation training, new insight regarding product design, strong distributional channel, effective promotional campaign, etc. 72.73% feel that customers need value added product. To meet the need of the customers, most of the T&CG/SHG members feel that they need to concentrate more on availability of product quality, product design, improved technology and superior quality raw material.

Financial Issues: All of the manufacturers of Baluchari Saree confess that they have not taken any financial training till now. But most of the manufacturers think that a further training is required to upgrade their economic condition.

SWOT ANALYSIS

Each business needs to evaluate its internal strengths and weaknesses (Kotler, Keller and Jha, 2007, p. 49). Business does not have to correct all its weaknesses, nor should it gloat about all its strengths. Here the big question is: whether the business should limit itself to those opportunities where it possesses the required strengths or whether it should consider opportunities that mean it might have to acquire or develop certain strengths (Stalk, Evans and Shulman, 1992). On the other side, a business unit has to monitor key macroenvironment forces and significant microenvironment actors that affect its ability to earn profits. A major purpose of external environmental scanning is to discern new opportunities (Kotler, 1999). Further, some developments in the external environment represent threats. An environmental threat is a challenge posed by an unfavourable trend or development that would lead, in the absence of defensive marketing action, to lower sales or profit. Therefore, business should monitor the status of internal and external marketing environment (SWOT analysis). Table 4 presents the overall evaluation of strengths, weaknesses, opportunities and threats of manufacturing of Baluchari Saree in Bishnupur.

TABLE 5
A SWOT Analysis of the Baluchari Industry of Bishnupur

Strength	**Weakness**
Land	Lack of entrepreneurship
Human resources	Agro-climatic condition
Connectivity	Educational and research organization
People's participation in development	Illiteracy
Opportunity	**Threat**
Plantation and horticulture	Drought
Sericulture development	Lack of awarer.ess of changes
Women's empowerment and strong presence of T&CG/SHG	in technology and market trend

IDENTIFICATION OF PROBLEMS

Though Baluchari Saree is one of the most expensive and exclusive textiles of India, which contributes a huge proportion to the country's silk production and export, the industry faces many problems:

- *Middlemen*: Middlemen grab the better part of the profit leaving the producers and weavers in poverty. Since they help the producers to supply to the city stores, they charge a high commission. They also bring in tourists especially foreigners and charge them exorbitantly to increase their profit margins.
- *High cost of raw materials*: Most of the weavers are poor and face the problem of capital, a factor that gives inroad to the middlemen who take a major share of the profit.
- *Traditional Method of Production*: Product diversification in the form of design and variation in colour shades is a need of the hour for the Baluchari.
- *Outdated design and Non-standardization*: Of late, the market of Baluchari has started declining due to repetition of same design and non-standardization of colour.
- *Cost of Design*: One design sometimes costs as high as Rs. 40,000.
- *Lack of advertisements and promotions by the producer*: Producers of Baluchari Saree depend too much on the middlemen for the marketing of the products who keep on using the method of commission-earning by bringing in customers who are tourists and foreigners to the local producers. It is the middlemen who negotiate the price where the producer is but a dumb spectator.
- *Lack of mass awareness*: There is also no mass awareness of the producers, as they do not advertise or promote their products.
- *Poor access of producers to market*: Even if the customers want to go to the producers directly they cannot, since producers could not be easily located

or identified or accessed. Sometimes, a producer advertises his shop on the wall of the high school of the Bishnupur town.

DEVELOPMENT OF SUSTAINABLE MARKETING STRATEGY

The textile market in India and abroad is huge and the superior quality of silk that the craftsmen and weavers in West Bengal produce is any designer's dream. But still these works of art do not get the value of high-fashion, which is entirely due to promotion failure on the part of the Government as well as the existent malpractices of the middlemen. Still the Baluchari Saree has created a niche for themselves in the metro cities. But further innovation can make it more popular.

To tackle such threats and provide a stable market for the silk weavers, the National Handloom Development Corporation (NHDC) Limited, under the aegis of Development Commissioner for Handlooms (DCH), has designed a number of schemes for handloom weavers. It also provides assistance in the marketing of handloom products. The various schemes implemented by the Office of DCH address the needs of weavers who constitute the disadvantaged social strata and occupational groups, which are at the bottom of the economic hierarchy. Concerted efforts are being made through the schemes and programmes to enhance production, productivity, and efficiency of this sector and enhance the income and socio-economic status of the weavers by upgrading their skills and providing infrastructural support and essential inputs. It is the fact that the manufacturers are not expert at marketing and the marketers are not well-versed with manufacturing and mostly, the weavers are producing age-old designs, which may not be relevant for the market. It is, therefore, the responsibility of the government to bring these two face to face.

The study has here attempted to explore a sustainable marketing strategy for promoting and developing the Baluchari industry. The first phase, *choosing the value*, represents the "homework" marketing must do before any product exists (Porter, 1985; Hiebeler, Kelly and Ketteman, 1998; Keller and Lehmann, 2003). Marketer must segment the market, select the appropriate market target, and develop the offering's value positioning (Kotler, Keller and Jha, 2007, p. 35). The formula "segmentation, targeting, positioning (STP)" is the essence of strategic marketing. Once the business unit has chosen the value, the second phase is *providing the value.* Marketing must determine specific product features, prices, and distribution. The task in the third phase is *communicating the value* by utilizing the sales force, sales promotion, advertising, and other communication tools to announce and promote the product.

The subsequent section here presents how the STP strategy can be applied to rejuvenate the Baluchari industry in Bishnupur.

Segmentation: The Baluchari Sarees are expensive and not everyone can afford it. The price range starts from Rs. 4,000 and it can range to a maximum of Rs. 20,000. The sareees have a traditional appeal, hence preferred by married or middle-aged women (income range of above Rs. 30,000 and above). Hence in order to make it affordable, the quality shouldn't be compromised. Since it has buyers mostly in the cities as well as abroad it should segment its market into the following:

Segment/Tier	*Particulars*
Metro cities	Kolkata, Mumbai, Delhi, Chennai, Hyderabad, Bangalore, etc.
Second-tier cities	Guwahati, Pune, Allahabad, Ahmedabad, etc.
Abroad	especially Bengali-dominated places like New York, London, Chicago, etc.

TARGETING

The target customers for these expensive ṣarees are upper-middle class Indians especially Bengalis and tourists who love wearing traditional sarees. The age-group should be 30-65 years, as because the sarees are too traditional and heavily woven. Young women do not feel comfortable in such sarees and do not consider it to be fashionable. But in order to attract younger customers, the product needs to be diversified.

For example, the colour palette should change from rich to pastel shades, the designs should change from mythological to contemporary. The silks should also be available in salwar suit pieces or scarves that might suit their youthful image, yet add a touch of traditionality. Manufacturers are now planning to use the complicated baluchari motif onto salwar kameezes, skirts, scarves and churidars, apart from than sarees. This will ensure a wider market and acquaint the younger generation with the skills and finery of baluchari. The traditional motifs are woven around scenes from the Ramayan, Mahabharata and the Puranas. These may be replaced by more contemporary designs. "The state government is trying to revive this very intricate and beautiful art forms in order to preserve this national heritage," says Cottage and Small Scale Industries' Minister.

The marketers should also target the men by innovating their products. The silks can also be stitched into gents' kurtas, sherwanis or draped as dhotis. These things could be done by designers, but a lot of them have exploited this option. Only exception has been Bibi Russell from Bangladesh who has worked wonders with handloom materials and the second is Sharbari Dutta from Kolkata, who has designed traditional clothes for men using silks like Baluchari.

Positioning: Since the Baluchari Sarees are really expensive, exclusive as well as high-end products, the marketers should position it exclusively. The sarees can very well be sold in designer malls and boutiques. The sarees should not only be treated as 11 yards weave, but the buyers should be made aware of the different ways in which they can use the product, for example, as the interior decoration stuffs—like, pillow and cushion covers, wall hangings, etc. The marketers need to shed-off the traditional image of this weave and innovate it to suit the needs of a wide range of customers.

The subsequent section explores how the value of the Baluchari Saree can be communicated through advertising and promotion.

Advertising and promotion: It is the fact that days of the word-of-mouth publicity and hand bills for promoting a product are gone. The Baluchari Saree producers have heavily depended on the retailers in the city, who sell the sarees, and the guides and middlemen in the small towns and villages to bring in tourists. This form of promotion has resulted in loss for them. They should adopt the new-age media to promote and display their products. Since innovation is the watchword for today's world, the producers should maintain the tradition with innovation as well as adaptability for different types of buyers.

Since the Indian apparel or handloom industry is going the 'designer way', the Baluchari Saree manufacturers should attract the attention of designers both national as well international to showcase their creations on a popular platform. Fashion shows, trade-fairs, exhibitions, interactive workshops, tourism can popularize this traditional saree and attract customers. Nowadays, fashion designers source a lot of traditional fabrics for films, which instantly becomes a craze among the common masses. Association with such designers can help the traditional Baluchari Saree to attract attention of the masses. Films like 'Parineeta', Devdas', etc. have showcased Baluchari Sarees as part of the heroines wardrobe on screen. A recent movie called 'Morning Walk' starring Sharmila Tagore has shown the elegant actress wearing traditional Bengali textile like 'tant' as well as Baluchari. The producers of Baluchari can promote their range of sarees for middle-aged women, as Sharmila Tagore is a style-icon for aristocratic middle-aged women. Even, promotions through innovations and retailing of the innovations like wall hangings, pillow and cushion covers, sofa-covers, gift items, etc. can provoke the mass.

Recently a noble initiative was taken by Behala Club, a city cultural club located in the suburbs of Kolkata to promote the traditional Baluchari Saree—The Club in their annual Durga Puja of 2008 had taken up the theme of the Baluchari Sarees to promote the industry as well as the weavers who create such masterpieces but live in utter poverty. They decorated the 'pandal' with Baluchari Sarees and wall hangings and decorated the deity in a typical traditional saree.

The famed Baluchari silk saree of West Bengal is in the list of items for which the government will be seeking protection under the Geographical Indication (GI) Protection Act. According to K. Rangrajan, Head of the Indian Institute of

Foreign Trade (IIFT), the Baluchari Saree occupies the top priority among the list of products eligible for GI Protection. There are at present 82 registered GI products in India, out of which only one belongs to West Bengal-Darjeeling tea. Darjeeling tea is famed the world over for its unique aroma and flavour and the first product to get protection under the GI Act, which protects the uniqueness and the nature of a product that owes its origin and heritage to a particular geographical location. Similarly, the Baluchari Saree of West Bengal has enormous potential as products that could be registered under the GI protection Act.

CONCLUSION

The traditional textiles of West Bengal need an image make-over and they could achieve it only through visibility and publicity. The producers need to be more aware of the recent trends and fashions and also the business culture. They need to do away with the middlemen and take more initiative in marketing and advertising their products. They should associate themselves with fashion houses or designers for better visibility. The producers need to pay the weavers more in order to stop them from changing profession. Government should show more responsibility towards the textile industry. Institutional mechanism for delivery should be strengthened by capacity building through appropriate training of all stakeholders and channelising/linking all the schemes of Central and the State aimed at improving socio-economic condition of the urban poor through a nodal body which could be the Department of Municipal Affairs and Urban Development. The role of banks in providing loans to T&CG/SHG leaves much to be desired.

Moreover, Bishnupur—Bankura has vast tourism potential not only at domestic level, but also at International scale. It has great potential for promotion of heritage tourism on an International scale, if a proper tourism package with upgraded infrastructure could be worked out in conjunction with tourism Department and the Chairmen of these two Municipalities with a view to providing a ready market at the doorsteps for Baluchari micro-enterprises. Even, it has been suggested that as the Baluchari Saree of West Bengal has enormous potential, it could be registered under the GI protection Act.

REFERENCES

Hiebeler, R., Kelly, Thomas, B. and Ketteman, C. (1998), *Best Practices: Building Your Business with Customer-Focused Solutions,* New York: Simon and Schuster.

Keller, Kevin L. and Lehmann, Don (2003), "How do Brands Create Value", *Marketing Management,* May/June, pp. 27-31.

Kotler, Philip (1999), *Kotler on Marketing,* New York: The Free Press.

Kotler, P., Keller, K.L., Koshy, A. and Jha, M. (2007), *Marketing Management—A South Asian Perspective,* 12th ed., New Delhi: Pearson Education.

Porter, Michael, E. (1985), *Competitive Advantage: Creating and Sustaining Superior Performance,* New York, The Free Press.

Stalk, George; Evans, Philip and Shulman, Lawrence E. (1992), "Competing Capabilities: The New Rules of Corporate Strategy", *Harvard Business Review,* March-April, pp. 57-69.

WEBSITE REFERENCES

http://www.thaindian.com/newsportal/india-news/famous-bankura-horse-of-west-bengal-may-become-history_10046858.html

(accessed on August, 2009).

www.bankura.org (accessed on August, 2009).

6

Consumer Perception Towards SMS Advertisements

N. Anitha and C. Selvaraj

ABSTRACT

It is a global fact that Mobile phones have made a revolutionary contribution in fulfilling the anywhere and anytime connectivity marketers. Predominant developments in information and communication technologies are offering new marketing channels to marketers. The high penetration rate of mobile phones has resulted in the increasing use of handset devices to deliver advertisements for products and services. Short Messaging Service (SMS) in particular, has been very successful across nations. The use of Short Messaging Service to access customers through their handset devices is gaining popularity, making the mobile phone the ultimate medium for one-to-one marketing. More than 100 billion SMS messages were sent worldwide in a single year. The present research investigates consumer's attitude towards SMS advertising through mobile phones.

Key Words : Revolutionary contribution, Mobile Phone Medium, Mobile Marketing, Short Messaging Services.

SMS ADVERTISEMENTS

Attitude of people towards advertising have been a focus of attention for long time. Although some earlier literature reported positive attitudes toward advertising, most of researchers have found that consumers generally have negative attitudes toward ads.

SMS has become a technological buzzword in transmitting B2C messages to such wireless devices as mobile phones. Many brands and media companies include text message numbers in their advertisements to enable interested consumers to obtain more information. This mode of advertising takes advantage of valuable channels of wireless communication to enhance customer relationships, and to carry out direct marketing and promotional activities. Moreover, MMS has provided more visual and active messages. Marketers can benefit from the use of photos, music, logos and animation, videos by advertising to consumer's mobile phones. SMS and MMS advertising are expected to achieve higher response rates than that of e-mail or television, because all advertisements can be sent personally.

Location-based advertising is regarded as one of the most interesting opportunities mobile commerce has to offer. Because of its impact on the perceived informational utility of the location-aware advertisement. By providing interactivity, the advertiser attempts to increase viewer involvement by creating a two-way communication in real time, instead of the usual one-way connection in media advertising.

Mobile marketing via SMS has expanded rapidly in Europe and Asia as a new channel to reach the consumer. SMS initially received negative media coverage in many parts of Europe for being a new form of spam, as some advertisers purchased lists and sent unsolicited content to consumer's phones. However, as guidelines are put in place by the mobile operators, SMS has become the most popular branch of the Mobile Marketing. Mobile advertising and Internet advertising have many features in common. Both are emerging Medias used to deliver digital texts, images, and voices with interactive, immediate, personalized, and responsive capabilities. Mobile advertising relaxes the mobility constraint associated with fixed-line Internet access. One may expect mobile advertising to be more favorable to consumers for location-sensitive and time-critical events.

LITERATURE REVIEW

The Mobile Marketing Alliance defines mobile marketing as "the use of the mobile medium as a communications and entertainment channel between a brand and an end-user. Mobile marketing is the only personal channel enabling spontaneous, direct, interactive and/or targeted communications, any time, any place".

Mobile marketing is the marketing of products and services through the use of a mobile communication channel. It is a personal, time and location sensitive channel, which can reach its intended audience instantaneously with direct, interactive, or targeted communication. Mobile marketing should always be used with the utmost care, so as not to compromise the integrity of the receivers of these messages. It is potentially a great new marketing tool, but it must always be integrated with other channels

Attitude is an important concept in research on marketing and information systems. SMS campaigns are proliferating around the world. In an empirical study of the state of interactive marketing in five large developed markets (United States, Japan, Germany, UK, and France) and two key emerging markets (China and Brazil). Barwise and Farley (2005) found that 19% of the participant firms were already using text messaging either as a direct response or as a "push" channel. Nevertheless, the academic literature is short of empirical studies investigating the importance of the factors that determine SMS advertising effectiveness.

ATTITUDE OF CONSUMERS TOWARDS SMS ADVERTISEMENTS

Fishbein defined an attitude as "a learned predisposition of human beings". Based on this predisposition, "an individual would respond to an object (or an idea) or a number of things (or opinions)". Kotler stated, "an attitude is a person's enduring favorable or unfavorable evaluations, emotional feelings, and action tendencies toward some object or idea". Since researchers have been studying the subject for a very long time, there is a large body of literature dealing with consumer attitudes toward advertising in general and toward advertising on the Internet.

Consumer attitudes toward advertising in general have long been found to be negative. Zanot, for instance, found that attitudes toward advertising became increasingly negative after the 1970s.

Bauer and Greyser reported that more people held favorable attitudes toward advertising than unfavorable attitudes. The trend changed after 1970. Harris and Associates, for example, found that a majority of respondents considered TV advertising to be seriously misleading. Later studies have provided more evidence of the unfavorable public attitude toward advertising.

Perceived clutter, hindered search, and disruption were related to less favorable attitudes and greater ad avoidance. These effects varied in different media. Bogart also reported the differences in the way different media affects consumer attitudes. Television ads often have a higher degree of irritation than radio ads, which are less irritating because radio programs usually serve as background music.

Internet, some surveys report that respondents viewed Internet advertising as more informative and trustworthy than a demographically similar sample found in general advertising.

Schlosser and colleagues reported that attitudes toward Internet advertising are affected by enjoyment, informativeness, and the ad's utility for making behavioral (purchasing) decisions.

Permission-based advertising differs from traditional irritative advertising in that messages about specific products, services, or content are sent only to individuals who have explicitly indicated their willingness to receive the message. Consumers often impatiently ignore the message when interrupted by an advertisement.

Incentive-based advertising provides specific financial rewards to individuals who agree to receive promotions and campaigns. For example, mobile phone companies may reward customers with free connection time for listening to voice advertisements. Both permission-based and incentive-based advertising mechanisms are feasible for mobile advertising because the wireless technology makes it possible to identify individual users. Consumer attitudes toward mobile advertising are generally negative, but are positive if permission is obtained, and entertainment is the most important attribute affecting consumer attitudes toward mobile advertising.

Mobile Advertising: A key component of mobile marketing communication is advertising, either in a push or pull mode. After obtaining the consumers permission, push advertising sends relevant but not explicitly requested text and video messages. Quah and Lim (2002) argue that the push model will dominate mobile advertising since it saves consumers. Time and money compared to browsing content. SMS and MMS messages are main mobile advertising systems.

Individuals are interested in deriving some monetary benefit from direct marketing programs (Milne and Gordon, 1993). In a Nokia-sponsored survey, conducted by HPI Research Group, almost nine out of ten participants (86%) agreed that there should be a trade-off for accepting advertisements on their mobile devices (Pastore, 2002). Prior research proposes that price discounts are particularly effective in inducing effects, such as purchase acceleration and product trial (Shi, Cheung, and Prendergast 2005).

The study of attitude toward advertising in general may be especially significant because it influences attitudes toward a specific ad, an important antecedent of brand attitudes (e.g., Alwitt and Prabhaker, 1992; Mackenzie and Lutz, 1989). Tsang, Ho, and Liang (2004) also found that consumers have generally negative attitudes toward mobile advertising unless they have specifically consented to receive the advertising messages. Thus, it is possible that attitudes toward specific mobile advertisements are influenced by attitudes toward advertising via cellular phones in general.

Research → Analysis → Discussion

To find out the attitude of mobile users towards SMS advertising, 150 samples have been selected for data collection. Out of 150, only 128 have given the proper reply. Hence 128 respondent's data is utilized for further analysis. Convenient sampling technique is used for data collection. The research is restricted only to Chennai city and mobile users.

- 30% of respondents accepted that the SMS advertisements are less informative to them. 50% do not have clear idea over that. It shows that the SMS advertisements are yet to reach the mobile users. Only 20% disagreed that the transmitted SMS advertisements are informative to them.
- 53% of respondents have the opinion that the SMS advertisements are not suitable for their personal needs and only 30% only disagreed with that. Still the advertisements have to be personalized to the mobile users.
- 40% of respondents agreed that the advertisements through SMS are relayed on time. It shows that people do not like the advertisements through SMS during their busy hours.
- 40% of respondents agreed that too much of mobile SMS ads create confusion to them. Only 13% disagreed with it.

FIG. 1
Suitability of SMS Advertisements

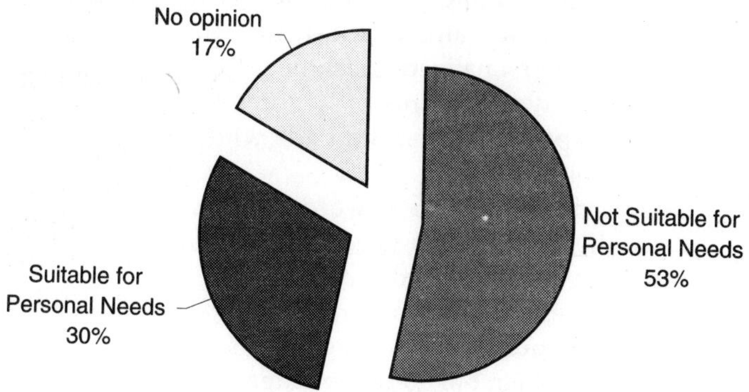

FIG. 2
Confusion Created by SMS Advertisements

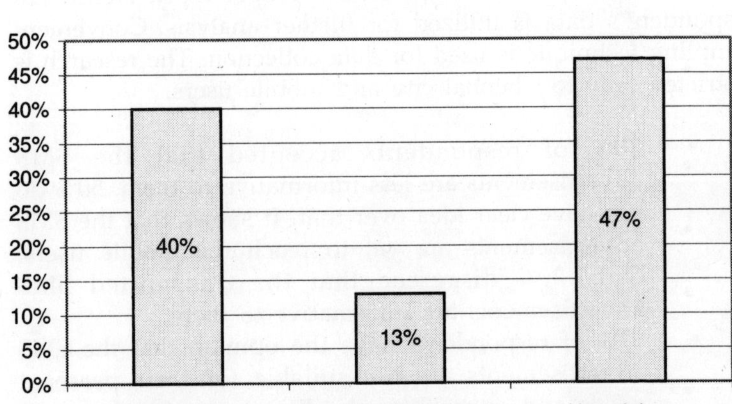

- 50% of respondents agreed that the sms ads create lot of disturbance during their work. The marketers have to take into consideration this particular point.
- Most of the respondents felt that it is time-consuming process to go through the sms ads. It shows that people are yet to acknowledge the sms advertisements.
- Only 37% of the respondents agreed that the SMS ads are helping them to recall the brands of product or services.
- 47% agreed stating the SMS ads create the sense of Loss of Privacy among the mobile users. Since the mobile is personalized instrument, people do not like the sms advertisements.
- 43% accepted that that SMS ads with text message is acceptable to them.
- People do not like to forward a message or ads, if it costs them. There is a need of some kind of incentive for them to forward the message.
- 47% of respondents are ready to receive the SMS advertisements, provided the service provider discounts their bill to some extent.

- People are ready to receive message like traffic update, even though they are in travel or work. It shows that the SMS ads must be useful to the individual.
- People do not like social messages during working hours. 33% of respondents agree to this. 40% people do not have any idea on this concern.
- Most of the respondents are in the age group of 20-30.48% of respondents belong to this age group.
- 32% of respondents are employed people. 25% are into their own business and 16% are students.
- Most of the respondents are having the family income more that Rs. 15,000 per month. 60% of the respondents belong to this category.
- 69% of the respondents are using entertainment type of mobile phones. It shows that people giving much important to the entertainment aspect in mobile also. Only 6% are having the business type of mobile phone like Blackberry, i-mate, HTC, etc.
- 63% of respondents are spending more than Rs. 500 for their mobile phone in a month and 7% spend below Rs. 300.
- 55% of mobile users regularly download the caller tunes. 47% downloads wallpapers/themes and 35% Ringtones. If the service providers give discounts/freebies on this category then it is easy for them to send sms advertisements.

CONCLUSION

SMS advertisements are yet to make inroads in India. Still people are not matured enough or not having sufficient knowledge to make use of the SMS ads. Most of the respondents feel that the advertisements received through sms are not suitable to them and creating lots of disturbances. Entertainment-oriented mobiles are largely attracted by our respondents. If the service providers sponsor freebies like entertainment incentive to the customers, then SMS advertisements will gain some momentum in India. Consumer's expenditure on mobile phone is also very low.

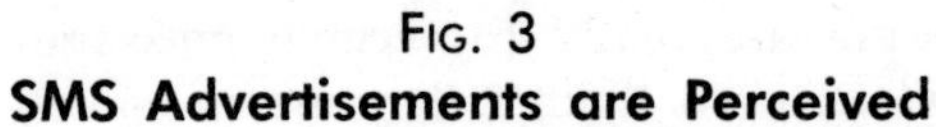
FIG. 3
SMS Advertisements are Perceived

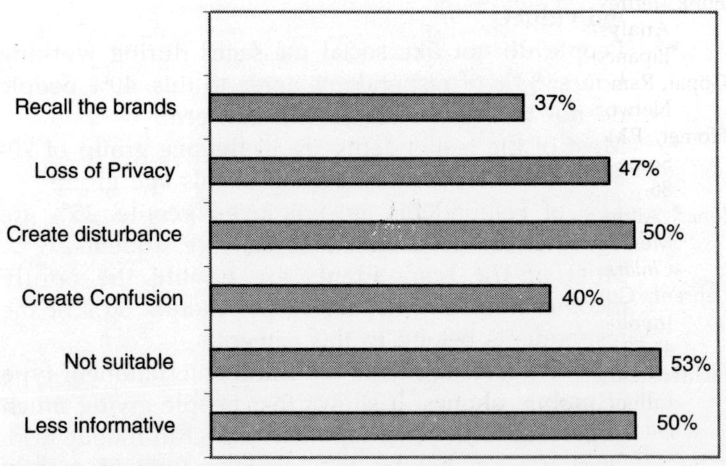

SMS ads are missing with audio and video features. It is also a major problem for the marketers. Still people are giving much importance to television ads. Creating awareness and lot of incentives to the users will owe success to the SMS advertisements strategies in India.

REFERENCES

Journals, Newspapers and Websites

Barnes, Stuart J. (2002a), "Wireless Digital Advertising: Nature and Implications", *International Journal of Advertising*, 21(3), 399-420.

Barwise, Patrick (2001), "TV, PC, or Mobile? Future Media for Consumer e-Commerce", *Business Strategy Review*, 12(1), 35-42.

Chen, Shih-Fen S., Kent B. Monroe, Yung-Chien Lou (1998), "The Effects of Framing Price Promotion Messages on Consumers' Perceptions and Purchase Intentions", *Journal of Retailing*, 74(3), 353-72.

Choi, Sejung Marina, and Nora, J. Rifon (2002), "Antecedents and Consequences of Web Advertising Credibility: A Study of Consumer Response to Banner Advertisements", *Journal of Interactive Advertising*, 3(1) (accessed on 3/15/2006).

Dahlen, Micael (2001), "Banner Advertisements through a New Lens", *Journal of Advertising Research*, 41(4), 23-30.

Danaher, Peter J. and Guy, W. Mullarkey (2003), "Factors Affecting Online Advertising Recall: A Study of Students", *Journal of Advertising Research*, 43(3), 252-67.

Funk, Jeffrey L. (2005), "The Future of the Mobile Phone Internet: An Analysis of Technological Trajectories and Lead Users in the Japanese Market", *Technology in Society*, 27(1), 69-83.

Gopal, Ram D. and Arvind, K. Tripathi (2006), "Advertising via Wireless Networks", *International Journal of Mobile Communications*, 4(1), 2-16.

Homer, P.M. (1990), "The Mediating Role of Attitude toward the Ad: Some Additional Evidence", *Journal of Marketing Research*, 27(1), 78-86.

Jones, Andrew (2002), "Wireless Marketing: The Linking Value of Text Messaging", *International Journal of Advertising and Marketing to Children*, 3(2), 39-44.

Laurent, Gilles and Jean-Noël Kapferer (1985), "Measuring Consumer Involvement Profiles", *Journal of Marketing Research*, 12 (February), 41-53.

Lichtenstein, Donald R. and William, O. Bearden (1989), "Contextual Influences on Perceptions of Merchant-supplied Reference Prices", *Journal of Consumer Research*, 16(1), 55-66.

Liu, Scott S. and Patricia, A. Stout (1987), "Effects of Message Modality and Appeal on Advertising Acceptance", *Psychology and Marketing*, 4(3), 167-87.

Lohtia, Ritu, Naveen Donthu, and Edmund, K. Hershberger (2003), "The Impact of Content and Design Elements on Banner Advertising Click-through Rates", *Journal of Advertising Research*, 43(4), 410-18.

Long, Ju, Andrew B. Whinston, and Kerem Tomak (2002), "Calling All Customers", Marketing Research, 14(3), 28-35.

Malhotra, Naresh K. (2005), "Attitude and Affect: New Frontiers of Research in the 21st Century", *Journal of Business Research*, 58(4), 477-82.

Pastore, Michael (2002) "Incentives Still Key to Mobile Advertising" http://www.clickz.com/stats/sectors/wireless/article.php/10094_965061 (accessed on 05/20/2006).

Petty, Richard E. and John T. Cacioppo (1986), Communication and Persuasion: Central and Peripheral Routes to Attitude Change, New York: Springer-Verlag.

Shavitt, Sharon (1990), "The Role of Attitude Objects in Attitude Functions", *Journal of Experimental Social Psychology*, 26 (March), 124-48.

Stewart, David W. and Scott Koslow (1989), "Executional Factors and Advertising Effectiveness: A Replication", *Journal of Advertising*, 18(3), 21-32.

Tsang, Melody M., Shu-Chun Ho, and Ting-Peng Liang (2004), "Consumer Attitudes toward Mobile Advertising: An Empirical Study", *International Journal of Electronic Commerce*, 8(3), 65-78.

APPENDIX

CONSUMER PERCEPTION TOWARDS SMS ADVERTISEMENTS

1. What is your opinion on Advertisements received through mobile phones?
   - Less informative on product and services to me
     i. Agree ii. Neither Agree nor Disagree iii. Disagree
   - Not suitable for my personal needs
     i. Agree ii. Neither Agree nor Disagree iii. Disagree
   - The messages are relayed at the wrong time
     i. Agree ii. Neither Agree nor Disagree iii. Disagree
   - It creates confusion as a result of too many advertisements
     i. Agree ii. Neither Agree nor Disagree iii. Disagree
   - It is Causing disturbance at work
     i. Agree ii. Neither Agree nor Disagree iii. Disagree
   - I find it time consuming to go through advertisements
     i. Agree ii. Neither Agree nor Disagree iii. Disagree
   - It is useful for me to recall of brands
     i. Agree ii. Neither Agree nor Disagree iii. Disagree
   - SMS advertisements are creating the feeling of "Loss of privacy"
     i. Agree ii. Neither Agree nor Disagree iii. Disagree
2. How for you agree with the following statements?
   - Receiving an advertising message within a text message would be acceptable
     i. Agree ii. Neither Agree nor Disagree iii. Disagree
   - I would send a text message including a 1 line advertising message providing I could send it for free
     i. Agree ii. Neither Agree nor Disagree iii. Disagree
   - I would agree to receive advertising text messages in exchange for discount phone call
     i. Agree ii. Neither Agree nor Disagree iii. Disagree
   - I would forward a text message 'voucher' to my friends, allowing them a discount on specific goods or services

i. Agree ii. Neither Agree nor Disagree iii. Disagree

- It would be acceptable to receive a text message service (e.g. local traffic update) while at work or travel

  i. Agree ii. Neither Agree nor Disagree iii. Disagree
- I would like to keep work text messages limited to work hours, and social text messages for other times

  i. Agree ii. Neither Agree nor Disagree iii. Disagree

3. Personal Details

   i. Age:
   ?15-20, ? 20-25, ?25-30, ?30-35, ?35-40, ?40-45, ?45-50, ?50 and above

   ii. Occupation:
   ?Business ? Employed ?Students ?Others

   iii. Monthly Income:
   ?Less than 5000 Rs. ?5000-10000 ?10000-15000 ?15000-20000 ?20000 and above

   iv. Type of Mobile Phone, you have:
   ?Basic Phone ?Entertainment Phone (FM, MP3, Camera etc.) ?Business Phone

   v. Approximate Expenses on monthly expenses:
   ?Less than 300, ?300-400, ?400-500, ?500-600, ?600-700, ?700-800, ?800 and above

   vi. Do you have the habit of downloading the following elements from mobile phone?
   ?Ring tones Yes/No
   ?MP3 songs Yes/No
   ?Wall Papers/Themes Yes/No
   ?Caller tunes Yes/No
   ?Browsing Yes/No

CRM
A Tool for Sustaining Competition

B. Neeraja and Arti Chandani

ABSTRACT

CRM (Customer Relationship Management) has become a buzz word in the present day business. There has been a continuous surge in the number of companies resorting to CRM as a tool for gaining competitive advantage thus to be able to sustain the stiff competition. In the present day, the companies are faced with tremendous competition, which was absent two decades ago. The companies are trying and ready to work hard in this changed scenario not only to sustain competition but also to gain superiority by using various tools. CRM has thus become a tool for gaining superiority in today's world.

CRM encompasses marketing, customer service, loyalty programs, and ongoing communications with customers, cross-channel recognition of customers—and on and on. In short, customer relationship management covers all the ways and times that a retailer interacts with a customer. "CRM is a business strategy to build loyalty and sales with one's best

customers," says Janet Murphy, president of Morristown, N.J.-based consultants Ogden Associates Inc.
CRM helps companies to hold the customer and thus bring the customer loyalty towards the company. This also helps them in earning a good name in the corporate world. It does not take place overnight; CRM is the result of the exercise carried out by the company in maintaining the database of the customer. The foundation of the CRM is the database. The role of technology or IT is of paramount importance in CRM. We can not think of CRM without technology, thus IT is the backbone for CRM.
The paper tries to highlight the importance of CRM for a business, in a highly competitive world. The paper also focuses on the ever changing role of IT in the field of CRM. The benefits and challenges being brought about. CRM is also a matter of discussion.
Key Words: CRM Model, Customer retention management, Role of IT, Customer Loyalty.

INTRODUCTION

CRM Customer Relationship Management is one of the most recent innovations in customer service today. It helps the management and customer service staffs cope with customer concerns and issues. CRM involves gathering a lot of data about the customer. The data is then used to facilitate customer service transactions by making the information needed to resolve the issue or concern readily available to those dealing with the customers. This results in more satisfied customers, a more profitable business and more resources available to the support staff. Furthermore, CRM Customer Relationship Management systems are a great help to the management in deciding on the future course of the company.

CRM is important not only for the marketing department but also for the top management as it provides the vital information about the customers which ultimately helps them in formulating the strategies for the future. CRM also helps in understanding as to what the company should do, if there is dissatisfaction among the customers. The top management is in the continuous need of the information about CRM so that they can formulate the strategies o stay ahead in the competition.

The NRF survey reveals that 54% of retail companies have already implemented at least one CRM application; another 39% expect to do so within two years. And many see true payback possible: 72% said they view CRM as a way to extend their business and generate revenue. Among the biggest uses that retailers plan to put CRM to be analyzing and understanding customers better, tracking results of marketing efforts and keeping track of customer contacts.

The NRF survey is backed up by a survey that Jupiter Research released in February predicting that CRM spending by retailers will nearly double from $ 1.7 billion in 2001 to $ 3.2 billion in 2006. Jupiter reported that 26% of businesses will spend $ 500,000 or more on customer relationship management over the next two years. Many also view CRM as more important than other technology initiatives; 23% are planning to spend $ 500,000 in web content management and 19% on supply chain efforts.

These facts speak for itself about the growing importance of CRM. In the times to come, CRM will be become just like a marketing tool such as advertising, sales promotion. As any company can't stay in the competitive world without advertising and sales promotion, the same way in the next decade, all the companies will have CRM as one of their marketing strategy. The only thing which will make the difference is as to how effective and efficiently the company can use its CRM to yield the desired results.

Of course, any good businessman has always understood the importance of developing and nurturing strong equations with the customers. This is as true of large conglomerates such as the Detroit auto majors and the Tatas as it is of a small neighborhoods and grocer who spends the time of day chatting up the families in the locality.

One may encounter a situation where one visits a regular grocery shop and the show owner orders his attender to keep the merchandise in the car number so and so. Similarly, if you visit a small shop and the shopkeeper gives you coke when you ask for cold drink (as he knows that you drink only coke, not Pepsi nor thumps up). These are just few of the examples of CRM exhibited by the next shop. We don't use word CRM for these activities as these don't maintain a proper record of the customers but definitely all these are part of CRM. The similar activities are performed by big companies but in more systematic and professional manner.

CRM has become as one of the important business strategy for the long-term survival and success of the any organization. This need has been rightly understood by the organization and they are getting ready to brace the CRM.

IMPORTANCE AND FUNCTIONS OF CRM

There is no denial that the customer still holds the position of a king. The customer not only wants that the goods desired by him but also the manner in which he wants them to reach him. CRM is aimed to bring value for the customer as the same time helps in building the image for the company. The NRF survey says 57% of retailers expect to spend more on CRM this year than last and 60% expect further increases next year. Those figures underscore how CRM is spreading throughout retailing.

Functions of CRM

The above diagram explains the importance of CRM for a company. The CRM is aimed at bringing the customer loyalty for the company with the help of various programmes. A company desirous of implementing the CRM program as a strategy should undertake the above steps to make it work. The company should bring about the reward program, and customer service as an important ingredient for the success of CRM. The customization of the product is also an important aspect of the CRM which delivers the product accommodating the changes required by him.

CRM can help the organization in the following ways:

1. It helps in identifying the buying pattern, thus helping a company to segment its customers in the segments such as frequent, average, low buyer. So the company can focus on the frequent buyer or customers.
2. It also helps in maximizing the per customer profits by showing how to reduce the cost of sales to the customers.
3. CRM not only helps in interacting with the existing customer but also with the prospective customers in an efficient manner.
4. It is all about understanding, creating and delivering value to the customers.
5. CRM software can help business in applying 80:20 concept, i.e. 20% of its customers brings 80% of the revenue.
6. It is also important for the company to retain its customer.
7. It helps customers as their needs are properly understood by the company and they get the product which is desired by them.
8. The company can differentiate itself in the competitive market based on the different strategies of handing and managing customers.

Key Elements of CRM

- Business vision—View the whole business where it is going.

- Competitive characteristics—What can you add as unique.
- Increase shareholder Value—remember the shareholder.
- The right sort of customers—What measures of CRM to what customer.
- Segment customers—What potential value do them give the business.

No matter how well a business grasps customer's desires and needs the way its people produce, create, offer and deliver products and services, add probably more value to the total customer experience.

Steps in Implementing CRM Programme

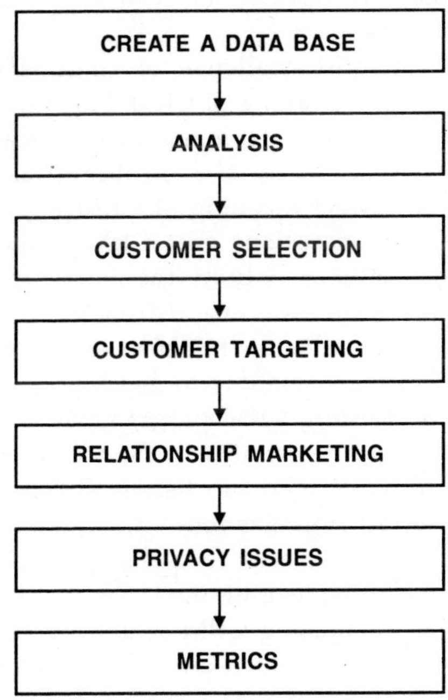

CRM is not an overnight process. The above diagram shows the steps involved in starting a CRM programme. The first step towards the CRM is creating database of the existing customer as well as of the prospective customer. IT becomes important here. After this the analysis takes part, to understand and segment the customer based on the value and well as on the volume basis. After that the customers are selected and targeted. Here the actual relationship marketing starts.

CHALLENGES OF CRM

In the present scenario, the IT brings benefit not only to one company; it is available to all in the market. When we are talking about CRM, it is not only one company is having CRM. All the players will start having CRM, if it appeals to them, as a tool for long-term strategy. Here, now the crux lies as to how effectively a company can use its CRM model to differentiate from its competitors.

First and foremost challenge of CRM is that different people have different meaning of CRM. For some people CRM means direct mails, for some it is mass customization. Here the company is poised with the problem as to how to communicate the correct meaning of CRM.

There are misconceptions that CRM is more related to technology and it is used only by the people in the top level with big business. It is very difficult to make people understand even a vendor at the street end in trying to have customer relationship in his day-to-day business.

Presently implanting CRM programmes is a costly affair and it demands huge investment in the technology as well as on the human resource who can handle CRM activities in an organization. Not all organizations can undertake this costly activity. It will take some time to spread the technology when it will become affordable and then we can see number of companies going for bracing CRM with their open arms.

One more challenge which one may encounter is that not many packages are available to handle CRM which may suit all the companies. Presently, there is a standard package available (tailor made is very expensive) which may not suit to the requirement of all the companies in different fields and industries. Therefore, this is a very big challenge for the vendor with CRM packages to serve the demands of their customers according to their requirements.

ROLE OF INFORMATION TECHNOLOGY IN CRM

We are living in the e-world where we start our day with electronics and end with electronics. The technology or popularly known as internet, has become an inseparable part of our daily life. The importance of IT or internet is much more for a company than what a person may think of. The globalization is the result of the web or information technology. Had the internet would not be there, we can't think of buying stock of company in NYSE sitting in India. Similarly, the Indian stock market would not have shaken when the result of Dubai Company having difficulty in paying its debt, came. All are the result of the information technology. In today's world there is hardly a field which has not been touched by IT. Name any field and you find involved there just bringing strength to the field. The field of CRM is also not untouched by this revolution.

The web plays a key role in implementing a customer relationship management strategy. It is an easy way to gather information about customers, often requiring only that the retailer ask the customer for information in return for discounts or notices of special sales. Because e-mail is inexpensive relative to other ways of communicating with customers, it facilitates keeping in touch. And the web is an effective way to move customer information among all the channels where sales associates might need it.

Various CRM packages are available in the market but buying the best and latest will not yield the desired result. The company has to analyze or set the objective as to what does it want to achieve with the CRM package. Once the objectives are set, then the company can go ahead for hunting the package which helps in achieving those stated objectives in the best possible manner. The CRM should ultimately help in creating and delivering value for the customer.

Beyond that, today's increasingly sophisticated and easy-to-use CRM software gives midsize businesses a wide range of ways to identify their most profitable customers. Customers will recognize benefits, too, as CRM helps businesses better understand them and determine how to reward their loyalty.

Microsoft Dynamics CRM, for instance, can record all details of customer transactions—purchases, sales and service calls, and more. You may also customize customer profiles, to allow for the deletion of irrelevant information or the addition of unique customer attributes. You can then export that data to Microsoft Office Excel or other tools for analysis. As well, you can run reports on customer revenue and costs.

CRM packages come in many sizes—from full-service offerings to small applications that solve one particular need or the other. The industry continues to grow, but sometimes suffers because managers tend to think the software can solve all the requirements. The software can only be a tool that can execute what a customer-oriented team of managers can think of offering as a service.

A typical CRM software package offers the following facilities:

1. Stores individual details of a huge number of customers.
2. Tracks transactions with these customers.
3. Records, across multiple points of interaction with the customer (call-centre, sales points, service centers), details of each fresh transaction.
4. Analyses this database to group customers based on their demographic profile, preferences, behavior patterns and profitability.
5. Flags problem areas such as a reduction in the business from a particular customer.
6. Alerts/reminds operatives of issues such as customers' birthdays.
7. Alerts or reminds operatives of more important issues such as payment reminders to enable cross-selling of services to the customer and has rigorous security mechanisms in place to ensure that such vital information cannot be misused.

FUTURE OF CRM

Until now, CRM vendors have concentrated on the United States and western world but this cant last as mergers and acquisitions continue all over the globe companies are more likely to be multinational and to serve a growing base of international customers. CRM vendors and users alike will need to account for the requirements of their international customers. Global CRM usually doesn't apply to sales-force automation or to marketing these types of CRM are normally executed locally. Instead global CRM focuses on customer support process. Business people who plan to launch CRM programmes into their business should make sure that their employees understand that by implementing CRM programmes they can actually:

- Develop information flows between customers and supply chain partners.
- Can collect and analyse customers and sales data more effective.
- Implement faster, more efficient internal processes of serving their customers.
- Allow a greater degree of collaboration to benefit everyone in the chain of service.
- Updated technology to face any crisis and unforeseen competition.
- Be in touch across the globe.

The task of getting things done is the quality of good manager. It is his job to get the full acceptance of his employees group to understand the importance of CRM implementation in the organization and make them understand that by doing so they can withstand the challenges and sustain the competition. CRM is only a tool to update them with the global environment. By using CRM strategy and the internet (IT) the business can also improve relationship with the traditional customers and simultaneously have a set of online customers. This would also increase their customer group and the sales of the company. The changing tastes and demands of customers force every company to implement CRM programmes into their business strategies. If not the company will be an odd man out in the competitive world.

CONCLUSION

CRM is one of the latest innovations in the present day of business on the global front. Few organizations have not only used CRM as a tool to create and deliver value thus satisfies the customer but also to use it in building the long-term relationship. CRM is carried out by an organization with an objective of satisfying the customer needs and expectation so that the organizations can have the same customer for their lifetime.

CRM is a blend of strategies, policies, processes undertaking by an organization to for tracking customer information related to the purchase and others. CRM includes many aspects which relate directly to one another including front office operations; direct interaction with customers, e.g. face to face meetings, phone calls, e-mail, online services, etc.

CRM involves gathering a lot of data about the customer. The data is then used to facilitate customer service transactions by making the information needed to resolve the issue or concern readily available to those dealing with the customers. This results in more satisfied customers, a more profitable business and more resources available to the support staff.

In the present time when the CRM has kicked off, it is not viable and feasible for all the organizations due to cost constraint and the availability of technology. It would not be incorrect to say that in the next 10 years it will be difficult to find a company which does not implement CRM. Implementing CRM package is a must for every company be it big or small if it has to sustain the challenges and competition in the 21st century. Without updating with CRM programmes in the company, it may be lost within a span of few years. To sustain the challenges and survive in the competitive era every company has to take a pledge to implement CRM strategy in their business.

References

Customer Relationship Management Essentials by John, W. Gosney and Thomas, P. Boehm.

Customer Relationship Management Emerging Concepts, Tools and Applications by Jagdish N. Sheth, Atul Parvatiyar and G. Shainesh.

The CRM Handbook by Jill Dyche.

http://skadiyala.blogspot.com/2008/01/crm.html

https://crmasiasolutions.wiki.zoho.com/Importance-of-CRM-in-a-Recession.html

http://www.internetretailer.com/internet/marketing-conference/35899-growing-importance-crm.html

http://www.thehindubusinessline.com/manager/2009/10/12/stories/2009101250331000.htm

ICONOCAST, January 4, 2001.

Richard, L. Oliver, *Satisfaction: A Behavioral Perspective on the Consumer,* (Boston,

MA: Irwin McGraw-Hill, (1997), and Valarie A. Zeithaml and Mary Jo Bitner, *Services Marketing,* (Boston, MA: Irwin McGraw-Hill, 2000) are good examples.

Frederick, F. Reichheld, *The Loyalty Effect,* (Cambridge, MA: Harvard Business School Press).

8

A Study on Corporate Social Responsibility

M. DEEPA

INTRODUCTION

Corporate Social Responsibility (CSR), also called corporate responsibility, corporate citizenship, and responsible business, is a concept whereby organisations consider the interests of society by taking responsibility for the impact of their activities on customers, suppliers, employees, shareholders, communities and other stakeholders, as well as the environment. This obligation is seen to extend beyond the statutory obligation to comply with legislation and sees organisations voluntarily taking further steps to improve the quality of life for employees and their families as well as for the local community and society at large.

CSR is the commitment of businesses to contribute to sustainable economic development by working with employees, their families, the local community and society at large to improve their lives in ways that are good for business and for development. It is about business giving back to society.

Corporate social responsibility (CSR) is about how businesses align their values and behaviour with the expectations and needs of stakeholders—not just customers and investors, but also employees, suppliers, communities, regulators, special interest groups and society as a whole.

Key CSR issues include governance, environmental management, stakeholder engagement, labour standards, employee and community relations, social equity, responsible sourcing and human rights.

THIS PAPER FOCUSES ON FOLLOWING OBJECTIVES

(1) Define the term Corporate social responsibility.
(2) To state Corporate Social Responsibility in India.
(3) To give suggestions on corporate Social Responsibility.

DEFINITION OF CORPORATE SOCIAL RESPONSIBILITY

Corporate social responsibility can be defined as the assumption of rights and obligations due to the economic, political, and social activity performed by organizations. In other words, this is to create and develop values, such as protection, sustainability, compromise, and acting responsibility and economically as far as the environment is concerned. This is also applicable to the people and society in general, both short and long-term, and independently of the distance (here it applies "thinking locally and globally at the same time"). The final goal has to be the increase of the humanity welfare:

- a voluntary approach that a business enterprise takes to meet or exceed stakeholder expectations by integrating social, ethical, and environmental concerns together with the usual measures of revenue, profit, and legal obligation.

- Business decision-making linked to ethical values, compliance with legal requirements, and respect for people, communities, and the environment around the world. (Aaronson, 2003)
- Open and transparent business practices that are based on ethical values and respect for employees, communities, and the environment. It is designed to deliver sustainable value to society at large, as well as to shareholders. (Aaronson, 2003)
- *European Commission* : A concept whereby companies decide voluntarily to contribute to a better society and a cleaner environment. (European Commission, 2001)

IMPORTANCE OF CSR

Social responsibility is the deliberate effort of a firm to increase its positive impact on society. Socially responsible business people behave in an ethical manner, the business environment, the organization and an individual's own moral philososphy influence ethical and unethical behaviour. Firms can encourage ethical behaviour through education and by developing and enforcing social responsibilities.

- An organization's obligation to maximize its positive impact.
- Fosters a reciprocal relationship between the corporation and community.
- Includes legal, ethical, economic, and philanthropic (discretionary) dimension.

CSR IN INDIA

While CSR has garnered significant amount of importance and momentum in the Indian corporate framework—several companies in fact, on running a successful and sustainable CSR program within their business environments.

India has been named among the top 10 Asian countries that are paying an increasing importance towards corporate social responsibility (CSR) disclosure norms, a survey says.

Indian companies are now expected to discharge their stakeholder responsibilities and societal obligations, along with their shareholder-wealth maximisation goal.

Nearly all leading corporates in India are involved in corporate social responsibility (CSR) programmes in areas like education, health, livelihood creation, skill development, and empowerment of the weaker sections of the society. Notable efforts have come from the Tata group, Infosys, Bharti Enterprises, Coca Cola India, Pepsico and ITC Welcome group, among others.

Corporate India has spread its CSR activities across 20 states and Union territories, with Maharashtra gaining the most from them. About 36 per cent of the CSR activities are concentrated in the state, followed by about 12 per cent in Gujarat, 10 per cent in Delhi and 9 per cent in Tamil Nadu.

Assocham's 'Eco Pulse Study' on CSR for 2009-10, released in June 2009, says some 300 corporate houses, on an aggregate, have identified 26 different themes for their CSR initiatives. Of these 26 schemes, community welfare tops the list, followed by education, the environment, health as well as rural development.

Of the 300 corporate houses, 74 are from the chemical sector, contributing 12 per cent to the overall CSR initiatives. As many as 62 companies in the FMCG and consumer durable sector are placed at second position with a CSR initiative contribution of 10.15 per cent.

Further, according to a survey carried out in June 2008 by TNS India (a research organisation) and the Times Foundation, over 90 per cent of all major Indian organisations surveyed were involved in CSR initiatives. The leading areas that corporations were involved in were livelihood promotion, education, health, environment, and women's empowerment.

In another study undertaken by automotive research company, TNS Automotive, India has been ranked second in global corporate social responsibility. The study was based on a public goodwill index and India received 119 points in the index against a global average of 100.

BEST CSR INTIATIVES OF CORPORATE INDIA

Reliance Industries and two Tata Group firms—Tata Motors and Tata Steel—are the country's most admired companies for their corporate social responsibility initiatives, according to a Nielsen survey.

- The Indian paints industry is making its products more environmentally friendly by opting for water-based paints and making it carcinogen-free.
- The heating, ventilation, air-conditioning and refrigeration (HVAC) industry is working to get rid of its 'global warmer' stigma through greater use of gases with zero ozone depletion potential (zero ODP).
- Sustainable Technologies and Environmental Projects Ltd (STEPS) is planning to start a project to change plastic, organic and electronic waste *into petroleum* without the usual harmful residue.
- In an effort to modernise rural health services in India, GE Healthcare now wants to focus on maternal health.
- SREI Sahaj e-Village Ltd will set-up 25,000 IT kiosks to be known as common service centres (CSC) across West Bengal, Bihar, Orissa, Assam, Uttar Pradesh and Tamil Nadu by 2010.
- ITC's e-Chaupal has been a great developmental initiative which has also added value to its own agricultural products. It comprises improving the lives of farmers and villagers.
- HDFC has started a 'village adoption' scheme to improve the investment climate in Indian villages.
- Mahindra Shubhlabh, the agricultural business arm of Mahindra & Mahindra, aims to use especially cultured seeds to improve contract-farming productivity.

RECENT TRENDS IN CSR

- Increasing awareness among consumers.

- Stakeholders expect corporate to participate in social welfare activities beyond profits.
- Government recognizes CSR initiatives of Corporates.
- Participation of college and school students in CSR activities.
- Famous personalities in Politics, Film, Sports are interested to take part in CSR activities to increase awareness among public.

ROLE OF GOVERNMENT OF INDIA ON CSR

1. December 2007—*RBI* Notification to all Banks and Financial Institutions recommending that Non Financial Reporting (NFR) be undertaken as a step towards 'Responsible Banking'.
2. June 2008—*Ministry of Corporate Affairs* has stated that it would like to encourage all companies to "disclose on their balance sheets the social work that they do".
3. September 2008—*Government of Gujarat*: mandates CSR expenditure—directs 6 PSUs to set aside 30% of their profit before tax to carry out welfare activities across Gujarat Draft industrial policy of Gujarat Government mandates CSR for industry associations and corporate houses in the state.
4. February 2009—*Petroleum Ministry* says that it will be mandatory for public sector oil companies to spend a minimum of 2% of their net profits on CSR activities.

CONCLUSION

Enlightened businesses world, to realize that responsible practices enhances good image and ensure long-term survival. Larger companies increasingly behaviour on social responsibility memoranda. Many companies believe that charity and sponsorship as CSR. Very few companies openly state about the process they follow on CSR. The amount used for CSR activities is minimum. Whereas Small and medium industries does not take part as much on CSR as they have thought only large and MNC companies should take part in Social responsibility. Despite of different aspects lot more to go on corporate social responsibility as country like India with huge population requires more participation of corporate sector in social development.

9

Demarcating the Financial Products

A Strategy during Recession

C. SELVARAJ AND MRS. R. PRIYA

ABSTRACT

Business and consumers are cutting back on discretionary spending which could mean lower response rates for products. On top of that many marketing budgets are being cut. This combination has sent many marketers into a panic. 15 September 2008 is a date that is scorched onto the brains of many executives as one of the darkest days in the history of the financial markets. On that day US investment bank Lehman Brothers failed into bankruptcy, sending investors around the world into a tailspin. On the same day Bank of America agreed to buy Merrill Lynch for $ 50 billion, and just like that two of the world's biggest finance brand disappeared into thin air.

In Asia, analyst feared the worst if American banks were collapsing and European banks were only being kept alive by government intervention. How could Asian Finance companies survive the crisis? Financial Markets executives faced a demoralizing challenge. They needed to assure their customers that the institution would not be the domino to crash, while persuading customers to keep trusting them with their money at a time in personal wealth was falling thanks to devalued stocks, rising unemployment, higher inflation, weaker export and devaluing currencies. Nearly a year since the fateful day which Asian finance brands have fared the worst?

This paper puts an attempt to understand the effects of global recession and it will also put a light on the marketing strategies employed by the financial institution to overcome the fever of recession.

INTRODUCTION

Economically, if a nation has gone through two incessant quarters of downbeat GDP growth, it is said to be in Economic Recession . . . parting out all such states and difficult explanation, what has happened in the economy is that people are tremendously indisposed to spend. Banks are indisposed to lend, consumers are tapering their folder fearing tougher days ahead, limited investment comes to stock market, businesses are cutting down on various projects—All in all, the circulation of money in economy has come down to a large extent.

The global fiscal structure plainly went into a cardiac capture after the Lehman Brothers Holdings Inc. fall down and a meltdown was hardly avoided through very belligerent policy responses. Unfortunately, the worst is ahead of us. The entire global economy will deal in a cruel and prolonged U-shaped global recession that happening a year ago.

The recession in the US market and the universal meltdown termed as Global recession have engulfed total world economy with an unstable degree of recessional impact. World over the impact has expanded and can be observed from the very fact of falling Stock market, recession in jobs accessibility and companies following cut backing in the existing available staff and cutting down of the perks and salary corrections.

India could also not escape from this mayhem. Part and partially it turned out to be a sufferer to this crisis. It suffered less of losses because of its stern economic policies. The BFSI

(Banking, financial sector, Insurance) sector has taken a hit with the financial sector getting affected in US. The rise and fall conditions in the market have to go on. But with this the economy has to follow. Business has to come out with answers. Solutions have to be determined out from the problem itself. The need of the day for the global recession is to employ strong marketing strategies for capable sectors.

GLOBAL CIRCUMSTANCES

In today's arena the most common word we come across are recession and downturn. Recession or disaster is the part of the normal cycle of business. It is sure that they will earlier or later on occur. Recessions are the result of decrease in the demand of products in the global market. Recession can also be connected with declining prices known as depression due to lack of demand of products. Again, it could be the result of inflation or a mixture of escalating prices and sluggish economic growth in the west. Recession has been defined in the marketing literature as a "process of decreasing demand for raw materials, products and services, including labor" (Shama, 1978) or as a "state in which the demand for a product is less than its former level" (Kotler, 1973).

Recession is a happening of decreasing demand for raw materials, products, and services. Technically, its beginning, progress, and ending depend on the equipped measures used by different researchers and national agencies. The worst ever financial crisis to destroy the United States since the Great Depression of 1930s, has taken a heavy charge on the world's largest economy.

IMPACT OF RECESSION

It all started in the US; the boom in the housing sector was taking the economy to a new level. A mixture of low interest rates and large inflows of overseas funds helped to create easy credit circumstances where it became quite easy for people to take home loans. As there was sufficient money to lend to probable borrowers, the loan agencies started to extend their loan disbursement reach and relaxed the loan conditions.

As a result, many people with low income and shocking credit were given housing loans in disregard to all principles of financial cautiousness. These types of loans were known as sub-prime loans as those were are not part of prime loan market. With stock markets thriving and the system redden with liquidity, many big fund investors like hedge funds and mutual funds saw sub-prime loan portfolios as good-looking investment opportunities. Hence, they bought such portfolios from the novel lenders. Major (American and European) investment banks and institutions greatly bought these loans (known as Mortgage Backed Securities, MBS) to expand their investment portfolios. Owing to heavy buying of Mortgage Backed Securities (MBS) of sub-prime loans by major American and European Banks, the problem, which was to remain within the confines of US promulgated into the word's financial markets.

In spite of efforts by the US Federal Reserve to offer some financial assistance to the besieged financial sector, it has led to the collapse of Bear Sterns, one of the world's largest investment banks and securities trading firm. Bear Sterns was bought out by JP Morgan Chase with some help from the US Federal Bank. The crisis has also seen Lehman Brothers—the fourth largest investment bank in the US and the one, which had survived every major upheaval for the past 158 years—file for bankruptcy. And slowly this recession started to creep into other countries like a contagious disease.

RECESSION IN INDIA

India is not de-linked from the world, and the financial meltdown has surely impacted us. In the age of globalization, no country can remains secluded from the fluctuations of world economy. Heavy losses suffered by major International Banks is going to affect all countries of the world as these financial institutes have their investment interest in almost all countries.

As of now India is facing warm on three grounds: (1) Our Share Markets are falling everyday, (2) Rupee is declining against dollars, and (3) Our banks are facing severe cash munch resulting in deficiency of liquidity in the market.

Actually all the above three problems are interconnected and have their extraction in the above-mentioned global crisis. For the last two years, our stock market was creating new pinnacles, which was mainly due to heavy investments by Foreign Institutional Investors (FIIs). However, when the parent companies of these investors (based mainly in US and Europe) found themselves in severe credit turmoil as a result of sub-prime jumble, the only option left with these investors was to pull out their money from Indian Stock Markets to meet responsibilities at home. FIIs were the main buyers of Indian Stocks and their exit from the market is certain to cause disaster in the market. FIIs, who were on a buying bender last year, are now in the mood of selling their stocks in India. As a result, our Share Markets were rousing new squat everyday.

Since, the money, which FIIs get after selling their stocks, needs to be transformed into dollars before they can sent it home, the demand for dollars abruptly amplified. As more and more FIIs are buying dollars, the rupee is loosing its power against dollar. As long as demands for dollars linger high, the rupee will keep loosing its potency against dollar.

The current financial crisis has also started dircctly touching Indian Industries. For the past few years, the two most preferred method of raising money by the companies were Stock Markets and external borrowings on low interest rates. Stock Markets were falling everyday and it was not possible to raise money there. Concerning external borrowing from world markets, this option has also become difficult.

In the last fiscal year alone, India borrowed $29 billion from foreign lenders and got $34 billion of foreign direct ventures. A global recession has injured external demand. International lenders who have become awfully risk aversive can limit access to international capital. If that happens, both India's financial markets and the real economy will be wound in the process. Suddenly, the 9% growth target does not seem 'feasible' any more; we should be happy to clock 7% this fiscal year and the next.

However, one positive point in favour of India is the fact that Indian Banks are more or less protected from the sick effects of sub-prime disorder. A quick look at Indian banks' balance sheets would show that their exposure to multifaceted instruments like CDOs is almost nil. In India, still the major banking operations are in the hands of Public Sector Banks who exercise extreme cautions in disbursing loans to needy people/companies. As a result, we are not likely to see a recur of sub-prime crisis in India. Though there have been an occurrence of big US/European Banks in India and even some Indian banks (like ICICI) have some foreign subsidiary with stake in the sub-prime losses, there presence is much small as compare to the overall size of Indian banking industry. So at least on this major obverse we need not worry much.

Negative impressions, shortage of cash, fall in demands, dropping growth rate and suspicions in the market are some of the most observable aspects of an economic gloominess. What started as a small matter of sub-prime loan defaulters has now become a subject of global discussion and has engulfed the global economy scenario?

PRESENT SCENARIO

Without doubt we are in the middle of a severe recession, the most terrible since the great depression. A large part of the prosperity we thought we had has departed. For example, the value of corporate equities has come down significantly during the past decade, from $19.4 trillion in 1999 to $ 15.2 trillion in 2008. Households (including non-profit organizations) net worth in the US has gone up from $ 42.1 trillion in 1999 to $ 51.7 trillion in 2008. However, the consumer price index (CPI) increased by 29% from 1999 to 2008, and the number of domestics in the US increased to 117 million in 2008 from 104 million in 1999. Hence, in real provisions (1999 dollars) the net worth per household declined sharply from $ 402,000 in 1999 to $ 343,000 in 2008, i.e., a 15% drop during the past decade. Averages mask the magnitude of the sobering of the loads. The unemployment rate captures the difficult times even better: it has gone up from 4.4% in 1999 to 7.2% in 2008—and currently estimated to be 9.5% (July 2009.)

In a closed economy, it is a simple book-keeping identity that the sum of domestic speculation must equal domestic savings in each period. In a world of open economies, this identity (between sources and uses) must still hold, even if at a global level. What changes in an open economy is that individual countries momentarily can run a current account spare or current account deficit, may be due to excess saving and due to excess spending/investment. In the absence of transactions costs and other frictions like taxes, entry barriers, governmental involvement in markets etc., and when competitive markets for all goods, services and securities exist, this should in general produce global competition for investment flows and lead to more earliest use of resources, with capital flowing to those regions where it is most fruitful. In fact, the group of budding and mounting countries run large current account deficits until the late 90's as a result of extensive investment in infrastructure and industrial capacity. As a result, the emerging economies in Asia as a group consistently practiced real GDP growth rates in excess of 7% over the period 1982-2008, largely driven by exports.

INSTITUTIONS AFFECTED BY A RECESSION

Banks: The major UK banks would definitely survive a recession. However, their profits would be reduced. A recession is likely to cause a further rise in bankruptcies, mortgage defaults and loan defaults. Therefore, UK banks would have to write-off a lot of bad debts.

Estate Agents: If the UK experiences a recession, it is most likely to come from a noteworthy fall in house prices. This would affect firms related to the housing sector. Estate agents would see lower revenue of houses and make smaller commissions on declining house prices. Home building firms would perhaps suffer from a decline in orders.

Share Prices and Shareholders: After the recent falls in the stock market, it may be that a recession wouldn't cause a momentous further fall in share prices. This is because an economic slowdown has already been built into the lower share prices. However, falling profits would lead to lower dividends. There would also be a fall in profits from share dealing and a decline in some of the 'bonus payments' that have characterized in recent years.

IMPACT OF THE ECONOMIC RECESSION IN FINANCIAL INSTITUTIONS

The financial crisis and the economic downturn are having an adverse impact on financial institutions. Loan losses are increasing and funding is still difficult to obtain. A number of financial institutions need fresh capital. The authorities have taken extensive action to mitigate the impact of the crisis.

Substantial losses on securities and lending have resulted in lower profits for banks compared with the preceding years and Banks' overall profits were 32% lower in 2008 than in 2007. About half of the banks recorded negative results in 2008 Q4. The decline in profits was primarily due to losses on securities and lending. Banks' results improved somewhat in 2009 Q1, but prospects remain weak.

Assets that are exposed to market fluctuations (securities recognised as current assets) accounted for 11% of banks' total assets at end-2008. In spite of the relatively modest share, losses on securities contributed over half of the reduction in profits from 2007 to 2008. These losses were a result of higher credit premiums on corporate bonds and the fall in equity prices. Losses due to lower equity prices were less severe after some banks made use of the option to reclassify securities as "held to maturity", as provided by the new guidelines of 16 October 2008. The reclassification was recognised on balance sheets as of 30 June 2008. The book value of these securities is thereby no longer directly influenced by changes in market value. Six banks reported that they had used the reclassification option. Without this option, banks' overall profits would have been 18% in 2008.

Banks' loan losses increased in 2008, particularly in 2008 Q4, and were the highest in any one quarter since 2002 Q4. Losses decreased somewhat in 2009 Q1, but projections of banks' loan losses based on economic developments show an increase ahead.

Loan losses rose considerably more than the stock of non-performing loans, which only showed a marginal increase in 2008 banks had set aside substantial funds to cover expected future losses on loans to industries with weak prospects (collective write downs) in 2008 compared with previous years. While a higher number of defaults increases individual writedowns, banks can take collective writedowns when there are clear indications that they will lose on loans to a group of customers, for example, in a specific industry. In 2008 the proportion of collective writedowns recognised by banks in Norway as a whole was almost as high as individual writedowns, although the distribution of collective and individual writedowns varied across banks.

In the course of 2008, financial institutions took on a more prominent role in bond markets. Credit premiums on bank bonds have declined somewhat since the beginning of November as a result of the swap arrangement for covered bonds. Risk premiums on subordinated loan capital have decreased somewhat but they remain high. This may indicate that market participants perceive a risk of banks' losses exceeding their equity capital.

Bank's surveys of the liquidity situation indicate that in autumn 2008 it was difficult for banks to comply with internal limits for long-term funding. Banks reported that funding with a maturity of more than one year had become particularly expensive and difficult to obtain. At the end of April 2009, banks reported that the funding situation had improved. Stable sources of funding and illiquid assets are more evenly balanced in small banks than in larger banks.

THE STUDY

In this current throat-cut setting where nothing is stable but everything is potential and flexible. It is very rough task to create strategy. The term strategy is generally used for future scheduling and working of the organization in corporate vista, Generally, in this competitive environment firms/companies/organizations are trying to achieve success by overcoming their best closest competitors through their good strategies.

In this current era of corporate primacy where we are searching for most adoptive strategy for the world. Though it is not clear that which decision option is good for a particular business. Researchers are searching for some strategies, which are easy to adopt and simple to implement with low cost and favourable results.

Strategies

As long-term factor: Strategies are generally long-term plans for the organization. In this current competitive global era strategies are generally very common tolerable concepts. Without strategies, planning for the organization is day-dreaming or outlandish. Especially when we are talking about the financial decisions like project selection decisions, pricing decisions, dividend decisions, cost decision, and other market and competitors' decision. We have to concentrate more and more on the decisions, which are very essential and helpful for the organization. In the project selection or we can say capital budgeting decisions it is very important task of the finance manager to maintain the level of decision for the ongoing health of the organization. The cost involvement in the project is very important factor.

Why Demarcating?

McGraw-Hill Research published a study of 600 companies in 16 industries over a 5-year period that included a recession. Researchers concluded that firms that chose to maintain or increase their marketing budgets experienced sales growth that was 256% higher than those companies whose advertising suffered. Furthermore, those who cut back on their advertising realized a small increase of only 19% in that same time period.

Here is another lesson learned from the last recession: The 25% of companies that increased their marketing budgets saw an increase in market share that was 2.5 times greater than competitors who cut back. But that's not all you need to know. Here's what I've learned from past recessions:

- Companies that don't adjust their marketing to the new economic environment suffer.
- Businesses that follow the direct marketing model trump those who rely on traditional advertising.

Traditional strategic planning models will not be very useful and relevant during a recession, wherein companies fight for survival on two fronts: Dwindling demand and sales and dwindling cash—both thanks to dwindling credit and confidence. Unless strategies are quickly and correctly aligned, even good and great companies can tumble in a meltdown.

Predictable competitive strategy and analysis teach how to steal market share from competitors and outflank them with so-called differentiating and niche strategies, or leaving them behind to decimate each other, as you swim to your Perfect blue ocean.

Michael Porter suggests that to compete efficiently, an organization must focus either on low costs or on demarcation. A low-cost strategy relies on a relatively homogeneous product, and the organization offers value through low costs and thus low prices. The differentiation-based approach means that the organization offers a product that is unique and offers value to the customers because of the range of features it possesses. For differentiation to be successful, the higher price received by the organization must offset the costs of supplying the differentiated product. At the same time, the customer must feel that it is worth paying extra for the distinctive image of the product and the additional features offered.

Differentiation leadership. A differentiation-based strategy means trying to offer something that is seen as unique and distinct. An apparent uniqueness and the linked customer loyalty protect the firm from its competitors, the threat of doorway and substitute products. HSBC, Citibank and American Express may all attempt to claim an apparent uniqueness based on their global presence and experience. However, research in the financial services sector suggests that this goal may be difficult to attain for many contributors. Devlin and Ennew (1997) have painted the difficulties that UK providers of financial services experience in frustrating to create a clear competitive advantage based on either price or differentiation in a mass market, and also the greater opportunities associated with either focus or niche-based strategies.

DEMARCATING STRATEGIES

Review your Unique Selling Proposition (USP)

A powerful USP will grab prospects' attention, distinguish you from competitors and draw them into your story. Now is the time to review and revise your USP. If it doesn't tell your prospects how they will benefit from your product in today's downturn and distinguish you from the competition, chances are you'll become irrelevant. Your USP needs to be prominent, easily found and up-to-date in all of your marketing—TV, direct mail, website, you name it.

Address Marketing Evils with Preemptive Copy

Marketing evils are the barriers that stand between your customer and their decision to buy from you. They create disbelief toward your product. Today's marketing evils include:

- Economic crisis
- Recession
- Competition
- Legal and regulatory changes
- Budget cuts
- Unemployment

When money is tight, fear of making a poor purchasing decision is high. Prospects will question what you say and raise more objections that prevent them from buying. Don't ignore the suspicions, fears and concerns that are epidemic your prospect. Instead, use anticipatory copy to address and overcome prospects' disbelief.

Well-executed copy for this recession will achieve the following 4 goals:

1. Address and dismiss your prospects' objections.
2. Demonstrate how your product solves their most pressing problems.
3. Explain why your product is absolutely necessary—even in an economic downturn—and why it's in your prospect's best interest to buy now.

4. Clearly exhibit why an alternative choice is not going to cut it.

Reevaluate your offer and make it Preemptive

In this recession, consumers are searching for the best way to get more for their money. It's tough to update your value proposition so that it's powerful and preemptive. It should answer prospects' questions before they ask them and overcome their objections. Remember, your offer is not about the product—it about the prospect and what the prospect gets. The strongest offers reinforce value. They focus on the deal that the prospect will receive and present a get-more for-your-money image.

Here are 3 components of a successful offer:

1. *A discount or price reduction*: Right now people are looking for value, and a discount is the simplest way to deliver it. Just look at the most successful catalogs, emails and mailing pieces; you'll find discounts in every one.
2. *A premium*: It's a gift, a bribe, and a strong inducement. Add value by giving something away. This can help you justify a higher price if you are unable to offer a heavy discount.
3. *A guarantee*: Reassure your prospects that they have nothing to lose. If you don't have a guarantee, now is the time to start one.

Reevaluate Your Media

Be sure to put your recession appropriate USP to work in all campaigns—including online and broadcast media.

1. *Direct mail*. You're still able to produce a low cost per lead or sale with this highly targeted medium...even in a recession. It should be a major component of any marketing mix.
2. *Email*. The days of sending a sales letter via email are over. Sales hype will not work. Instead, use an information-driven, content-rich email. Remember value.

3. *TV and radio*: Rates for prime airtime have been dipping, so now's your chance to renegotiate rates and retest your options, such as time of day.

Invest in Your Customers

Now they need you most. Loyalty hangs in the balance.

Downturns provide the opportunity to strengthen relationships with customers thereby improving customer loyalty. At a time when consumer sentiment is nearly at an all-time low, rather than reduce customer service, use this time to get closer to your customers, connect with them on a deeper level, and show them what's possible—what the future will hold.

Rather than Reduce Price, Offer more Value to Your Customers

During difficult economic times, consumers use greater discretion in making purchasing decisions. Every dollar matters and therefore every decision a customer makes are examined more closely. If your product or service isn't extraordinary, your customers will be more likely to delay purchasing it.

Look for Creative Ways to Extend Your Current Products

Consider adding value-added services to your products, and brainstorm ways to provide new customer experiences. Think in terms of other uses for your existing products. If your customers know that your products provide greater utility than those of your competitors, you'll be more likely to win their business. Also, look for incremental improvements to your products that can significantly increase their value, at a minimal additional cost. Finally, take a fresh look at some of the incremental improvements or R&D projects you may have shelved before the downturn because the timing wasn't right; some of them may do a great job of meeting customers' current needs.

Keep your Current Customers Near and Dear

You've probably heard this before, but it bears repeating: It costs 10 times more to acquire a new customer than to sell to an existing one, so do all you can to solidify your customer relationships.

- Send your customer's emails on a regular basis—to thank them, announce a special offer, or share tips and hints.
- Keep your customers engaged—and bring in new customers—with a "refer-a-friend" program, offering a free gift or a discount for referrals.

Insurance company Aviva says understanding consumers are key to winning back their trust. As a result, the company has invested in substantive global and local research to address the needs of its consumers, which has triggered the launch of services such as the Money banter website (http://www.moneybanter.com.sg/), a forum for Singaporean consumers offering advice and information.

Brush up your social skills

If you've got some time on your hands, ramp up your networking to create top-of-mind awareness for you and your business.

- Attend Chamber of Commerce and other business breakfasts, socials and forums.
- Volunteer for community and charity work.
- Explore some of the new social networking websites geared for businesses, such as Twitter, Plaxo, Yelp and LinkedIn. Most are free to join.

Appeal to the Nervous Buyer

A recession can mean more risk-adverse buyers, which may lead to a tendency to go with "safe" solutions. This is fine for large established companies, but it means younger companies need to do more than ever to reassure and build trust.

Focus on Family Values

When economic hard times loom, we tend to retreat to our village. Look for cozy hearth-and-home family scenes in advertising to replace images of extreme sports, adventure and rugged individualism. Zany humor and appeals on the basis of fear are out. Greeting card sales, telephone use and discretionary spending on home furnishings and home entertainment will hold up well, as uncertainty prompts us to stay at home but also stay connected with family and friends.

PROVIDE OPTIMAL PACKAGING

This is so important because the packages are competing on the shelf for attention and consideration. Is your package doing the best job of communicating the brand, what it stands for, the variety/flavor of the product, and key benefits of the product? Right now especially, you cannot afford to have the wrong size, wrong graphics, or wrong key benefits on your packages.

Adopt Cutting Edge Technologies

One of the best ways to stay ahead of your competitors is by keeping up with current technology.

CONCLUSION

The market for financial services has become increasingly aggressive in recent years. In such an environment, success requires a designed and strategic approach to marketing. Developing a unique plan to guide marketing is of extensive value, because it encourages watchful thought and analysis. In building choices about products and markets, it is essential that the organization try to develop a match between its own particular strengths and the needs of the different segments of the market. There are many different tools available to help an organization develop its unique marketing plan and its demarcating strategy. So institutes which lead uniqueness in their marketing strategy wins the race.

References

http://www.indianembassy.org.sa/
International Monetary Fund, World Economic Outlook, December 2001.
http://www.aspo-usa.org/index.php/category/commentary/
Business world. Business line.

10

A Factor Analytic Investigation of Management Attitudes Towards Internees' Performance

A Study on Opinions Survey of Chief Executive Officers (CEO)/ Managers in Bangladesh

MD. ABU TAHER AND BALASUNDARAM NIMALATHASAN

ABSTRACT

The present study is initiated on factor analytic investigation of management attitudes towards internees' performance in different organizations in Bangladesh. Random and purposive sampling is used for drawing samples for this study. The questionnaire is designed by the researchers a five point Likert scale (1-excellent; 2-very good; 3-good; 4-average; and 5-unsatisfactory) to identify the management attitudes (MA) towards internees' performance (IP). In the present study, we,

therefore, used Cronbach's alpha scale as a measure of reliability. Its value is estimated to be 0.900. Sophisticated statistical model as 'Exploratory Factor Analysis (EFA)' has been used. The results show that management attitudes group extracted from the analysis that together accounted 60.452 percent of the total variance. Finally, on the basis of factor score these groups were ranked (1) Ability to work independently (AWI); (2) Job interest (JI) and constitute the key dimensions of management attitudes towards internees' performance.
Keywords: Management Attitudes (MA); Internees' Performance (IP); Exploratory Factor Analysis (EFA).

1. INTERNSHIP PROGRAMME—AN OVERVIEW

Every year, Department of Management Studies (DMS), University of Chittagong, Bangladesh is allowed internship training program with live practical exposure for Master of Business Administration (MBA) graduates. The basic objective of internship is to provide practical exposure to the students in a working environment. Internship can be really helpful to any MBA graduates, who are looking for hands-on expertise. As an intern, they can widen knowledge, competencies, and experience related to their career. DMS provides internship program to help students to assimilate information and bridge gap between academics and career. This is helpful for the student as pre-work experience that employers are looking out for in a candidate. It provides a supervised pre-professional learning experience, in which students apply their skills and knowledge in a professional setting. After completion of MBA written exam, the internees are required to undergo internship program with business organizations, autonomous and governments' enterprises, multinational companies (MNCs) and other research bodies or development projects where the students get an opportunity for translating theoretical conception into real life situation.

2. LITERATURE REVIEW

In general terms, an internship is viewed as a short-term practical work experience in which internees receive training and gain experience in a specific field or career area of their interest. The internship experience enables internee to apply classroom theory within the actual world of work thus bridging the gap between theory and practice. The value of internships is well documented in research literature (Kok, 2000). Internships provide real world industry demands and hands on learning needed to rekindle skills and update their knowledge. Boyle & Crosby (1997) said that internships for both faculty and students should be required to adequately evaluate the quality of educational programmes. Department or faculty internships were important for those who teach courses that are vocationally-oriented (Baha & Glon, 1988). Samenfink (1995) noted that internships are outlets that should be used to invigorate faculty and bring excitement back to the classroom as well as stimulate new research interests. This idea is mirrored by other researchers that believe vocationally-oriented faulty tend and starve for the excitement of guest service and fast-paced production missing in their teaching careers (Chesser, Ellis & Rothbery, 1993). Failure to create and support opportunities for faculty to re-enter the industry squelches the overall motivation for these individuals to perform in the classroom, seek outside experiences for the students, and contributes to little or no interest in researching the issues facing the industry.

Various studies (Petrilose & Montgomery, 1998; Gabris & Mitchell, 1989; Downey & DeVeau, 1987) outline the value and variety of the benefits enjoyed by those internee participating in internships, including a better understanding and knowledge of the tasks and practices performed by industry professionals, improved self-confidence, enhanced employment and professional growth opportunities, the ability to network within the industry by creating personal contacts, exposure to management activities, and the development of skills relevant to their particular career choice. Therefore, the present study is initiated to identify dimensions of management attitudes towards internees' performance.

3. OBJECTIVES

The following two objectives are taken for the study:

1. To identify the factors which determine the MA.
2. To recognize the factors that determines the MA.

4. MATERIAL AND METHODS

1. Sampling Strategy

The internees were underwent internship program with the business organizations, autonomous, government enterprises, MNCs, other research bodies and development projects. These enterprises have been selected through random and purposive sampling. Hence, ultimate sample is seventy-five organizations.

2. Data Sources

Given the nature of the present study, it was required to collect data from the primary and secondary sources. During data collection, the authors were always careful of the objectives and hypotheses of the study and collected data accordingly to achieve those objectives. Primary data were collected through the questionnaire. Secondary data were collected from research studies, books, journals, newspapers and ongoing academic working papers. The collected data may be processed and analyzed in order to make the study useful to the practitioners, researchers, planners, policy-makers and academicians.

3. Instrumentation

The questionnaire was administrated to Chief Executive Officer (CEO)/General Managers in different organizations which were attached the internees in Bangladesh. It has been prepared based on five Likert scale (1 = Excellent; 2 = Very Good; 3 = Good; 4 = Average; and 5 = Unsatisfactory) to identify the management attitudes towards internees' performance.

4. Reliability and Validity

The reliability value of our surveyed data was 0.900 for management attitudes variables. If we compare our reliability value with the standard value alpha of 0.7 advocated by Cronbach (1951), a more accurate recommendation (Nunnally

& Bernstein's, 1994) or with the standard value of 0.6 as recommendated by Bagozzi & Yi's (1988). Researchers find that the scales used by us are highly reliable for data analysis.

Validation procedures involved initial consultation with experts (i.e., academic committee) from Department of Management Studies (DMS), University of Chittagong. The experts also judged the face and content validity of the questionnaires as adequate. Hence, researchers satisfied content and construct validity.

5. Statistical Tools Used

In the present study, we analysed the collected by employing descriptive statistics (i.e., mean, standard error, standard deviation) and inferential statistics (i.e., EFA). For the study, entire analysis is done by personal computer. A well-known statistical package like 'Statistical Package for Social Sciences' (SPSS) 13.0 version was used in order to analyze the data.

6. Sample Description

After collection of data, all numerical values indicating level of agreement for different questions have been used to calculate means, standard errors and standard deviations. Table 1 shows the respective means, standard errors and standard deviations of each question asked to compute the level of job satisfaction. Standard error of means range from 0.071 to 0.093 which confirms that sample means of different variables are close to population means.

5. ANALYSIS AND DISCUSSION

Before applying factor analysis, testing of the reliability of the scale is very much important as it shows the extent to which a scale produces consistent result if measurements are made repeatedly. This is done by determining the association in between scores obtained from different administrations of the scale. If the association is high, the scale yields consistent result, thus is reliable. Cronbach's alpha is most widely used method. It may be mentioned that its value varies from 0 to 1 but, satisfactory value is required to be more than 0.6 for the

TABLE 1
Description of Sample

Variables	*IN*	*RE*	*JI*	*AC*	*AOUP*	*T*	*AWI*	*MA*	*EFF*	*CRE*	*IP*
(1)	(2)	(3)	(4)	(5)	(6)	(7)	(8)	(9)	(10)	(11)	(12)
Mean	1.77	1.84	1.67	1.81	1.95	1.88	1.81	1.93	1.73	1.99	1.65
Std. Error	0.072	0.087	0.072	0.082	0.071	0.093	0.080	0.074	0.074	0.086	0.082
Std. Deviation	0.628	0.754	0.622	0.711	0.613	0.805	0.692	0.644	0.644	0.744	0.707

Source : Survey data.

scale to be reliable (Malhotra, 2002; Cronbach, 1951). In the present study, we, therefore, used Cronbach's alpha scale as a measure of reliability. Its value is estimated to be 0.900. If we compare our reliability value with the standard value alpha of 0.6 advocated by Cronbach (1951), a more accurate recommendation Nunnally and Bernstein (1994) or with the standard value of 0.6 as recommendatcd by Bagozzi and Yi's (1988) we find that the scales used by us are highly reliable for factor analysis. After checking the reliability of scale, an examination of the correlation matrix (For details please see Table 2) reveals moderately significant correlations between some of the variables. These are *IN* with JI; *RE* with T, MA; *AOUP* with AWI and MA; *T* with EFF and CRE; *AWI* with EFF and CRE; *MA* with EFF and *EFF* with CRE.[1] But no correlation comes out as damaging as to cause multicolinerity and so, the matrix is suitable for factoring

TABLE 2
Correlation Matrix

	IN	*RE*	*JI*	*AC*	*AOUP*	*T*	*AWI*	*MA*	*EFF*	*CRE*
IN	1									
RE	0.294	1								
JI	0.600	0.288	1							
AC	0.449	0.423	0.499	1						
AOUP	0.495	0.420	0.449	0.349	1					
T	0.427	0.569	0.405	0.386	0.453	1				
AWI	0.337	0.460	0.293	0.368	0.550	0.445	1			
MA	0.430	0.562	0.416	0.386	0.642	0.428	0.457	1		
EFF	0.417	0.496	0.450	0.362	0.477	0.590	0.524	0.511	1	
CRE	0.341	0.381	0.253	0.327	0.443	0.516	0.520	0.365	0.500	1

Source : Survey data.

After checking the reliability of scale and correlation matrix, we tested whether the data, so, collected is appropriate for factor analysis or not. The appropriateness of factor analysis is dependent upon the sample size. In this connection, MacCallum, Windaman, Zhang & Hong (1999) have shown that the minimum sample size depends upon other aspects of the design of the study. According to them, as communalities become lower the importance of sample size increases. They have advocated that if all communalities are above 0.6 relatively small samples (less than 100) may be perfectly adequate. In this regard communalities of management attitudes have been shown in Table 3.

TABLE 3
Communalities

Sl. No.	*Management Attitudes*	*Initial*	*Extraction*
1.	Initiative	1.000	0.701
2.	Resourcefulness	1.000	0.567
3.	Job interest	1.000	0.774
4.	Ability to Communicate	1.000	0.516
5.	Ability to Operate Under Pressure	1.000	0.572
6.	Timeliness	1.000	0.587
7.	Ability to Work Independently	1.000	0.605
8.	Maturity	1.000	0.556
9.	Efficiency	1.000	0.608
10.	Creativity	1.000	0.560

Source : Survey data; Extraction Method: Principal Component Analysis.

The appropriateness of factor analysis is dependent upon the sample size. In this connection, Kaiser-Meyer-Olkin (KMO) measure of sampling adequacy is still another useful method to show the appropriateness of data for factor analysis. The KMO statistics varies between 0 and 1. Kasier (1974) recommends that values greater than 0.5 are acceptable. Between 0.5 and 0.7 are mediocre, between 0.7 and 0.8 are good, between 0.8 and 0.9 are superb (Field, 2000). In this study, the value of KMO for overall matrix is 0.879 (For details please see Table 4), thereby indicating that the sample taken to process the factor analysis is statistically significant.

TABLE 4
KMO and Bartlett's Test

Kaiser-Meyer-Olkin Measure of Sampling Adequacy.		.879
Bartlett's Test of Sphericity	Approx. Chi-Square	310.594
	Df	45
	Sig.	.000

Source : Survey data.

Bartlett's test of sphericity (Barlett, 1950) is the third statistical test applied in the study for verifying its appropriateness. This test should be significant i.e., having a significance value less than 0.5. In the present study, test value of Chi-Square 310.594 is significant (as also given in Table 4) indicating that the data is appropriate for the factor analysis.

After examining the reliabity of the scale and testing appropriateness of data as above, we next carried out factor analysis to indentify the variables for management attitudes. For this, we employed Principal Component Analysis (PCA) followed by the varimax rotation, [Generally, researchers' recommend as varimax—Ather & Nimalathasan (2009); Taher, Rahman and Ferdausy, (—)]. Statistical Package for Social Science (SPSS) software (version 13.0) was used for this purpose. When the original ten variables were analysed by the PCA. Two variables extracted from the analysis with an Eigen value of greater than 1 (i.e., 'rule of thumb'), which explained 60.452 percent of the total variance (For details please see Table 5). The first component explains the most and about 35.421 percent and second component explains 25.031 percent. The remaining variance, as we know, is explained by other components.

The PCA are further Orthogonally Rotated using Varimax with Kaiser Normalization algorithm. It is worth mentioning out here that factor loading greater than 0.30 are considered significant. 0.40 are considered more important and 0.50 or greater are considered very significant. The rotated (Varimax) component loadings for the two components (factors) are

Table 5
Total Variance Explained

Component	*Extraction Sums of Squared Loadings*			*Rotation Sums of Squared Loadings*		
	Total	*% of Variance*	*Cumulative %*	*Total*	*% of Variance*	*Cumulative %*
1	4.968	49.680	49.680	3.542	35.421	35.421
2	1.077	10.772	60.452	2.503	25.031	60.452

Source : Survey data.

presented in Table 6. For parsimony, only those factors with loadings above 0.50 were considered significant (Pal, 1986; Pal & Bagi, 1987; Hair, Anderson, Tatham and Black, 2003).

Table 6
Rotated Component Matrix for Management Attitudes

Variables	*Components*	
	1	2
AWI	0.759	
CRE	0.739	
RE	0.726	
EFF	0.703	
T	0.699	
MA	0.612	
AOUP	0.602	
JI		0.865
IN		0.804
AC		0.652

Source : Survey data.

Each of two management attitudes listed in Table 6 is labelled according to the name of the value that loaded most highly for those attitudes. The higher a factor loading, the more would its test reflect or measure as characteristics

(Pallant, 2005; Hema, Anura, Tilak and Basil, 2000). The management attitudes getting highest loading becomes the title of each group of management attitudes, e.g. AWI—title of management attitudes group I and the like.

Management attitudes group-I: AWI—These attitudes are represented by seven variables with factor loadings ranging from 0.759 to 0.602. They are ability to work independently; creativity; resourcefulness; efficiency; timeliness; maturity and ability to operate under pressure

Management attitudes group-II: JI—Three management attitudes' variables ranging from 0.865 to 0.652 belong to job interest; initiative and ability to communicate.

TABLE 7
Ranking of Characteristics According to their Importance

Key Characteristics of Entrepreneurs	*No. of. Variables*	*Factor Score*[1]	*Rank*
Management Attitudes group-1 : AWI	07	1.097	1
Management Attitudes group-II : JI	03	1.020	2

[1]Factor score = 'Composite scores estimated for each respondents on the derived factors. The Factor scores for the ith factor may be estimated as follows: $F_i = W_{i1}X_1+W_{i2}\ X_2+W_{i3}X_3+ \text{———} +W_{ik}X_k$

Where

F_i= estimate of ith factor; W_i = Weight or factor score coefficient;

K = number of variables; and

*Factor Score = Factor loadings × Component Score Coefficient.

Source : Survey data.

As depicted in Table 7, the management attitudes: 'AWI; and JI got the ranks of first, second, respectively and constitute the key dimension of management attitudes.

6. CONCLUSION

Sophisticated statistical model as EFA has been used. The results show that two management attitudes groups extracted from the analysis that together accounted 63.632 percent of the total variance. Finally, on the basis of factor score these groups were ranked (1) AWI; (2) JI. Moreover, outcome of the research would be helpful to the practitioners, researchers, planners, policy makers and academicians for formulating effective policies and strategies.

Note

1. *IN:* Initiative; *RE:* Resourcefulness; *JI:* Job interest; *AC*: Ability to Communicate; *AOUP*: Ability to Operate under Pressure; *T*: Time; *AWI*: Ability to Work Independently; *MA*: Maturity; *EFF*: Efficiency; *CRE*: Creativity.

References

Ather, S.M. and Nimalathasan, B. (2009). Factor Analysis: Nature, Mechanism and Uses in Social and Management Researches. *Journal of the Institute of Cost of Management Accountant of Bangladesh*, XXXVII (2), 12-17.

Baha, Z. and Glon, P.L. (1988). Faculty Industry Internship as an Important priority in Construction Education, in ASC Proceedings of the 24th Annual Conference, California Polytechnic State University, San Luis Obispo, A, April, 83-87.

Bartellet, M.S. (1950). Tests of Significance in Factor Analysis. *British Journal of Statistical Psychology*, 3, 77-85.

Bagozzi, R.P. and Yi, Y. (1988). On the Evaluation of Structural Equation Models. *Journal of the Academy of Marketing Science*, 16(1), 74-95.

Boyle, M.A. and Crosby, R. (1997). Academic Program Evaluation: Lessons from Business and Industry. *Journal of Industrial Teacher Education*, 34(3), 81-85.

Chesser, J.W., Ellis, T. and Rothbery, R. (1993). Hospitality Faculty: A Motivational Challenge, Cornell Hotel and Restaurant. *Administration Quarterly*, 34(4), 69-74.

Cronbach, L.J. (1951). Coefficient Alpha and the Internal Structure of Tests. *Psychometrika*, 6(3), 297-334.

Downey, J.F. and De Veau, L.T. (1987). Coordinating the Hospitality Internship. The Cornell Hotel and Restaurant. *Administration Quarterly*, 29(3), 18-21.

Gabris, G.T. and Mitchell, K. (1989). Exploring the Relationships between Intern Job Performance, Quality of Education Experience, and Career Placement. *Public Administration Quarterly*, 12(4), 481-504.

Hair, J.F., Anderson, R.E., Tatham, R.L. and Black, W.C. (2003). Multivariate Data Analysis, New Delhi: Pearson Education, 5e.

Hema, W., Anura, D.Z., Tilak, F. and Basil, P. (2000). Factors Contributing to the Success of Manufacturing Enterprises in Sri Lanka: An Empirical Investigation. *Sri Lankan Journal of Management*, 5(1&2), 110-30.

Kasier, H.F. (1974). An Index of Factorial Simplicit. *Psycometrica*, 39, 31-36.

Kok, R.M. (2000). Outside the box: Creating Your Own Internship Opportunities. *Journal of Hospitality and Tourism Education*, 12(3), 21-23.

Malhotra, N.K. (2002). Marketing Research: An Applied Orientation, (3rd ed.), New Delhi, Pearson Education Asia.

MacCallum, R.C., Windaman, K.F., Zhang, S. and Hong, S. (1999). Sample Size and Factor Analysis, *Psychological Methods*, 4, 84-99.

Nunnally, J.C. and Bernstein (1994). Ira Psychometrics Theory, New York: McGraw-Hill,

Pallant, J. (2005). SPSS Survival Manual, Sydney: Allen and Unwin.

Pal, Y. (1986). A Theoretical Study of Some Factor Analysis Problems and Pal, Y. and Bagai, O.P. (1987). A Common Factor Better Reliability Approach to Determine the Number of Interpretable Factors", a paper presented at the IX Annual Conference of the Indian Society for Probability and Statistics held at Delhi, University of Delhi, India.

Pal, Y. (1997). A New Factoring Criterion Based on Principal Factor Reliability Coefficients and its Comparison, with some well known Factoring Criteria. *Indian Psychological Review*, 48(3):187-200.

Pertillose, M.J. and Montgomery, T. (1998). An Exploratory Study of Internship Practices in Hospitality Education and Industry's Perceptions of the Importance of Internships in Hospitality Curriculum. *Journal of Hospitality and Tourism Education*, 9(4), 46-51.

Samenfink, W.H. (1995). International Exchanges for Hospitality Educators: Are You Ready?. *Hospitality and Tourism Educator*.

Taher, M.A., Rahman, M.S. and Ferdausy, S. (—). Knowledge Management in Small and Medium-Sized Enterprises: Issues and Challenges in Bangladesh Perspective. *South Asian Journal of Management*, 9(4), 28-35.

———, Retrieved August 18, 2009, from http://www.igurutraining.com/internship-training.php.

11

Entrepreneurship Development Potentiality in Bangladesh
Lessons for Sri Lanka

MD. ABU TAHER, ARUMUGAM SUBRAMANIAM AND BALASUNDARAM NIMALATHASAN

ABSTRACT

Entrepreneurship Development (ED), proved to be critical resources, is an important factor in economic uplift and growth of developing countries. There is a paramount importance of the subject for the employment generation and increasing productivity. The study highlights entrepreneurship development potentiality in Bangladesh and pointing out lesson that Sri Lanka can take. The research is based on desk study. For the betterment of ED both Government and opposition parties should develop consensus on policy matters as well as improved law and order situation followed by some recommendations which would be helpful to the practitioners, researchers, planners, policy-makers and academicians in the concerned area.

Keywords: Entrepreneurship Development (ED); Economic growth; Productivity.

1. INTRODUCTION

Irrespective of their nature, most of the developing countries are characterized by overpopulation, limited resource endowments, unemployment and underemployment which, in turn, lead to minimum consumption, malnutrition, low propensity and rate of savings and dearth of capital formation. Increasing concern over widespread poverty is the self-evident economic reality, which deserve special attention for planned intervention to improve the situation. The cross-country analysis shows that economic growth of all these countries is worsened for the uneven distribution of income. At present, world is considered as 'Global village' with strong network and information system. In the present scenario industrialization is the only hope of the third world especially for developing countries.

The recent experiences from developing countries all over the world favours the hypothesis that entrepreneurship can be developed through planned efforts. There also has been wide recognition that the ED is essential not only to solve the problem of economic development but also to solve the problems of unemployment, unbalanced areas development, concentration of economic power, and diversion of profits from traditional avenues of investment. Therefore, one can notice some attempts by the government's development agencies and other institutions to undertake the task of entrepreneurial promotion.

Bangladesh is a country with a high density of population, low per capita income, and low agricultural productivity. A large number of populations are unemployed due to weak industrial base, and lack of employment opportunities. The rapid population growth, resulting in addition to the civilian force, is posing a great threat to the economic development process of the country.

Since pre-liberation days, the then Government of Bangladesh encouraged entrepreneurship by offering various facilities and incentives to the private sector, with the realization of the needs of the country. Government emphasized on micro-enterprises development after its independence.

1. Objectives

The study has the following objectives :

- To find out the scope and role of entrepreneurship for attaining economic development in developing countries;
- To focus on present scenario of ED policy in Bangladesh;
- To identify the promoting entrepreneurship organizations in Bangladesh and its activities; and
- To suggest some possible solution for developing and improving the entrepreneurial environment to Sri Lanka from Bangladesh perspectives.

2. Methodology

Given the nature of the present study, it was required to collect data from the secondary sources. The authors were always careful of the objectives of the study and collected data accordingly to achieve those objectives. Secondary data were collected from research studies, books, journals, newspapers and ongoing academic working papers. The collected data may be processed and analysed in order to make the present study useful to the practitioners, researchers, planners, policy-makers and academicians of the concern area.

2. ANALYSES AND FINDINGS

The analyses of findings have been discussed under the following sub-heads.

1. Entrepreneurship

Cunningham and Lischeron (1991) in their article, "Defining Entrepreneurship" stated that the term entrepreneurship is derived from the French verb 'entreprendre' and the German word 'Unternehamen', both of which mean 'to undertake'. According to Robbins and Coulter (1998) entrepreneurship is a process of identifying the profitable opportunities from the environment, exploiting those opportunities through the successful organisation of business operations, handling the risks and uncertainties carefully and managing the operations systematically to help attain the objectives of a firm.

Glos and Lowery (1980) tried to define entrepreneurship through four common characteristics of entrepreneurs, viz., (1) Purposeful (i.e., sets goals and strives diligently and continually to accomplish them, setbacks and disappointment do not halt him towards goal attainment); (2) Persuasive (i.e., influences others to assist in reaching desired goals); (3) Presumptuous (i.e., strikes out boldly and acts when others hesitate to do so, is willing to take calculated risks and to accept innovative approaches); (4) Perspective (i.e., understands how each separate decision relates to accomplishing the established goals). On the other hand, Cole (1942) indicated that entrepreneurship is the purposeful capacity of individual or a group of associated individuals, who undertake to initiate, maintain or organize some profit-oriented business units for the production or distribution of economic goods and services.

McClelland (1961) explored that entrepreneurship indicates risk taking, which is responsible for end results in the form of profit or loss. According to him the function of an entrepreneur is to promote economic ventures and take decisions on vital issues concerning production, finance, personnel and marketing; and bear the risk arising out of business operations of an organization. Rashid (as quoted in Nazma, 1994) identified that entrepreneurship is a purposeful activity of initiating, promoting and managing economic activities for the production and distribution of wealth. It consists of perceiving new opportunities for profit, marshalling and assembling financial and other resources for exploiting the perceived opportunities and responding positively to changes in the same.

Rahman (1997) concluded in his paper that entrepreneurship is the function specific to the entrepreneur and it indicates the ability to organise and use the factors of production—land, labour, capital, and management, in order to produce new goods and services. Further he mentioned that entrepreneurship might be defined as a kind of behaviour of a person displaying perception of new economic opportunities, initiative, creativity and innovation. Kao (1989) argued that entrepreneurship is adventurism, risk taking and thrill seeking. He stated that entrepreneurship is an attempt to create value through recognition of business opportunity, and through the communicative and management skills to mobilize human, financial, and material resources necessary to bring a project to realization.

2. Entrepreneurship Development

ED refers to the process of enhancing entrepreneurial skills and knowledge through structured training and institution-building programmes. ED aims to enlarge the base of entrepreneurs in order to hasten the pace at which new ventures are created. This accelerates employment generation and economic development. ED focuses on the *individual* who wishes to start or expand a business. To develop entrepreneurship in a country requires comprehensive effort that covers various activities right from the stimulation to its long-term survival. The scheme of such a comprehensive intervention effort is suggested by Dr. M.M.P. Akouri, Former Executive Director of National Institute for Entrepreneurship and Small Business Development (NIESBUD) Delhi, in the form of entrepreneurship development cycle. The cycle identified three groups of activities concerning ED. They are :

(1) *Stimulating activities*: It comprises entrepreneurial education, provision of entrepreneurial opportunities and guidance in selecting industries, supply of techno-economic information, are needed to help emergence of entrepreneurship in the society. The support ensures a good supply of entrepreneurs to start a new venture and developed potentiality to succeed in a venture.

(2) *Supporting activities*: It refers to those which enable the entrepreneurs in setting up and running the enterprise successfully. They help in mobilizing resources and assistance. They include arranging finance, providing land, shed, power and other utilities, supply of capital machinery, scarce raw materials, offering management consultancy, help marketing products, etc.

(3) *Sustaining activities*: It includes the challenge of actual operation. Many enterprises starting well, meet immature death subsequently because of some problems. Such cases are many and they are particularly more significant in the field of small enterprises.

According to Rahman (1989) the above groups of activities play complementary roles to each other. Therefore, they should be developed in balanced way and of course not placing more emphasis on some activities while negligence to others.

3. Entrepreneurship Development Policy in Bangladesh

More than three decades have passed since Bangladesh achieved independence after bloody liberation war. The liberation generated great hope for accelerated economic growth through rapid industrialization. The successive governments in power in order to guide the emerging entrepreneurs announced Industrial Policies from time to time keeping in view the changing needs of the country. The first industrial policy was announced in 1972 heavily emphasised the role of public sector dealing as well the role of private sector. The private sector investment was restricted to the investment of only Taka 25 lacs ceiling since the announcement of first industrial policy. The policy was revised and changed several times. The last industrial policy was announced in 2005. In this policy the Government reiterated its firm commitment to rapid industrialization and extended more liberal support services to entrepreneurs and clearly stated in the policy the role of government which will be facilitator rather than regulator.

The Government of Bangladesh in its policies has awarded priority to privatisation especially to small, medium and micro industries development. Human resources development efforts to existing and potential entrepreneurs have to be supported by required appropriate implementation measures. The country features a number of innovative grassroots schemes for income-generating activities; however, entrepreneurship development programmes at more advanced level of business operations were found inadequate. It is important for creating incremental wealth by undertaking productive activities particularly industrialization. Rapid industrialization is an inescapable necessity to generate employment opportunities to meet crucial educated unemployment and underemployment problems.

4. Organizations Involved in ED Programme (EDP) in Bangladesh

There are many Government, non-government organizations (NGOs) and professional organizations involved in EDP in Bangladesh in which the industrial policy remains the major guide for the purpose. These are:

1. Government Organizations

Bangladesh Small and Cottage Industries Corporation (BSCIC)

The main objectives of BSCIC are to strengthen the Small and Cottage Industry (SCI) by providing support services, including infrastructural facilities to small and tin entrepreneurs. Services include pre-investment counselling; supply of techno-economic information; credit arrangement; infrastructural facilities management and skill development training; arranging for raw materials; diagnostic studies; market studies; sub-contracting arrangement; inter-organizational co-ordination; and product development.

The BSCIC provides services to entrepreneurs under different schemes through its central office and its institutional network, which regularly covers all districts in the country. The BSCIC offers training support mainly through the

Bangladesh Small and Cottage Industries Training Institute (BSCITI), established in 1984. The main aims are to meet the training needs of small entrepreneurs, as well as staff from BSCIC, and other promotional agencies. Training programmes for both women and men include entrepreneurship development training for skilled technicians, engineers, wage earners, and their dependants; for starting a small business; and for non-farm employment of rural women. The SCITI also organizes training courses in industrial management, financial management, marketing management, and general management for entrepreneurs and their employees.

Bangladesh Rural Development Board (BRDB)

BRDB target beneficiaries are landless and assetless rural women and men. Two self-employment programmes provide assistance: Bittaheen Samabaya Samity (BSS), for assetless persons; and Mahila Bittaheen Samabaya Samity (MBSS), for poor women. BRDB programmes activities focus on training of functionaries. Skill training is organized for members of cooperatives according to their specific needs. Materials are provided on credit for members who have undergone skill training. The BRDB Training Materials production Unit (operated by professional staff) develops audio-visual materials for use in various training activities.

Bangladesh Institute of Management (BIM)

BIM was established in 1961. An autonomous organization under the Ministry of Industries, BIM entrusted with responsibility for developing and improving skills and techniques at various level of management. Training is at the core of BIMs activities. Each year the centre organizes more than 100 short courses, some are related to areas such as starting a small business, establishing a new industry, and entrepreneurship development for women.

Directorate of Women Affairs (DWA)

Following the 1971 war, the women's development programme, first taking the form of rehabilitation of war-affected women, was formally initiated under government sponsorship. DWA function is now the provision of vocational training and assistance in achieving economic solvency. DWA projects work mostly for poverty alleviation, increase of social awareness, employment generation, and technology extension for women. The main objective of the training programmes is to impart non-formal vocational, technical, and other skill development training to women of various categories who are interested in participating in income-generating activities. In addition, management and leadership development training are given to the employees of the Directorate and other agencies.

Department of Youth Development (DYD)

The Department of Youth Development was created in December 1981 with the aim of transforming unproductive youth into organized, disciplined, and productive human resources. DYD offers training to poor and unemployed youth in rural and urban areas in various trades and income-generating activities such as livestock, poultry, computer use, repair of electrical equipment, electrical and house wiring, refrigeration, and air-conditioning. Training also given in human development areas such as youth leadership, communication, motivation, personnel management, problem-solving, and decision-making.

2. *Non-government Organizations*

Micro-Industries Development and Assistance Services (MIDAS)

MIDAS is a company incorporated under the Companies Act of 1913. Since 1982, it has been working for the promotion and development of micro and small enterprises. Two of the organization's most important programmes for promoting entrepreneurship are the New Business Creation Programmes (NBC) and the Micro Industries Development Initiative (MIDI). The NBC aims to select train, motivate and assist potential and existing entrepreneurs who want to diversify or introduce new products. Its basic approach is to act as midwife for the energy and creativity that already exists in individuals wanting to establish small enterprises. The NBC programme is based on German GTZ's model of Creation of Enterprises and Formation of Entrepreneurship (CEFE), which was developed in Nepal as part of the multifaceted assistance scheme known as the GTZ Small Business Promotion Project. The duration of the course is one month. MIDAS promotes NBC training through advertisements in daily newspapers. Candidates are required to submit application forms. Prospective candidates are evaluated on the basis of NBC selection guidelines, which include goal clarity, financial capability, entrepreneurial history and characteristics, and for financial support. On request, MIDAS also conducts the NBC course for participants selected by other organizations. The course addresses all the essential training elements.

Bangladesh Rural Advancement Committee (BRAC)

Operating in Bangladesh since 1972, BRAC implements a number of multi-sectoral programmes in pursuit of its two major goals of poverty alleviation and empowerment of the poor. BRAC activities, directed towards poor, disadvantaged women, stem from the belief that people can change their own destiny through individual and cooperative action.

Training is an integral part of every BRAC programme, especially in the areas of human development and management and occupational skill development. Skill development training is provided in poultry and livestock development, fisheries, irrigation, afforestation, vegetable cultivation and sericulture. Programme duration varies from 1-30 days.

Gana Shasthya Kendra (GSK)

Given that women are among the most oppressed and have the lowest status in the family in terms of entitlement to food, education, income, security and treatment as independent human beings, the GSK started a women's emancipation programme in 1973.

This scheme aims (i) to establish the rights of women by promoting awareness building and changing women's status in society, and (ii) to empower the poor by promoting education, particularly among poor women and children. The GSK established a Nari Kendra (Women's Centre) in 1973 to train women in various traditional and non-traditional occupational skills to increase employment opportunities and capacity for income generation. Nari Kendra manages such production activities as laundry services, jute and bamboo products, a sewing centre, a bakery and poultry. All of these originated as training centres, later developing as training-*cum*-production units. In addition, the GSK has successfully demonstrated that women can be professionally trained in what is too often thought of as "men's work" and that they can do the work efficiently and responsibility.

Business Advisory Services Centre (BASC)

The BASC is a non-profit organization aiming to promote growth by providing technology and market information, training, consultancy and advisory services for business development. It undertakes special programmes related to women in business and micro-enterprise development. Established in 1991 under an agreement between the Government of Bangladesh and USAID, BASC provides services to business enterprises, entrepreneurs, financial institutions, development agencies, and private voluntary organizations. BASC offers customers a wide range of services. It conducts training programmes in entrepreneurship development, business management, skill development, training of trainers and human resources development.

3. *Private-Sector Membership Associations*

National Association of Small and Cottage Industries of Bangladesh (NASCIB)

A private-sector trade association for the promotion and development of the small cottage industries (SCI) sector, NASCIB is the apex organization of entrepreneurs. NASCIB offers its members a range of services including credit availability; infrastructure support; SCI sector policy formulation; technological support; marketing assistance; training; database activity; and dissemination of information.

NASCIB programmes are directed at assisting existing SCI entrepreneurs.

The New Business Creation (NBC) course is basically organized for NASCIB members, who are already entrepreneurs, to help expand or diversify their businesses. The NBC is a three-day programme covering entrepreneur identification, project idea selection, location of business, preparation of business plan, technical know-how and marketing. It includes a field visit to a small industrial unit to collect practical ideas about marketing, technical, financial and organizational management. Counselling and guidance, however, are provided upon request to participants in such areas as marketing, technology, business information, and infrastructures support.

Bangladesh Employers' Federation (BEF)

The BEF is an all-country organization representing nearly every established employer in the private sector and all sector associations and autonomous bodies. This is the only recognized organization of employers, and enjoys representation on all national committees and boards concerned with labour-management relations. The BEF provides comprehensive services to member firms covering all aspects of industrial relations. Management training is a regular feature of its activities. BEF promotes women entrepreneurship by organizing various training programmes and workshops. It maintains close links with international organizations such as the International Labour Organizations (ILO) and the International Organization of Employers (IOE).

Women Entrepreneurs' Association (WEA)

WEA, Bangladesh was formed as a follow-up of a seminar on "Women Entrepreneurship Development: Women in Business", jointly organized by the Bangladesh Employers' Association and ILO/UNDP in 1994. Major WEA activities include workshops and seminars to create awareness and an enabling environment for women entrepreneurship development; linkages of members with support service organizations; fairs and exhibitions promoting female entrepreneurs products; sharing successful experiences of entrepreneurs at home and abroad; training and consultancy services and dissemination of information concerning available support services (training, credit, marketing channels, technology, etc); liaison with similar organizations in other countries; and research on related issues. Most of the members received training on entrepreneurship; marketing; accounting and production management from different organizations.

4. *Professional Associations*

Dhaka Chamber of Commerce and Industry (DCCI), Chittagong Chamber of Commerce and Industry (CCCI), Sylhet Chamber of Commerce and Industry (SCCI) and the National Association of Small and Cottage Industries of Bangladesh (NASCIB) organized ED training programme in a limited scale. However, these programs in true sense of the term provide training assistance which is a part of the total entrepreneurship development programme.

4 Lessons for Sri Lanka from Bangladesh Perspectives: A Discussion

Bangladesh has also been working to develop entrepreneurial resources in the country. Various Government, private sector membership organization, and NGOs have been working side by side to promote entrepreneurship skills especially among the different segments of its people. These organizations are basically working in the ED with different degrees of success.

Sri Lanka is primarily an agricultural country with a wide range of crops ranging from tropical to semi-temperate, grown on about 1/3rd of the country. The chief crop is rice, which is the staple diet of the people. Tea, rubber, coconut and spices are important agricultural crops. The country has a reasonably well-developed economic infrastructure whilst continuing to be an export-import economy. At present entrepreneurship training is conducted by several governmental, non-governmental and private sector agencies in Sri Lanka. However, the system has not been properly utilized due to the lack of co-ordination in the sector itself as well as with other sectors, and the lack of relevant policy to stimulate growth in this sector. The identification of various business linkages is a crucial prerequisite to introducing proper co-ordination and relevant policies. In this situation, micro, small and medium enterprises in Sri Lanka mostly depend on business owners' (entrepreneurs) relationships and contact with other institutions and organizations.

3. POLICY IMPLICATIONS FOR SRI LANKA

The following policy implications may be helpful to promote the entrepreneurship to practitioners, researchers, planners, policy-makers and academicians of Sri Lanka.

Development of Entrepreneurship and Managerial Talent

The main input for development of entrepreneurship and management talent is training program which increases motivation and changes attitude of both entrepreneurs and executives. It focuses and teaches on how to appraise projects, manage projects, and manage finance, and have to use effectively the essential of management techniques in the business. Such training programmes for entrepreneurship development can be designed so that entrepreneurial qualities; intelligence; industrious; innovate, enterprising talent and risk taking capability and so on can be enhanced. To achieve these, Government organisations, NGOs, Universities and trade associations can play a vital role for the development of entrepreneurs and managerial talent with frequent and goal-oriented training programme. Timely evaluation of the programmes is also essential to make them objective and requirement-based.

Research and Development Forum

Entrepreneurs, bankers and policy-makers need information about potential and existing competitors, finance, market and technology as well. A research cell involving representatives from concerned agencies including universities can be engaged in finding innovative plans and ideas refining information, developing new method of production and collecting the news about the advent of new technology in business. This type of cell may be formed either at private level or at Government level of both, so that all interested groups can get information for the development of business and activities upon request on fee basis.

Educational Policy

To develop entrepreneurship, Government should change her present education policy. In this regard Government should introduce some courses relating to entrepreneurship development in various levels (Especially in higher level of education). Government should encourage business associations to establish training institutions to start consultancy services and to introduce training programmes in district as well as provincial-wise.

Entrepreneurship Development Institute

The Government should establish similar institutes in other areas of the country at least one in each assistant government divisions. In this connection the examples of India may be mentioned where there are a number of Government sponsored institutes or centres offering entrepreneurship development programmes at national level and state levels. For example, Entrepreneurship Development Institute of India (EDII), Ahmedabad, National Institute of Entrepreneurship and Small Business (NIESBUD), Delhi, Small Industries Service Institutes (SISI), National Institute for Small Industry Extension and Training (NISIET), National Science and Technology Entrepreneurship Development Board (NSTEDB), etc. at national level and Institutes of Entrepreneurship Development (IED) and Centre for Entrepreneurship Development (CED) at state levels work for the training and promotion of entrepreneurship throughout the country. A directory of industrial, technical and management experts is to be prepared so that prospective entrepreneurs can make use of their expertise at various stages of establishing the units.

Integrated Package Assistance

Integrated package assistance, viz., stimulative, supportive and sustaining services may be offered by the governmental and promotional agencies to the sample entrepreneurs in order to develop entrepreneurship in study areas. For this purpose, clear-cut policy decisions may be advocated.

Development of Financial Sector

For the development of entrepreneurship and entrepreneur in Sri Lanka financial sector should be developed through creating mobility, framing realistic policy and making administration. Loan should be given to the real entrepreneurs (free from political and trade union pressure). Professional and efficient bankers should be appointed in top positions for managing and administrating the financial sector. At the time of sanctioning loans, nepotism, favouritism, political pressure should be avoided. The real entrepreneurs should get loan after proper appraisal of their projects within a limited period of time.

There should be certain cells in every bank for appraisal of projects, sanctioning of loans and recovery of the same. These cells will complete their work within a short period of time and then comment whether the project is acceptable or not. In this regard, it may be pointed out that the bank authority should take every possible step, so that the entrepreneurs are not harassed unnecessarily.

Monetary, Fiscal, Import and Export Policy

The Government should frame and declare such a monetary policy as to stabilize the rate of interest, create savings, encourage investment and also develop capital and money markets. Government should take care for the development and encouragement of the entrepreneurs as well as local industries while framing fiscal, import and export policies. The Government also should control smuggling, remove red tapism and administrative complexity. The Government must be willing to help the entrepreneurs so that they can easily and timely get their projects passed from the concerned departments. It will help the entrepreneurs to implement their projects in time and thus overall entrepreneurship will develop automatically. In short, the role of the Government should be promotive as well as supportive.

Government and opposition in the parliament on the basis of consensus should frame relevant policies permanently through revision of existing polices in order to (a) bring back the confidence of entrepreneurs of SMEs in Government policies; (b) ensure consistency in all projects; (c) protect the interest of SME by removing or minimising tariff wall; (d) make SMEs competitive in domestic and foreign market; (e) establish a special tribunal to dispose the pending cases quickly regarding loan defaulting.

Information Regarding Current Changes

Information regarding current changes in the national and global scenario of business and trade should be provided to the entrepreneurs in time. The different information technology i.e., fax, telex, telephone, internet, e-mail and computer networks may be used by supporting agencies for the purpose.

The Labour-Management Relations

The labour-management relations of the enterprises should be made cordial. This would help to make a congenial working environment, which in turn contributes to the achievement of organizational targets. Understanding of human behaviour and knowledge about human relations may be effective for the purpose.

4. CONCLUDING REMARKS

Entrepreneurship is essential to wealth building *vis-a-vis* national development. It needs favourable environment basically the political, legal, socio-cultural and economic environment. Then the entrepreneur to turn those resources into productive and profitable resources. it is expected that the political environment will improve financial institutions will be able to supply sufficient loans to the real entrepreneurs, law and other order situations will improve, social attitude will be changed towards industrial entrepreneurship, economic infrastructure will be extended and human resources will be developed. As a result, the growth and development of entrepreneurship will be ensured. These recommendations would be helpful to the practitioners, researchers, planners, policy-makers and academicians, who are involved in the concern area.

References

Cole, A.H. (1942). Entrepreneurship as an Area of Research, the Task of Economies History.

Cunningham, J.B. and Lischerson, J. (1991). Defining Entrepreneurship. *Journal of Small Business Management*, 29, (1):44-61.

Glos, S. and Lowery. (1980). Business: Its Nature and Environment, (9th ed.), Cincinnati, Ohio: South- Klestern Publishing Co, 616-17.

McClelland, D.C. (1961). The Achieving Society, New York: D. Van Norstrand Co, 210-15.

Nazma, A.H. (1994). Women Entrepreneurs in a Poverty Ridden Society: A Case Study Bangladesh, Khair Jahan Sogra (Ed), Women in Management: Champions of Changes, Dhaka, Bangladesh: University Press Ltd., 108.

Robbins, S.P. and Coulter, M. (1998). Management, Prentice Hall, India: 19.

Rahman, A.H.M.H. (1997). Entrepreneurship Development as a Strategy for Promoting Development of Industrialization in Bangladesh, paper presented in seminar, July 3rd, University of Dhaka, Bangladesh.

Kao, J.J. (1989). Entrepreneurship, Creative and Organization, Text Cases and Readings. New Jersey: Prentice Hall.

Rahman, A.H.M.H. (1989). Profile of Bangladesh Entrepreneurs, Bangladesh Business Research Report, University Grants Commission, 1:67-80.

Rahman, A.H.M.H. (1979). Entrepreneurship Development as a Strategy for Promoting Development of Industrialization in Bangladesh, paper presented seminar, July 3rd.

12

Managing Business Intelligence in Internet Worked Knowledge Enterprises

A. SURYANARAYANA

ABSTRACT

In an economy where the only certainty is uncertainty, the one sure source of lasting competitive advantage is 'business intelligence'. When markets shift, technologies proliferate, competitors multiply, and products become obsolete almost overnight, successful companies are those that consistently create new knowledge, disseminate it widely throughout the organization, and quickly embody it in new technologies and products. To many companies today, this enduring competitive advantage can only be theirs if they become knowledge-creating companies or learning organizations. The rapid pace of change in today's business environment had made Information Systems (IS) and Information Technology (IT) vital components that help keep an enterprise on target to meet its business goals. IT has become an indispensable ingredient in several strategic thrusts that businesses have initiated to meet the challenge of change.

We are living in an emerging Global Information Society, with a global economy that is increasingly dependent on the creation, management, and distribution of information resources over interconnected global networks like the Internet. It is an indisputable fact information technologies can give a business a strategic technology platform that supports electronic commerce and enterprise collaboration among the internet-worked enterprises in today's knowledge driven global business environment. Business Process Reengineering is an example of how IT is being used to restructure work by transforming business processes. Using IT for globalization and BPR frequently results in the development of IS that help give a company a competitive advantage in the market place. In order to survive and flourish in a rapidly changing business scenario, more and more organizations are developing Knowledge Management Systems (KMS) to manage organizational learning and business intelligence.

Keywords: Business Intelligence; Knowledge Management; Global Information Society; Strategic Technology Platform; Business Process Reengineering; Expert Systems; Internet Value Chain; and Knowledge Management Systems.

INTRODUCTION

In an economy where the only certainty is uncertainty, the one sure source of lasting competitive advantage is '*Knowledge*'. When markets shift, technologies proliferate, competitors multiply, and products become obsolete almost overnight, successful companies are those that consistently create new knowledge, disseminate it widely throughout the organization, and quickly embody it in new technologies and products. These activities define the "knowledge-creating" company, whose sole business is continuous innovation.[1] To many companies today, this enduring competitive advantage can only be theirs if they become knowledge-creating companies or learning organizations.

Knowledge-creating companies exploit two kinds of knowledge. One is *explicit knowledge*—data, documents, things written down or stored on computers. The other kind is *tacit knowledge*—"the HOW-TOs" of knowledge, which reside in employees. Successful *Knowledge Management* (KM) creates techniques, technologies, and rewards for getting employees to share what they know and to make better use of accumulated workplace knowledge. In that way, employees of a company are leveraging knowledge as they do their jobs.[2]

New knowledge always begins with the individual. A brilliant researcher has an insight that leads to a new patent. A middle manager's intuitive sense of market trends becomes the catalyst for an important new product concept. A shop-floor worker draws on years of experience to come up with a new process innovation. In each case, an individual's personal knowledge is transformed into organizational knowledge valuable to the company as a whole. Making personal knowledge available to others is the central activity of the knowledge creating company. It takes place continuously and at all levels of the organization.[3]

THE ROLE OF INFORMATION SYSTEMS AND INFORMATION TECHNOLOGY IN BUSINESS INTELLIGENCE AND KM

Today's managers need all the help they can get. Their firms are being buffeted on all sides by strong, frequently shifting winds of change. Organizations' strategic objectives (chosen markets, product strategy, expected outcomes) and their business processes (such as Research and Development, Production, Cash-flow management, and Order fulfilment) are undergoing significant and volatile changes, placing great pressure on firms and their managers.[4] The rapid pace of change in today's business environment had made *Information Systems* (IS) and *Information Technology* (IT) vital components that help keep an enterprise on target to meet its business goals. IT has become an indispensable ingredient in several strategic thrusts that businesses have initiated to meet the challenge of change.

THE ROLE OF INTERNET IN A GLOBAL INFORMATION SOCIETY

We are living in an emerging *Global Information Society*,

with a global economy that is increasingly dependent on the creation, management, and distribution of information resources over interconnected global networks like the *Internet*. So information is a basic resource in today's society. People in many nations no longer live in agricultural societies, composed primarily of farmers, or even industrial societies, where a majority of the workforce consists of factory workers. Instead, much of the workforce in many nations consists of workers in service occupations or *Knowledge Workers*, that is, people who spend most of their time communicating and collaborating in teams and workgroups and creating, using, and distributing information. Business end users are knowledge workers who are part of a global information society. Knowledge workers include executives, managers, and supervisors; professionals such as accountants, engineers, scientists, stockbrokers, and teachers; and staff personnel such as secretaries and clerical office personnel. We are living in an IT era where information technology is internet-working enterprises and individuals where they may be creating a global internet-worked society of universal connectivity. In the immediate future, IT will exploit this connectivity, so that digital multimedia content will be available for all applications anywhere at any time to create a true global information society.

IT AS A STRATEGIC TECHNOLOGY PLATFORM FOR BUSINESS ENTERPRISES

IT is reshaping the basics of business. Customer service, operations, product and marketing strategies, and distribution are heavily, or sometimes even entirely, dependent on IT. The computers that support these functions can be found on the desk, on the shop floor, in the store, even in briefcases. IT and its expense have become an everyday part of business life.[5] Information systems can perform three vital roles in any type of organization viz., support of business operations, support of managerial decision-making, and support of strategic competitive advantage.

IT has become a strategic necessity. Believe it, act on it, or become a footnote in history.[6] Today, CEOs need to understand how IT is changing our business and must ensure that their organizations use technology effectively. Consequently, it is no surprise they may end up spending a lot of their time trying to understand the implications of new technologies. Even the CIOs are expected to have a rock-solid business view of technology and the line managers have to demonstrate that they not only understand IT but also apply it to their unique business situations and use it for the strategic success of their firms. IT, in all its forms, is expected to transform data resources into a variety of information products.

The revolution in business caused by the Internet and its related technologies demonstrates that IS and IT are essential ingredients for the success of today's internet-worked knowledge business enterprise. Therefore, all managers, entrepreneurs, and business professionals must learn how to use and manage a variety of information technologies to revitalize business processes, improve managerial decision-making, and gain competitive advantage. The imperativeness of the identification, acquisition, and application of areas of knowledge of information systems they need for 21st Century business end users can hardly be exaggerated. Businesses can use IT for strategic competitive advantage through enterprise internet-working, globalization, and business process reengineering.

It is an indisputable fact that Internet, intranets, and extranets, and many other information technologies, can give a business a *strategic technology platform* that supports electronic commerce and enterprise collaboration among the internet-worked enterprises in today's knowledge driven global business environment. In this context, this paper provides knowledge management perspective to the role of information systems and technologies in knowledge-intense firms by placing a major emphasis on the strategic role of IT in solving business problems, gaining competitive advantage, supporting business operations and managerial decision-making, and enabling electronic commerce and enterprise collaboration. Let us consider, in this context, the following statements:

- When IT *substitutes* for human effort, it automates a task or process.

- When IT *augments* human effort, it 'informates' a task or process.
- When IT *restructures,* it transforms a set of tasks or processes.[7]

Businesses have used IT for many years to automate business processes and support the analysis and presentation of information for managerial decision-making. However, *Business Process Reengineering* (BPR)—the fundamental rethinking and radical redesign of business processes to achieve dramatic improvements, such as cost, quality, service, and speed by questioning all assumptions about "the way we do business"—is an example of how IT is being used to restructure work by transforming business processes.

Using IT for globalization and BPR frequently results in the development of IS that help give a company a *competitive advantage* in the market place. These strategic information systems use IT to develop products, services, processes, and capabilities that give a business a strategic advantage over the competitive forces it faces in industry. These forces include not only a firm's competitors but also its customers and suppliers, potential new entrants into its industry, and companies offering substitutes for its products and services.

To confront each of these competitive forces facing a company, IT can support and enable a variety of competitive strategies and play a major role in implementing such strategies as well. They may include, *inter alia,* cost strategies, differentiation strategies, innovation strategies. In this context, names such as Levitz Furniture, Deere & Company, Navistar, Merrill Lynch, Federal Express etc., loom large to exemplify how companies used IT to implement strategies for competitive advantage.

EXPERT SYSTEMS/KNOWLEDGE-BASED INFORMATION SYSTEMS

The frontiers of information systems are being affected by development in *Artificial Intelligence* (AI). AI is an area of computer science, whose long-range goal is to develop computers that can think, as well as see, hear, walk, talk, and feel. For example, AI projects involve the development of natural computer interfaces, advanced industrial robots, and intelligent computer software. A major thrust is the development of computer functions normally associated with human intelligence, such as reasoning, learning, and problem-solving.

"AI is making its way back to the mainstream of corporate technology, this time at the core of business systems that are providing competitive advantage in all sorts of industries, including electronics, transportation, manufacturing, software, medicine, entertainment, engineering, and communication. Designed to leverage the capabilities of human rather than replace them, today's AI technology enables an extraordinary array of applications that forge new connections among people, computers, knowledge, and the physical world. AI-enabled applications are at work in information distribution and retrieval, database mining, product design, manufacturing, inspection, training, user support, surgical planning, resource scheduling, and complex resource management.

Indeed, for anyone who schedules, plans, allocates resources, designs new products, uses the Internet, develops software, is responsible for quality, is an investment professional, heads up IT, uses IT, or operates in any of a score of other common capacities and arenas, new AI technologies already may be in place and providing competitive advantage".[8]

One of the most practical applications of AI is the development of *Expert Systems* (ES). An expert system is a knowledge-based information system; that is, it uses its knowledge about a specific area to act as an expert consultant to users. The components of an expert system are a knowledge-base and software modules that perform inferences on the knowledge and offer answers to a user's questions. ES are being used in many different fields, including medicine, engineering, the physical sciences, and business. For example, ES now help diagnose illnesses, search for minerals, analyze compounds, recommend repairs, and do financial planning. They can support either operations or management activities. The benefits of such systems such as preservation and replication of expertise must be balanced with their limited applicability in many problem situations.

Role of Knowledge Engineers: A knowledge engineer is a professional who works with experts to capture the knowledge (facts and rules of thumb) they possess. He then builds the knowledge-base (and the rest of the expert system if necessary), using an iterative, prototyping process until the expert system is acceptable. They perform a role similar to that of systems analysts in conventional information systems development. Obviously, such professionals require people skills, as well as a background in AI and IS.

KNOWLEDGE MANAGEMENT SYSTEMS (KMS)

Many companies today realize that they must become knowledge-creating companies or learning organizations in order to survive and flourish in a rapidly changing business scenario. That means constantly creating new business knowledge, disseminating it within the organizations, and quickly building it into new products and services. The knowledge-creating company must find ways to use knowledge management techniques and IT to encourage employees to share what they know and make better use of accumulated workplace knowledge.

More and more organizations are developing Knowledge Management Systems (KMS) to manage organizational learning and business know-how. KMS help knowledge workers create, organize, and share important business knowledge wherever and whenever it is needed. For example, many KMS rely on Internet and intranet Web sites, knowledge bases, and discussion forums as key technologies for gathering, storing, and disseminating business knowledge. In this way, KMS facilitate organizational learning and knowledge creation and dissemination within the enterprise. For example, the data mining process can transform data in a data warehouse into knowledge.[9]

KM has thus become one of the major strategic uses of IT. Many companies are building KMS to manage organizational learning and business know-how. This includes processes, procedures, patents, reference works, formulas, "best practices," forecasts, and fixes. KMS use a variety of information technologies to collect and edit information, assess its value, disseminate it within the organization, and apply it as knowledge to the processes of a business. They are sometimes called adaptive learning systems as they create cycles of organizational learning called learning loops, where the creation, dissemination, and application of knowledge produces an adaptive learning process within a company.

KMS can provide rapid feedback to knowledge workers, encourage behaviour changes by employees, and significantly improve business performance. As the organizational learning process continues and its knowledge-base expands, the knowledge-creating company integrates its knowledge into its business processes, products, and services. This makes it a highly innovative and agile provider of high quality products and customer services, and a formidable competitor in the marketplace.[10]

CONCLUDING REMARKS

Companies need a *strategic framework* that can bridge the gap between simply connecting to the Internet and harnessing its power for competitive advantage. The most valuable Internet applications allow companies to transcend communication barriers and establish connections that will enhance productivity, stimulate innovative development, and improve customer relations. Implementing such applications requires more than technical expertise. Managers must understand the competitive forces influencing electronic commerce today, evaluate the strengths and weaknesses of the commercial Internet, and analyze the internal factors that will generate momentum and support for [Internet-based] programs.[11]

Though Internet can be used strategically for competitive advantage, in order to optimize this strategic impact, a company must continually assess the strategic position of its Internet-based applications. A *strategic positioning matrix* can help a company identify where to concentrate its use of the Internet. In such a matrix, while collaboration, information, application requirements, and cost containment act as the internal drivers, customer connectivity, competition, and technology act as the external drivers to produce four alternative positioning strategies. They may be in the form of cost and efficiency improvements, performance improvement in business effectiveness, global market penetration, or product and service transformation.

Trying to come up with an *Internet Value Chain* would be a good idea as it demonstrates the strategic business value of Internet-based applications that focus on a company's relationships with its customers. For example, company-managed Internet newsgroups and Web sites are powerful tool for market research and product development, direct sales, and customer feedback and support. If the same are used with suppliers, they can substantially lower costs, reduce lead times, and improve the quality of products and services. Similarly, the company's internal operations can also benefit strategically from them.

For example, communication costs can be drastically reduced while improving the quality and amount of communications within a company, and with its customers, suppliers, and business partners. This can result in new strategic alliance with business partners and extensive use of virtual teams and telecommuting via online collaboration technologies like discussion forums and videoconferencing. Dramatic increases in flexibility, agility, and responsiveness in developing and supporting new products and services can provide significant opportunities for competitive advantage.

However, one should bear in mind that sustained success in the strategic use of information technology is not a sure thing. Success depends on many environmental and foundation factors, but also on the actions and strategies of a company's management team. For 21st Century knowledge managers, developing strategic business uses of IT shall remain one of their biggest managerial challenges and opportunities.

Notes and References

1. Nonaka, Ikujiro, "The Knowledge Creating Company". *Harvard Business Review,* November-December 1991.

2. *Ibid.*
3. *Ibid.*
4. Cash, James I., Jr., Robert G. Eccles; Nitin Nohria; and Richard L. Nolan. *Building the Information—Age Organization: Structure, Control, and Information Technologies.* Burr Ridge, IL: Richard D. Irwin, 1994.
5. Keen, Peter G.W., Shaping the Future: *Business Design through Information Technology.* Cambridge: Harvard Business School Press, 1991.
6. Champy, Jim, "Now Batting Cleanup: Information Technology". *Computerworld,* October 28, 1996.
7. Cash, James I., Jr.; *et al.*
8. Winston, Parick, "Rethinking Artificial Intelligence", Program Announcement, Massachusetts Institute of Technology, September 1997.
9. Fayyad, Usama, Gregory Piatetsky-Shapiro; and Padhraic Smith. "The KDD Process for Extracting Useful Knowledge from Volumes of Data". *Communications of the ACM,* November 1996.
10. Nonaka, Ikujiro, *op. cit.*
11. Cronin Mary, *The Internet Strategy Handbook.* Boston: Harvard Business School Press, 1996.

13

Emotional Intelligence among HR Professionals
An Empirical Study

M. Manohar and A. Suryanarayana

ABSTRACT

Every professional receives an elaborate structure of technical skills to serve his or her clientele through the professional course he pursues. But, rarely do we come across the same professional courses addressing the issue of imparting them the all-important human skills to be able to eventually practice them in their careers. Every profession ordains that its members practice a code of conduct in the application of their technical and human skills. Professionals learn the soft skills mostly through experience to complement the technical aspects of organizational life. A few extraordinary professionals may attain success despite their arrogant interpersonal behaviour. But an average professional's success comes through a blend of human skills alongside the nitty-gritty of other techniques acquired in a Professional Institution. On the contrary, there are also instances of professionals, who are technically below-average, being able to achieve a high level of success solely because of their human skills. This calls for a special role for HR professionals in every organization and it is their Emotional Intelligence (EI) that becomes crucial for building the organizational competencies, of course, through their employees.

For instance, Technical knowledge may be adequate to conduct formal communication in a profession. But one needs to possess a degree of EI as well to conduct effectively with one's significant internal and external publics as they involve emotions in large measure. Members of Faculties in various professional courses are in a better position to inculcate the required intricacies among their students by honing their human skills involving emotional factors. The emergence of a 'knowledge workforce' with flat hierarchies has heightened the need for application of EI for effective learning. This study is an attempt to survey the usage of EI by HR professionals in various organizations. It also suggests a package of inputs that should go into formal education of HR Professionals, which in turn would equip them to select and groom better candidates for their organizations.

OBJECTIVES

The principal objectives of this empirical study are:

- To discuss the current scenario of application of EI by HR professionals in Hyderabad.
- To examine the challenges and issues facing the HR managers in Small and Medium Companies in the area of Change Management through application of EI.
- To identify the factors that make study and use of emotional intelligence an emerging discipline in study of professional management.

ASSUMPTIONS

- HR managers in Private Sector Companies have higher Emotional Quotient (EQ, an indicator of EI) than those in Public Sector employees.

- The EI increases proportionately with age and experience of the HR professional and is reflected in the EQ

HYPOTHESIS

Hypotheses of the study are formulated based on the objectives of the study and are stated below:

- There is a significant relationship between designation of HR Professional and degree of EI.
- There is a significant relationship between income of the HR professional and the degree of EI.

SURVEY OF LITERATURE

Stephen Covey in his book, "Seven Habits of Highly Effective People" did make an indirect reference to Emotional Intelligence (EI). For example, in his discussion on the very first effective habit, he observed the following responses coming from some typical personal cases:

1. "I achieved tremendous professional success, but it cost me my family life and personal freedom. Is it worth it?"
2. "I attended several Training Programs along with other employees but there seems to be no change. Employees continue to remain dependent and irresponsible.
3. I see my friends and relatives achieve a great degree of success. I smile and congratulate but inside, I feel jealous.

Stephen Covey's second effective habit speaks of human behaviour involving various emotions. They result in several behaviours such as Money-centered, Work-centered, Pleasure-centered, Friend-centered, Enemy-centered, Religion-centered, Self-centered, Spouse-centered, and Family-centered behaviours. All these are various sets of emotions, which when used intelligently can contribute to effective professional management. He even discusses about emotional bank account comprising of six major deposits. They are:

1. Understanding individuals
2. Attending to little things
3. Keeping commitments
4. Clarifying expectations
5. Showing integrity
6. Apologizing on mistakes

Stephen covey's fifth effective habit asks every person to understand himself first before being understood by the others. This also has reference to Emotional Intelligence concepts such as Empathetic listening and Diagnosis before prescription. In his book, "The art of winning", Jack Welch, the former CEO of General Electric, makes only a subtle reference to emotional intelligence. His concept of *differentiation* is crucial. Darwin also refers to Emotional Intelligence Management.

Companies transform from 'mediocre' to 'outstanding' state when they cultivate the strong performers and cull out the weak links. Companies suffer when they treat every one as equal. Winning leaders invest where the payback is the highest and they cut their losses everywhere else. Differentiation is a way to manage people and businesses. Every company has strong and weak product lines. Differentiation requires managers to know 'which is which' and invest accordingly. Not every soccer player can be a great football player. This is true of doctors, programmers, musicians, or poets. What is true in sports is true in business as well. If you want best people in your team you must face up differentiation because it means more transparency, fairness, and speed.

INTRODUCTION

In this paper, we have made an attempt to seek answers to the following questions:

- What is Emotional Intelligence (EI)?

- What are its components?
- Whether they can be observed and thereby controlled in a scientific manner?
- Whether EI is practiced by HR professionals?
- Whether it is possible to establish the linkage between EI and effective recruitment?
- Whether there can be a linkage between training and other HR Practices?

It is a well-known fact that effective inter-personal communication among the peers and subordinates contributes to *team spirit* and thereby leads to self-growth and development.

Every organization works on several projects simultaneously. There are several teams working simultaneously on several projects. Each project has several sub-systems. Each sub-system has several players on specific tasks. It is the emotional bonding or the fit between the coordinators of various projects that contributes to smooth functioning of an organization. This is true even in the case of HR professionals who need to gel well with professionals from various functional areas. This emotional bond or fit contributes to organizational loyalty and thereby facilitating the development of the organization. Therefore, it becomes imperative to study as to what machinery can be set-up to study and control the emotions of HR professionals to make organizations successful and effective. The emergence of Business Process Outsourcing (BPO) and Knowledge Process Outsourcing (KPO) organizations has further heightened the need for this study as today's management trainees are future employees of such emotionally stress-prone organizations. This is an attempt to build emotionally stable and winning culture-oriented employees for emotionally intelligent organizations.

Every profession has a sub-culture of its own depending on functions and factors such as rigor in curricula, criticality of professional relationship with beneficiaries, outcomes, and political power. Majority may live up to the expectations of their profession but there are deviants here and there who behave beyond the contours of their profession. You may find persons whom you feel would have been better as teachers than as engineers. Somebody would have been a better priest than a doctor. Problems arise in interpersonal communication when the personality orientations differ from professional expectations. In this context, we may recall the Pareto's Principle of 80/20. Such deviations may be only 20% of the organization but they may be affecting 80% of the organization's efforts or output. These factors are studied in this Paper as HR Professionals have to be constantly aware of them and their impact on prospective employees.

METHODOLOGY

A structured questionnaire was administered to a convenient sample of 100 respondents with equal representation from HR Executives, Assistant HR Managers, Senior HR Managers, AGM (HR) and VP (HR). In addition to this, unstructured interviews were also held with professionals with considerable experience and exposure. The data collected was analyzed through SPSS package. Chi Square tests were conducted and results tabulated for arriving at observations and conclusions.

About the Questionnaire

Many emotional factors, which are common at workplaces have not found a place and are deliberately set aside in the first half of the questionnaire. The questions are not arranged in any particular order. Several emotional factors such as arrogance, sincerity, honesty, patience, total work experience, dependency on repeated instructions to do the simple task, interacting with lady bosses, lady colleagues were excluded because of the sensitive nature of such topics. This subject is so vast and interesting that excluding some common factors has become essential to make the study manageable. Only a few important emotions relevant to HR professionals are included. The second half of the questionnaire is focused more on emotions at workplace.

About Respondents

Our data collection has begun with a premise that not many are emotional while working at office. But our experience after collecting responses to our questionnaire proved otherwise. Some of them were truly professional in answering the entire questionnaire in one go. Some of them took time to read it thoroughly before beginning to answer. Some respondents were reluctant to answer immediately. Some of them had not returned the questionnaire in spite of reminders. In fact, the questionnaire was pre-tested and the average time required to answer the four page questionnaire comprising of about 40 objective-type questions was around 10 minutes. Some senior people were reluctant to fill up minimum personal information alleging possible misusė or harassment by cell phone companies. This matter was specifically explained to some of the respondents that no personal information was being collected with any intention of passing it on to any other agency. Few of them were tactful in saying they would get back to us later but did not respond subsequently. While some very senior people could spare valuable time and helped us in our endeavor to study this subject. Hats-off to their professionalism in proving the old saying that people can spare time to do things they love to do. The Survey covered HR professionals working in the range of 8 hours to 16 hours per day. The organizations covered in the survey had an employee strength ranging from 30 employees to over 3500 employees. The turnover of organizations was in the range of Rs. 3 lakhs to over $ 900 million.

ASSUMPTIONS MADE BEFORE THE STUDY

Our Study started with the following premises:

- Younger HR professionals were more emotional.
- Elderly ones were less emotional in their official communication.
- Post-graduates were less emotional and therefore more effective in their daily routine.
- Private sector HR Professionals have no time for emotions in their communications.

- Emotional fatigue arising out of longer working hours in private sector was a major barrier for effectively discharging their duties.
- Professionals working on routine jobs had lower levels of emotional tolerance.
- And lastly, People working on extraordinary or rare jobs had more emotional bonding and thereby more effective while learning.

Sl. No.	*Emotional Factors*	*Never 0/10*	*Rarely 1-2/10*	*Some times 3-4/10*	*Mostly 5-6/10*	*Always 7-9/10*
1.	Helpful				20	80
2.	Selfish	70	30	20		
3.	Frank				30	70
4.	Tolerance of Indiscipline	30	10	30	20	10
5.	Tolerance of Inefficiency	12	64		12	12
6.	Team Focus				20	80
7.	Task Focus				20	80
8.	Details-oriented				25	75
9.	Summary Oriented				30	70
10.	Humour at office			20	20	60
11.	Gossip at office	35	45			20
12.	Blame others	48	30		10	12
13.	Praise others				75	25
14.	Frequency of seeking your advice			10	50	40
15.	Security at office	12	12		24	52
16.	Technology at office			25	25	50
	Competition at office	10	12		24	54
17.	Patience	40	30		20	10

Emotional Intelligence (EI) broadly includes the ability to perceive accurately, appraise and express emotion, the ability to assess and/or generate feelings, and the ability to understand and regulate emotions. EI operates at personal and social levels. An attempt is made to identify the crucial skill indicators for various emotional states that affect the relationships in a work environment. The study focuses not on the desirability but on the feasibility for better productivity in organizational set-up through control of emotions of team members. It also examines whether machinery for assessing the various emotional states of team members can be set-up, and if so, to what extent it can monitor and contribute to the success of the team-building as the main theme of the Paper.

Emotional Intelligence implies the following:

1. *Self-awareness:* Knowing one's internal states, preferences, resources, and intuitions.
2. *Managing self-emotions:* Managing one's internal states, impulses, and resources.
3. *Motivation:* Emotional tendencies that guide or facilitate reaching the goals.
   (Social Competencies):
4. *Empathy:* Awareness of others' feelings, needs, and concerns.
5. *Social skills:* Adeptness at inducing desirable responses in others

SELF-AWARENESS

In this paper, an attempt is made to identify some of the key indicators of self-awareness as a skill. High self-awareness refers to having an accurate understanding of how you behave, how other people perceive you, recognizing how you respond to others, being sensitive to your attitudes, feelings, emotions, intents, and general communication style at *any given moment,* and being able to accurately disclose this awareness to others.

MANAGING SELF-EMOTIONS

This is a skill and an attempt to identify some of the key indicators of that skill is made in this Paper. This is basically to know when you are: thinking negatively; becoming angry; interpreting events; currently using what senses; able to communicate accurately what you experience and when;

experiencing changes in your moods; becoming defensive; and finally the impact your behaviour has over others. An attempt is also made to assess and recognize one's feelings and emotions as they happen, others' perceptions of one's emotions and one's reactions to others' perceptions.

MOTIVATION

It is the ability to canalize emotions to achieve a goal; to postpone immediate gratification for future gratification; to be productive in low interest; to indulge in low enjoyment activities; to persist in the face of frustration, and to generate initiative without external pressure. It implies the presence of such abilities in all the members who form part of a winning team. However, the degree to which the members actually imbibe and practice may be different in different groups.

Findings

Age Group

Age (In yrs.)	*Number of respondents*
< 25	10
<35	35
<45	45
>45	10

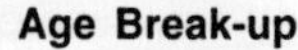

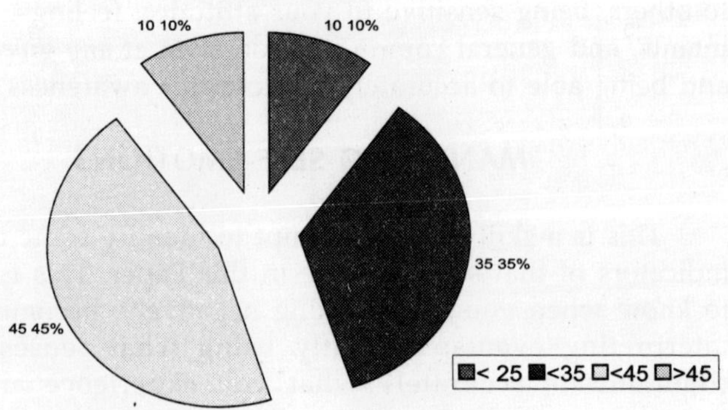

SELF-AWARENESS

In response to the question, "What upsets you?" the respondents across the disciplines have shown marked preference for criticism (32%), followed by frustration (30%) and anger (22%). Only 16% of the respondents have given 'none of the above disturbs them' as their response.

What upsets you?

Anger	25
Frustration	50
Criticism	25

What upsets you?

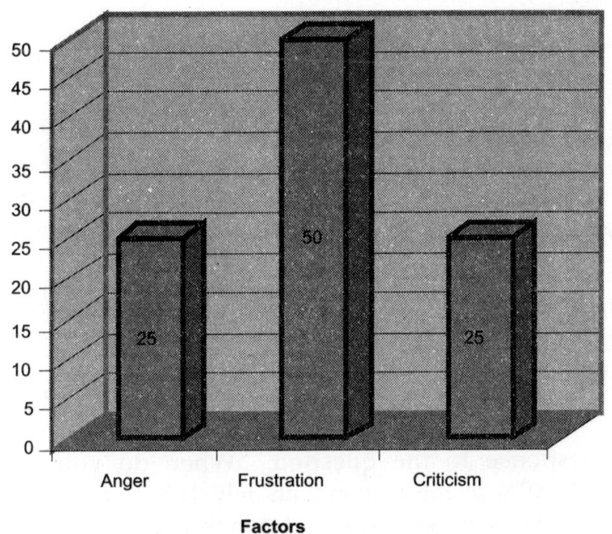

In response to the question, "What changes your moods?" 44% of the respondents blamed the work environment, 22% of the respondents felt that it was the company itself. Only 6% felt it was time of the day or week, and 2% opted for place as the reasons for the changes in their moods.

What Changes Your Moods?

Time	7
Place	13
Environment	30
Company	37
All	13

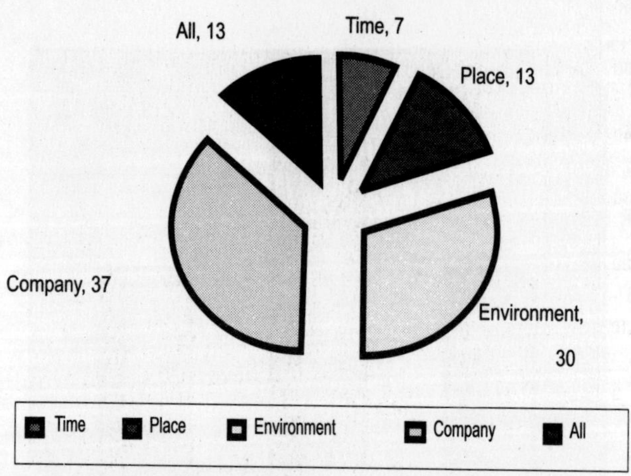

In response to the quęstion, "When do you become defensive?" 40% of the respondents felt that it was 'Offensive Language' that makes them defensive and 60% of the respondents believed that it was others' actions that make them defensive against others.

70% of the respondents preferred to ignore others' perception and only 15% preferred to listen and another 15% preferred to react violently.

MANAGING EMOTIONS

In response to the question, "How do you shake off anxiety, gloom, despair, or irritability?" Various professionals have responded as below:

Shaking-off Emotions

Sharing with others	60
Inner strength	30
Others	10

Shake-off Emotions

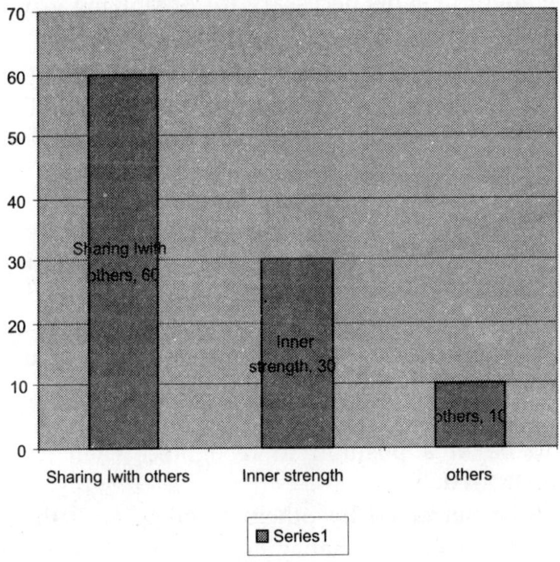

How often do you use anger productively?

Always	25
Often	50
Not so Often	25

SELF-MOTIVATION

What inspires you?

What Inspires You?

Ideals	18
Achievement	54
Work	18
Money	10

Empathy

It is the ability to exchange information at a meaningful level, to be adept in skills necessary for organizing groups and building teams, negotiating solutions, mediating conflict among others, building consensus, and making personal connections. Here again the hypothesis is that empathy of different professionals is independent of the professional backgrounds they come from.

Social Skills

It is the skill to be aware of other people's feelings and emotions; of being able to listen to their feelings; to help others' deal with their feelings and emotions in productive ways and assist them in increasing their awareness about their own impact on others.

Skill Indicators in this context are as follows:

- To be in a position to recognize when others are distressed.
- To be perceived by others as being empathic.
- To be skillful in managing the emotions of others.
- To be able to know when your boss is angry, sad, and anxious?
- To be comfortable with your feelings?

EMOTIONALLY INTELLIGENT ORGANIZATIONS

The emotionally intelligent work group or organization

has a culture that exhibits: Organizational self-Awareness of its internal and external needs; Management of organizational emotions through leadership, Celebration and environment; Organizational Motivation through meaningful work and the delivery of incentives; Organizational Empathy by maintaining effective and meaningful relationships with consumers and employees; Mentoring of Organizational Social Skills through training, productive personnel selection practices, and performance appraisal, and movement towards perfection with regard to emotional intelligent organization.

Communication in Organization

	Harsh	*Soft*	*Mixed*
Superiors	10	70	20
Subordinates	30	40	30
Colleagues		55	45
Clients		70	30

In response to question about Communication with superiors 10% of the respondents have chosen harsh option and 70% have chosen soft option and 20% have chosen mixed mode. This shows that softer communication is effective while dealing with superiors. In relation to subordinates, 40% of the respondents preferred soft way of communication. 30 % preferred mixed mode and 30% preferred 'Harsh' mode of communication. With regard to communication with colleagues 55% preferred soft mode and 45% preferred mixed mode. With regard to communication with clients 70% of the respondents have chosen Soft mode and 30% preferred mixed mode indicating that they were some times harsh and some times soft in dealing with clients.

Nearly 70% of the respondents have a tendency to react faster in their official communication with regard to advice form of communication and 30% preferred to go slow even if it was advice mode of communication.. If it were order form of communication 30% of the respondents tended to be slow to react and 70% were fast to react to order form of communication. 80% of respondents were fast to react to request form of communication indicating their sensitive nature to emotions. There are variations in relation to speed of communication depending on whether it is in the form of advice or order or request.

CONCLUDING REMARKS

Emotions vary with age, experience, designations, specialization of HR professionals, size of organizations, number of employees, timing of communication, number of working hours, freshness or tiredness of the employees, and tone of communication. Emotional fatigue arising from different factors was also blocking effective communication in organizations. Another observation that came to light through discussions with senior executives was that the five senses were the blocking factors for effective communication. Closed mindedness (eyes), thick skin nature, deaf ears, abusive tongue, and trouble smelling nature (nose) were contributing to the emotional disturbances and thereby to ineffective communication and learning in organizations.

Most Professionals are upset by criticism than by anger. This study has once again proved that with age and experience, irrespective of their background, professionals have learnt to mask their emotional injuries in order to ease the process of interpersonal communication and effective learning. Respondents also stated that they undergo a change of mood in large measure due to conditions in the work environment. It may vary on account of the time constraints or the client pressure, or the lack of receptive ability on the part of the recipients of communication. Moreover, a large number of respondents emphatically revealed that it was the offensive language, more than anything else, which makes them defensive in interpersonal relationships. Seventy percent of the respondents preferred to ignore others' perceptions and only 15% preferred to react violently.

Chi-square Test conclusively proves the hypothesis that emotions such as productive anger, inspiration, and ability to shake-off emotions are independent of specializations in HR profession. The study clearly draws the conclusion that

Emotional Intelligence factors examined in the study are common to all HR Professionals. The findings prove the hypothesis that professionals use the Emotional Intelligence factors, in large measure, in their interpersonal communication more due to learning by experience than formal training. Large majority of respondents felt that they would have been better equipped to handle their interpersonal communication had there been inclusion of Emotional Intelligence factors in their professional curriculum.

REFERENCES

Cooper, R.K., and Sawaf, A., 1997. *Executive EQ: Emotional Intelligence in leadership and organizations*. Grosset/Putnam, New York.

Goleman, D. 1998. *Working with Emotional Intelligence.* Bantam Books, New York

Weisinger, H., 1998. *Emotional intelligence at work: The untapped edge for success.* Josey-Bass, San Francisco

www.eiconsortium.org

www.dshs.state.tx.us.

14

Performance of Exchange Traded Funds in the Indian Capital Market

Ms. Sira Sivaraj

INTRODUCTION

An Exchange Traded Fund (ETF) is a type of investment whose objective is to achieve the same return as a particular market index. It is similar to an index fund in that it will primarily invest in the securities of companies that are included in a selected market index. An ETF may invest in either all of the securities or a representative sample of the securities included in the index. Just as their name implies it is a basket of securities that are traded, like individual stocks on the exchange. Unlike regular open-ended mutual funds ETF can be bought and sold throughout the trading day like stock. An ETF combines the benefits of equity, derivative and mutual funds. The unique structure of ETF offers investors with the flexibility to buy or sell on real time prices, very close to its fair value. This is possible due to its unique "in kind" mechanism of creation and redemption through authorized participants. This feature also makes it one of the ideal long-term investment tool as it insulates long-term holders from effects of short-term flows in and out of the fund.

STATEMENT OF THE PROBLEM

ETFs are the leading financial innovation of the last decade. They are a new addition to vocabulary of the Indian investor in the domestic financial markets and a new species in the kingdom of the innovative financial instruments that have become buzzwords in the turbulent stock markets. They provide several advantages such as lower costs, transparency, all day tracking and trading, buying and selling flexibilities and a wide array of investment strategies.

ETFs have gained popularity as an alternative investment instrument since its launch in late 1993. Technically ETF started in India on Dec. 2001, when Benchmark Asset Management Company introduced its fund known as Nifty Bees. Because of its scintillating performances ETFs became popular right from its infant stage. Although ETFs are fairly new investment tools, they are growing and making their mark in the investment world. ETF assets have grown by about 38.2% in 2007 and the number of ETFs available have gone from 359 to 586 in 10 months.

In this present scenario, the study which focuses on the performance of ETF's will definitely help the investors to find out where these funds stand on the basis of its performance. It will also help the investors to understand the various factors that need to be considered for the evaluation of the performance of this fund.

OBJECTIVES OF THE STUDY

- To evaluate the performance of four of the Exchange Traded Funds which are been traded in Indian Stock Market.

- To compare the weekly percentage returns of ETF with its benchmark returns percentage.
- To make a comparative weekly return analysis of ETFs.
- To compare the performance of ETFs on the basis of their tracking error.
- To rank the ETFs based on the Tracking error, Sharpe Ratio, Treynor ratio and Sortino Ratio.
- To evaluate the correlation among the different performance measures of ETFs using Spearman's Rank Correlation.
- To evaluate the performance persistence of ETFs using Winner-Loser Approach.

HYPOTHESIS

The following hypotheses were framed to analyze the performance of ETFs:

Ho: There is no persistence in the performance of the ETF Nifty Bees.

Ho: There is no persistence in the performance of the ETF Nifty Junior Bees.

Ho: There is no persistence in the performance of the ETF Bank Bees.

Ho: There is no persistence in the performance of the ETF UTI Sunder.

Sample Design

There are 15 ETF's listed and traded in the capital market segment of the NSE. Out of this 4 ETF's were randomly selected for the purpose of the study. The ETFs selected are: Nifty Bees, Junior Nifty Bees, Bank Bees, UTI Sunder.

METHODOLOGY AND DATA COLLECTION

Primary data was collected by means of interaction with the members and brokers of Cochin Stock Exchange. Secondary data was collected from various websites and journals.

TOOLS OF ANALYSIS

For analyzing the performance of ETFs the following tools were used.

Return Analysis: Return analysis was done by calculation of thc percentage change in NAV.

Percentage change in NAV
= [{NAV (t)–NAV (t–1)}/NAV (t–1)]*100

where NAV (t) = NAV as on Date.
NAV (t–1) = Entry Value.

Tracking Error Analysis: Tracking error is defined as the annualized standard deviation of the difference in return between the Index fund and its target index. Lower the tracking error, closer are the returns of the fund to that of the target Index.

Tracking Error = √[Σ(Rp–Rb)2/(N–1)]

where Rp = Return of the fund.
Rb = Return of the Benchmark.
N = Number of weeks for which returns are calculated.

Performance Analysis: The performances of the ETFs are compared with the performances of its benchmark. The performance was also analyzed using Sharpe's Ratio, Treynor Ratio and Sortino Ratio.

Sharpe Ratio (SR) = [Σ(Rp–Rf)]/S

where Rp = Realized return on the portfolio.
Rf = Risk free rate of return.
S = Standard deviation of the return.

Treynor Ratio (TR) = [Σ(Rp–Rf)]/β

where Rp = Realized return on the portfolio.

Rf = Risk free rate of return.
β = Systematic Risk.

Sortino Ratio = [ΣRp–Rf]/S

where Rp = Realized return on the portfolio.
Rf = Risk-free rate of return.
S = Standard Deviation of Negative Asset Return.

Risk-free Rate: Risk-free rate is taken as 4.4056%. The risk-free rate is estimated as the yield on 364 days Treasury Bills.

Spearman's Rank Correlation Coefficient: Spearman's Rank Correlation is a ranking order test. This method works by assigning a rank to each observation in each group separately. For the purpose of our study ranks have been assigned on the basis of Sharpe Ratio, Treynor Ratio and Tracking Error. Then the Spearman's Rank Correlation coefficient is calculated.

$R = 1-6[\Sigma D^2]/n(n-1).$

D = Is the difference between the ranks of corresponding values of X and Y.
N = Number of Observations.

Winner-Loser Approach: Winner-Loser Approach is used for evaluating performance persistence. It is used to identify the frequency with which funds are defined as winners and losers over a time period. In this approach each fund is either a winner or a loser. Winner is a fund with returns above the median and a loser as a fund with returns below the median. To test for the independence in the results the statistical test Repeat Winner Approach was used.

1. Repeat Winner Approach

The proportion of repeat winners (WW) to winner-losers (WL).

Percentage Repeat Winners = WW/(WW+WL)

2. Z-test for Repeat Winners

= [WW–0.5(WW+WL)]/√ (WW+WL)*O.5*O.5

where WW = A winner in the first period that remains the winner in the future period.

WL = A fund that moves from being a winner (W) to a loser (L) is a Winner-Loser

LW = A fund shifts from a Loser (L) to a Winner (W) it is a Loser-Winner (LW).

LL = A loser (L) in the first period is also a loser (L) in the future period, is a (LL).

OPERATIONAL TERMS AND DEFINITIONS

1. NAV

The NAV of an ETF is determined in a manner consistent with other mutual funds. It is calculated by taking the total assets of the ETF, less liabilities, divided by the number of ETF shares outstanding.

2. Nifty Bees

An ETF launched by Benchmark Mutual Fund in January, 2002.

3. Nifty Junior Bees

An ETF based on CNX Nifty Junior launched by Benchmark Mutual Fund in February, 2003.

4. Bank Bees

An ETF launched by Benchmark Mutual Fund in May, 2004.

5. UTI SUNDER

An Exchange traded fund launched by UTI in July, 2003.

6. S&P CNX Nifty Index

The Standard and Poor's CRISIL NSE Index 50 is the leading index for large companies on the National Stock Exchange of India. It is a well diversified 50 stock index accounting for 22 sectors of the economy.

7. CNX Nifty Junior Index

The CNX Nifty Junior is an index for companies on the National Stock Exchange of India. It consists of 50 companies representing approximately 10% of the traded value of all stocks on the National Stock Exchange of India.

8. CNX Banking Index

CNX Banking Index is an index comprising of the most liquid and large capitalized Indian Banking Stocks. It consists of 12 stocks taken from the banking sector which trade on the National Stock Exchange.

SCOPE OF THE STUDY

The study deals with the analysis and interpretation of NAV of 4 ETF's over the period 1st December, 2008 to 24th April, 2009 resulting in 22 observations.

PERFORMANCE OF EXCHANGE TRADED FUNDS—AN ANALYSIS

From Table 1 it can be seen that there was a steep decline in returns of Nifty Bees and S&P CNX Nifty Index, by 7.1379% and 7.1871% respectively on 20th February, 2009. However the returns rose by 10.7024% and 10.7444% respectively for Nifty Bees and S&P CNX Nifty Index on 27th March, 2009. The percentage changes in returns of Nifty Bees are similar to its benchmark S&P CNX Nifty. The individual returns of Nifty Bees and S&P CNX Nifty Index are highly volatile and inconsistent.

The percentage change in returns of Nifty Junior Bees is similar to its benchmark CNX Nifty Junior Index. The individual returns of Nifty Junior Bees and CNX Nifty Junior Index are highly volatile and inconsistent.

It can be seen that there is slight difference in the percentage change in returns of Bank Bees and CNX Banking Index on 6th March, 2009 and on 13th March, 2009. The percentage change in returns were –12.7167% and –11.2283% for Bank Bees and CNX Banking Index respectively on 6th

TABLE 1
Weekly Returns of Nifty Bees and S&P CNX Nifty Index

Date	*NAV of Nifty Bees*	*Nifty Bees Return (%)*	*NAV of S&P CNX Nifty Index*	*S&P CNX Nifty Index Return (%)*
1-Dec. -08	270.6261		2682.90	
5-Dec.-08	273.6544	1.1190	2714.40	1.1741
12-Dec.-08	294.4252	7.5902	2921.35	7.6242
19-Dec.-08	310.0888	5.3201	3077.50	5.3451
26-Dec.-08	288.5506	-6.9458	2857.25	-7.1567
02-Jan.-09	307.5606	6.5881	3046.75	6.6323
09-Jan.-09	290.0630	-5.6892	2873.00	-5.7028
16-Jan.-09	285.5728	-1.5480	2828.45	-1.5506
23-Jan.-09	270.4832	-5.2840	2678.55	-5.2997
30-Jan.-09	290.7877	7.5068	2874.80	7.3267
06-Feb.-09	287.6074	-1.0937	2843.10	-1.1027
13-Feb.-09	298.2156	3.6884	2948.35	3.7019
20-Feb.-09	276.9293	-7.1379	2736.45	-7.1871
27-Feb.-09	279.6416	0.9794	2763.65	0.9940
06-Mar.-09	265.1547	-5.1805	2620.15	-5.1924
13-Mar.-09	275.1204	3.7584	2719.25	3.7822
20-Mar.-09	283.9419	3.2064	2807.05	3.2288
27-Mar.-09	314.3306	10.7024	3108.65	10.7444
02-Apr.-09	324.6281	3.2760	3211.05	3.2940
09-Apr.-09	337.8001	4.0576	3342.05	4.0797
17-Apr.-09	342.0332	1.2531	3384.40	1.2672
24-Apr.-09	351.7265	2.8340	3480.75	2.8469

Source : Secondary Data.

TABLE 2
Weekly Returns of Nifty Junior Bees and CNX Nifty Junior Index

Date	*NAV of Nifty Junior Bees*	*Nifty Junior Bees Return (%)*	*NAV of CNX Nifty Junior Index*	*CNX Nifty Junior Index Return (%)*
1-Dec.-08	39.0403		3808.30	
5-Dec.-08	41.3442	5.9013	4036.00	5.979
12-Dec.-08	44.2547	7.0397	4323.85	7.1321
19-Dec.-08	47.0877	6.4016	4603.10	6.4584
26-Dec.-08	4.2509	-6.0245	4325.25	-6.0361
02-Jan.-09	48.7508	10.1691	4769.75	10.2769
09-Jan.-09	45.0689	-7.5525	4408.80	-7.5675
16-Jan.-09	44.0678	-2.2213	4310.90	-2.2206
23-Jan.-09	40.8057	-7.4256	3989.40	-7.4578
30-Jan.-09	43.2465	5.9815	4230.15	6.0347
06-Feb.-09	42.3181	-2.1468	4138.15	-2.1749
13-Feb.-09	44.0382	4.0647	4307.35	4.0888
20-Feb.-09	40.7415	-7.4860	3981.80	-7.5580
27-Feb.-09	40 .7694	-0.0685	3980.55	-0.0314
06-Mar.-09	37.8034	-7.2751	3688.80	-7.3294
13-Mar.-09	38.9841	4.3323	3802.40	4.4017
20-Mar.-09	40.6730	3.1233	3969.75	3.0796
27-Mar.-09	44.8892	10.3661	4390.55	10.6002
02-Apr.-09	46.7893	4.2329	4579.15	4.2956
09-Apr.-09	49.9875	6.8353	4896.25	6.9287
17-Apr.-09	52.2189	4.4639	5118.00	4.5290
24-Apr.-09	54.9353	5.2019	5386.40	5.2442

Source : Secondary Data.

TABLE 3

Weekly Returns of Bank Bees and CNX Banking Index

Date	*NAV of Bank Bees*	*Bank Bees Return (%)*	*NAV of CNX Banking Index*	*CNX Banking Index Return (%)*
1-Dec.-08	419.7952		4124.30	
5-Dec.-08	443.0443	5.5382	4357.00	5.6422
12-Dec.-08	472.8343	6.7239	4655.30	6.8465
19-Dec.-08	521.6772	10.3299	5144.15	10.5009
26-Dec.-08	486.1682	-6.8067	4789.45	6.8952
02-Jan.-09	526.6876	8.3344	5195.10	8.4697
09-Jan.-09	497.8052	-5.4838	4906.70	-5.5514
16-Jan.-09	460.2138	-7.5514	4581.25	-6.6328
23-Jan.-09	410.2582	-10.8549	4081.15	-10.8944
30-Jan.-09	447.6606	9.1168	4456.55	9.1716
06-Feb.-09	435.3738	-2.7447	4334.15	-2.7465
13-Feb.-09	458.5090	5.3139	4565.85	5.3459
20-Feb.-09	395.3176	-13.7819	3934.40	-13.8298
27-Feb.-09	391.0807	-1.0718	3892.40	-1.8300
06-Mar.-09	341.3482	-12.7167	3455.35	-11.2283
13-Mar.-09	365.3389	7.0282	3632.75	5.1341
20-Mar.-09	371.1975	1.6036	3691.70	1.6227
27-Mar.-09	442.6595	19.2517	4406.80	19.3705
02-Apr.-09	444.5514	0.4239	4426.05	0.4368
09-Apr.-09	460.3763	3.5597	4584.80	3.5867
17-Apr.-09	507.5204	10.2403	5056.90	10.2973
24-Apr.-09	514.3185	1.3395	5125.35	1.3535

Source : Secondary Data.

March, 2009. On 13th March, 2009 the percentage change in returns were 7.0282% and 5.1341% respectively.

From Table 4 it can be seen that there are slight difference in the percentage change in returns of UTI SUNDER and S&P CNX Nifty Index on 26th December, 20th February, 6th March and 27th March 2009.

TABLE 4
Weekly Returns of UTI SUNDER and S&P CNX Nifty Index

Date	*NAV of UTI Sunder*	*UTI Sunder Return (%)*	*NAV of S&P CNX Nifty Index*	*S&P CNX Nifty Index Return (%)*
01-Dec.-08	281.8683		2682.90	
05-Dec.-08	285.0791	1.1391	2714.40	1.1741
12-Dec.-08	306.0824	7.3675	2921.35	7.6242
19-Dec.-08	322.0729	5.2242	3077.50	5.3451
26-Dec.-08	300.0997	-6.8224	2857.25	-7.1567
02-Jan.-09	319.4818	6.4586	3046.75	6.6323
09-Jan.-09	301.6777	-5.5728	2873.00	-5.7028
16-Jan.-09	297.0740	-1.5260	2828.45	-1.5506
23-Jan.-09	281.6978	-5.1759	2678.55	-5.2997
30-Jan.-09	302.4498	7.3668	2874.80	7.3267
06-Feb.-09	299.2142	-1.0698	2843.10	-1.1027
13-Feb.-09	310.0345	3.6162	2948.35	3.7019
20-Feb.-09	288.8423	-6.8354	2736.45	-7.1871
27-Feb.-09	291.1815	0.8099	2763.65	0.9940
06-Mar.-09	276.8674	-4.9159	2620.15	-5.1924
13-Mar.-09	286.6382	3.6118	2719.25	3.7822
20-Mar.-09	295.7099	3.1649	2807.05	3.2288
27-Mar.-09	326.9328	11.5731	3108.65	10.7444
02-Apr.-09	337.5253	3.2400	3211.05	3.2940
09-Apr.-09	351.0368	4.0031	3342.05	4.0797
17-Apr.-09	355.3418	1.2263	3384.40	1.2672
24-Apr.-09	365.3099	2.8052	3480.75	2.8469

Source : Secondary Data.

Table 5 shows the comparison of the ETFs on the basis of their weekly returns shows that Bank Bees have highest percentage change in returns, i.e 19.2517% on 27th March, 2009 and it also registered the lowest percentage change in returns, i.e 13.7819% on 20th February, 2009 when compared to the other ETF's. Hence, it can be inferred that Bank Bees provide investors with high risk and returns for their investments.

TABLE 5
Comparative Weekly Returns of ETF's

Date	*Nifty Bees (%)*	*Nifty Junior (%)*	*Banking Bees (%)*	*UTI Sunder (%)*
1-Dec.-08				
5-Dec.-08	1.1190	5.9013	5.5382	1.1391
12-Dec.-08	7.5902	7.0397	6.7239	7.3675
19-Dec.-08	5.3201	6.4016	10.3299	5.2242
26-Dec.-08	-6.9458	-6.0245	-6.8067	-6.8224
02-Jan.-09	6.5881	10.1691	8.3344	6.4586
09-Jan.-09	-5.6892	-7.5525	-5.4838	-5.5728
16-Jan.-09	-1.5480	-2.2213	-7.5514	-1.5260
23-Jan.-09	-5.2840	-7.4256	-10.8549	-5.1759
30-Jan.-09	7.5068	5.9815	9.1168	7.3668
06-Feb.-09	-1.0937	-2.1468	-2.7447	-1.0698
13-Feb.-09	3.6884	4.0647	5.3139	3.6162
20-Feb.-09	-7.1379	-7.4860	-13.7819	-6.8354
27-Feb.-09	0.9794	-0.0685	-1.0718	0.8099
06-Mar.-09	-5.1805	-7.2751	-12.7167	-4.9159
13-Mar.-09	3.7584	4.3323	7.0282	3.6118
20-Mar.-09	3.2064	3.1233	1.6036	3.1649
27-Mar.-09	10.7024	10.3661	19.2517	11.5731
02-Apr.-09	3.2760	4.2329	0.4239	3.2400
09-Apr.-09	4.0576	6.8353	3.5597	4.0031
17-Apr.-09	1.2531	4.4639	10.2403	1.2263
24-Apr.-09	2.8340	5.2019	1.3395	2.8052

Source : Secondary Data.

TABLE 6
Ranking of ETF's based on Tracking Error

Funds	*Tracking Error*	*Rank*
Nifty Bees	0.0650	1
Nifty Junior Bees	0.0770	2
Bank Bees	0.5908	4
UTI Sunder	0.1363	3

Source : Secondary Data.

Nifty Bees have the least tracking error that is 0.0650 and hence it has been assigned a rank of one. Bank Bees have the highest tracking error of 0.5908 and hence it has been assigned the least rank. Based on the value of tracking error it can be inferred that the return of Nifty Bees closely follow the returns of its benchmark S&P CNX Nifty Index while the returns of the ETF Bank Bees do not perfectly track its underlying Benchmark CNX Banking Index.

TABLE 7
Ranking of ETF's based on Sharpe Ratio

Fund	*Average Realized Return on The portfolio*	*Risk free Rate of Return*	*Standard Deviation of the Return*	*Sharpe Ratio*	*Rank*
Nifty Bees	1.6667	0.8811	5.0167	0.1566	2
Nifty Junior Bee	1.8054	0.8811	5.8308	0.1585	1
Bank Bees	1.3234	0.8811	8.3790	0.0528	4
UTI Sunder	1.4137	0.8811	4.9674	0.1072	3

Source : Secondary Data.

The table shows the value of Sharpe Ratio calculated for the four ETF's. Based on the value of Sharpe Ratio ranks have been assigned to each of the ETF's. Higher the value of Sharpe Ratio greater is the return that the investor gets for the risk that he/she undertakes. Out of the 4 ETF's Nifty Junior Bees is been ranked as the best performer while Bank Bees is ranked the least according to Sharpe Ratio. Hence it can be inferred that Nifty Junior is the best ETF for the Investors.

TABLE 8
Ranking of ETF's based on Treynor Ratio

Fund	Average Realized Return on the portfolio	Risk-free Rate of Return	Beta	Treynor Ratio	Rank
Nifty Bees	1.6667	0.8811	0.9954	0.7892	2
Nifty Junior Bee	1.8054	0.8811	0.9787	0.9605	1
Bank Bees	1.3234	0.8811	0.9623	0.4596	4
UTI Sunder	1.4137	0.8811	0.9869	0.5397	3

Source : Secondary Data.

Based on the values of the Treynor Ratio the ETF's have been ranked. It can be seen that Nifty Junior Bees has the highest value for Treynor Ratio and has been ranked as one. The value of the ratio is least for Bank Bees and as a result it has been given the least rank. Hence it can be inferred that Nifty Junior Bees gives more returns.

It can be seen that Nifty Junior Bees has been ranked as the best performing ETF while Bank Bees has been ranked the

TABLE 9 .
Ranking of ETF's-based on Sortino Ratio

Fund	Average Realized Return on The portfolio	Risk free Rate of Return	Standard Deviation of the Return	Sortino Ratio	Rank
Nifty Bees	1.6667	0.8811	3.9030	0.2014	2
Nifty Junior Bees	1.8054	0.8811	4.5561	0.2028	1
Bank Bees	1.3234	0.8811	6.1019	0.0725	4
UTI Sunder	1.4137	0.8811	3.6475	0.1460	3

Source : Secondary Data.

Table 10
Correlation between Sharpe Ratio, Treynor Ratio, Tracking Error Ranking

Sharpe Ratio (R_1)	*Treynor Ratio (R_2)*	*Tracking Error (R_3)*	$D_{12}=(R_1-R_2)$	$D_{13}=(R_2-R_3)$	$D_{23}=(R_3-R_1)$	D_{12}^2	D_{13}^2	D_{23}^2
(1)	(2)	(3)	(4)	(5)	(6)	(7)	(8)	(9)
2	2	1	0	1	-1	0	1	1
1	1	2	0	-1	1	0	1	1
4	4	4	0	0	0	0	0	0
3	3	3	0	0	0	0	0	0
			$D_{12}=0$	$D_{13}=0$	$D_{23}=0$	$D_{12}^2=0$	$D_{13}^2=2$	$D_{23}^2=2$

Calculations:

$R_{12}= 1 - 6\Sigma D_{12}^2/N(N^2-1) = 0$

$R_{13}= 1 - 6\Sigma D_{13}^2/N(N^2-1) = 0.80$

$R_{23}= 1 - 6\Sigma D_{23}^2/N(N^2-1) = 0.80$

least performer based on the value of Sortino Ratio. Hence it is inferred that Nifty Junior is the best ETF for investors who are willing to take high risk.

Spearman Rank Correlation was calculated to see whether there is a correlation between the ranking done on the basis of Sharpe and Treynor Ratio, Sharpe Ratio and Tracking error, Treynor Ratio and Tracking Error. Spearman Rank Correlation

TABLE 11

Winner-Loser Contingency Table for Nifty Bees

Date	*NAV of Nifty Bees*	*WW/WL*
1-Dec.-08	270.6261	L
5-Dec.-08	273.6544	LL
12-Dec.-08	294.4252	LW
19-Dec.-08	310.0888	WW
26-Dec.-08	288.5506	WW
02-Jan.-09	307.5606	WW
09-Jan.-09	290.0630	WW
16-Jan.-09	285.5728	WW
23-Jan.-09	270.4832	WL
30-Jan.-09	290.7877	LW
06-Feb.-09	287.6074	WL
13-Feb.-09	298.2156	LW
20-Feb.-09	276.9293	WL
27-Feb.-09	279.6416	LL
06-Mar.-09	265.1547	LL
13-Mar.-09	275.1204	LL
20-Mar.-09	283.9419	LL
27-Mar.-09	314.3306	LW
02-Apr.-09	324.6281	WW
09-Apr.-09	337.8001	WW
17-Apr.-09	342.0332	WW
24-Apr.-09	351.7265	WW

Source : Secondary Data.

coefficient among the performance measures Sharpe Ratio and Tracking Error, Treynor Ratio and Tracking Error is 0.80 which shows that there is a strong positive correlation between these performance measures. The Spearman Rank correlation coefficient among the performance of Sharpe and Treynor Ratio is Zero which shows that there is no correlation.

REPEAT WINNER APPROACH AND Z-TEST FOR REPEAT WINNERS

Hypothesis

H_0: There is no persistence in the performance of Nifty Bees.

H_1: There is persistence in the performance of Nifty Bees.

TABLE 12
Winner-Loser Table for Nifty Bees

Particulars	*Win*	*Loss*
Win	9	3
Loss	4	5

Percentage Repeat Winners = WW/(WW+WL)
= 0.7500 = 75%

Z-Test Repeat Winners = WW-0.5(WW+WL)/√ (WW+WL)*0.5*0.5 = 1.7320

The calculated value of percentage of repeat winners for Nifty Bees is 75%and the value for Z-test repeat winners is 1.7320. Since the percentage of repeat winners is above 50% and the Z-test value is above Zero we reject the null hypothesis. Hence it can be inferred that there is persistence in the performance of Nifty Bees.

TABLE 13
Winner-Loser Contingency Table for Nifty Junior Bees

Date	*NAV of Nifty Junior Bees*	*WW/WL*
1-Dec.-08	39.0403	L
5-Dec.-08	41.3442	LL
12-Dec.-08	44.2547	LW
19-Dec.-08	47.0877	WW
26-Dec.-08	44.2509	WW
02-Jan.-09	48.7508	WW
09-Jan.-09	45.0689	WW
16-Jan.-09	44.0678	WW
23-Jan.-09	40.8057	WL
30-Jan.-09	43.2465	LL
06-Feb.-09	42.3181	LL
13-Feb.-09	44.0382	LW
20-Feb.-09	40.7415	WL
27-Feb.-09	40.7694	LL
06-Mar.-09	37.8034	LL
13-Mar.-09	38.9841	LL
20-Mar.-09	40.6730	LL
27-Mar.-09	44.8892	LW
02-Apr.-09	46.7893	WW
09-Apr.-09	49.9875	WW
17-Apr.-09	52.2189	WW
24-Apr.-09	54.9353	WW

Source : Secondary Data.

Hypothesis

H_0: There is no persistence in the performance of Nifty Junior Bees.

H_1: There is persistence in the performance of Nifty Junior Bees.

TABLE 14
Winner-Loser Table for Nifty Junior Bees

Particulars	*Win*	*Loss*
Win	9	2
Loss	3	7

Percentage Repeat winners
WR = WW/(WW+WL) = 0.8181 = 82%
Z-TEST = WW-0.5(WW+WL)/Σ(WW+WL)*0.5*0.5 = 2.1106

The calculated value of percentage of repeat winners for Nifty Junior Bees is 82% and the value for Z-test repeat winners is 2.1106. Since the percentage of repeat winners is above 50% and the Z-test value is above Zero we reject the null hypothesis. Hence it can be inferred that there is persistence in the performance of Nifty Junior Bees.

TABLE 15
Winner-Loser Contingency Table for Bank Bees

Date	*NAV of Bank Bees*	*WW/WL*
(1)	*(2)*	*(3)*
1-Dec.-08	419.7952	L
5-Dec.-08	443.0443	LL
12-Dec.-08	472.8343	LW
19-Dec.-08	521.6772	WW
26-Dec.-08	486.1682	WW
02-Jan.-09	526.6876	WW
09-Jan.-09	497.8052	WW
16-Jan.-09	460.2138	WL
23-Jan.-09	410.2582	LL
30-Jan.-09	447.6606	LW
06-Feb.-09	435.3738	WL

(*Contd.*)

TABLE 15 (Contd.)

(1)	*(2)*	*(3)*
13-Feb.-09	458.5090	LW
20-Feb.-09	395.3176	WL
27-Feb.-09	391.0807	LL
06-Mar.-09	341.3482	LL
13-Mar.-09	365.3389	LL
20-Mar.-09	371.1975	LL
27-Mar.-09	442.6595	LL
02-Apr.-09	444.5514	LL
09-Apr.-09	460.3763	LW
17-Apr.-09	507.5204	WW
24-Apr.-09	514.3185	WW

Source : Secondary Data.

Hypothesis

H_0: There is no persistence in the performance of Bank Bees

H_1: There is persistence in the performance of Bank Bees.

TABLE 16
Winner-Loser Table for Bank Bees

Particulars	*Win*	*Loss*
Win	6	3
Loss	4	8

Percentage Repeat winners
WR = WW/(WW+WL) = 0.6666 = 67%
Z-TEST = WW–0.5(WW+WL)/Σ(WW+WL)*0.5*0.5 = 1.

The calculated value of percentage of repeat winners for Bank Bees is 67% and the value for Z-test repeat winners is 1.

Since the percentage of repeat winners is above 50% and the Z-test value is above Zero we reject the null hypothesis. Hence it can be inferred that there is persistence in the performance of Bank Bees.

TABLE 17
Winner-Loser Contingency Table for UTI Sunder

Date	*NAV of UTI Sunder*	*WW/WL*
01-Dec.-08	281.8683	L
05-Dec.-08	285.0791	LL
12-Dec.-08	306.0824	LW
19-Dec.-08	322.0729	WW
26-Dec.-08	300.0997	WL
02-Jan.-09	319.4818	LW
09-Jan.-09	301.6777	WW
16-Jan.-09	297.0740	WL
23-Jan.-09	281.6978	LL
30-Jan.-09	302.4498	LW
06-Feb.-09	299.2142	WL
13-Feb.-09	310.0345	LW
20-Feb.-09	288.8423	WL
27-Feb.-09	291.1815	LL
06-Mar.-09	276.8674	LL
13-Mar.-09	286.6382	LL
20-Mar.-09	295.7099	LL
27-Mar.-09	326.9328	LW
02-Apr.-09	337.5253	WW
09-Apr.-09	351.0368	WW
17-Apr.-09	355.3418	WW
24-Apr.-09	365.3099	WW

Source : Secondary Data.

Hypothesis

H_0: There is no persistence in the performance of UTI Sunder.

H_1: There is persistence in the performance of UTI Sunder.

TABLE 18
Winner-Loser Table for UTI Sunder

Particulars	*Win*	*Loss*
Win	6	4
Loss	5	6

Percentage Repeat winners

WR = WW/(WW+WL) = 0.6000 = 60%

Z-TEST = WW-0.5(WW+WL)/Σ (WW+WL)*0.5*0.5
= 0.6325

The calculated value of percentage of repeat winners for UTI Sunder is 60% and the value for Z-test repeat winners is 0.6325. Since the percentage of repeat winners is above 50% and the Z-test value is above Zero we reject the null hypothesis. Hence it can be inferred that there is persistence in the performance of UTI Sunder.

FINDINGS

The main findings of the study based on the analysis of data are presented here:

1. The study shows that weekly percentage returns of Nifty Bees and Nifty Junior Bees are symmetric with its benchmark returns. The returns are highly volatile and inconsistent for all the ETFs.
2. It can be seen that there are slight difference in the percentage change in returns of Bank Bees and UTI

Sunder from its benchmark CNX Banking Index and S&P CNX Nifty Index.

3. Bank Bees provide investors with high risk and returns for their investments.
4. Tracking error of ETFs has decreased. All funds have very low tracking error.
5. From the comparison of the ETFs based on the tracking error it can be found that the return of Nifty Bees closely follows the returns of its benchmark S&P CNX Nifty Index while the returns of the ETF Bank Bees do not perfectly track its underlying Benchmark CNX Banking Index.
6. Out of the 4 ETF's Nifty Junior Bees is been ranked as the best performer while Bank Bees is ranked the least according to Sharpe Ratio. This shows that Nifty Junior is the best ETF for the Investors.
7. Nifty Junior Bees has the highest value for Treynor Ratio and has been ranked as one. The value of the ratio is least for Bank Bees and as a result it has been given the least rank. Hence it is inferred that Nifty Junior Bees gives more returns.
8. Nifty Junior Bees has been ranked as the best performing ETF while Bank Bees has been ranked the least performer based on the value of Sortino Ratio. Hence it is found that Nifty Junior is the best ETF for investors who are willing to take high risk.
9. Spearman Rank Correlation coefficient among the performance measures Sharpe Ratio and Tracking Error, Treynor Ratio and Tracking Error is 0.80 which shows that there is a strong positive correlation between these performance measures. The Spearman Rank correlation coefficient among the performance of Sharpe and Treynor Ratio is Zero which shows that there is no correlation.
10. There is persistence in the performance of Nifty Bees.
11. It is found that there is persistence in the performance of Nifty Junior Bees.
12. It is found that there is persistence in the performance of Bank Bees.

13. It is found that there is persistence in the performance of UTI Sunder.

SUGGESTIONS

Based on the findings of the study, the following suggestions are made to improve the performance of ETF's:

1. ETF is a new financial instrument, so investors do not opt for them because of lack of awareness. It is essential to organize awareness programs for the potential investors as this would help in gaining popularity of ETFs.
2. Investors who are willing to take moderate rate of risk can invest in Nifty Junior Bees as they assure moderate level of returns.
3. The investors who are willing to take more risk could invest in the ETF Bank Bees.
4. An ETF is created through an Initial Public Offer (IPO) by the Asset Management Company (AMC) in which only Authorized Participants (AP's) i.e., institutional investors, mutual funds, insurance companies, etc. are allowed to participate. So, there is a need to popularize this among the retail investors.
5. AMC's need to reduce the size of creation unit. The creation unit size is so heavy that only institutional Investors can buy/sell the ETF units.
6. The expense ratio for the ETF's need to be uniform for all the ETF's.
7. With the above solution, the ETF industry can market itself aggressively as a very attractive scheme.

CONCLUSION

An exchange-traded fund (or ETF) is an investment vehicle traded on stock exchanges, much like stocks or bonds. An ETF holds assets such as stocks, bonds, or futures and offer the ability to be traded real-time like a stock, accessibility to investors with brokerage account and the transparency of the investment instrument. The ETF market provides advantages like liquidity, less risk, good return and flexibility in operation etc.

The aim of the study was to investigate the performance and persistence of four ETF's over the period December 2008 to April 2009. Our results show that the ETFs were on average, competent in mirroring their benchmark's performance. For all the funds, all performance estimates used in this study were found to support the hypothesis that there is persistence in the performance of Exchange Traded Funds. The weekly returns analysis of the ETFs show that Nifty Junior Bees have more consistent returns compared to other ETF's.

The market for ETF's is at a nascent stage in India. There are hardly any volumes in the market for the product. The prime reason for low volume is that market participants are of big size. Secondly, the brokers who are in direct touch with the market participants are also not advising the ETF products to the client. Thirdly, Regulations are a major hindrance for the development of ETF market. If the above problems could be tackled, the ETF industry can market itself aggressively as a very attractive scheme. In coming years, as more and more investors turn towards modern investment avenues, the market will also see a rise in trading of Exchange Traded Funds.

References

Allen, D.E. and M.L. Tan (1999), "A Test of the Persistence in the Performance of UK Managed Funds", *Journal of Business Finance and Accounting*, Vol. 26, pp. 559-93.

Amin, G.S. and H.M. Kat (2003), "Stocks, Bonds, and Hedge Funds", *Journal of Portfolio Management*, Vol. 29, pp. 113-20.

Gastineau, Gary L. (2004), "The benchmark Index ETF Performance Problem", *Journal of Portfolio Management*, Vol. 30, pp. 96-103.

Gastineau, Gary L. (2001), "Exchange-traded Funds: An Introduction", *Journal of Portfolio Management*, Vol. 27(3), p. 88

Punithavathy Pandian (2005), "Security Analysis and Portfolio Management", New Delhi: Vikas Publishing House Ltd.

Websites

www.bseindia.com
www.nseindia.com
www.benchmark.com
www.pruicici.com
www.utimf.com
www.mutualfundsindia.com
www.sensex.com
www.amfiindia.com

15

The Impact of Product Label's Colour on Quality Perception

A. Ananda Kumar

ABSTRACT

Marketers to incorporate pleasing attributes to differentiate their product and to feed into consumer's emotions when making purchasing decisions. Vision is the most important senses because marketers know a consumer's visual perception is the first introduction and this can highly influence whether a consumer will even consider the purchase of the product. This includes colour, shape, pattern, movement and scale of the product. Product labels are sources of information designed to attract consumers´ attention, to communicate a message that will motivate consumption. *Now-a-days* marketers spend considerable time and money on packaging the products in a manner that will attract consumer attention and promote its consumption. This study is to evaluate how consumers assess quality perception on product label's colour. This research utilized a focus to understand consumer behavior toward the impact of label's colour of various products. The challenge for researchers to identify at what extent that label's colour will affect for consumer quality perception and at what extent the level of purchasing decision. Results of the study might be useful to academicians, manufacturers, and other applied researchers.

Keywords: Consumer, colour, purchase decision, marketers, perception, product label, quality.

INTRODUCTION

The study of consumers helps firms and organizations improve their marketing strategies by understanding issues such as (Lars Perner, 2008).

- The psychology of how consumers think, feel, reason, and select between different alternatives (e.g., brands, products);
- The psychology of how the consumer is influenced by his or her environment (e.g., culture, family, signs, media);
- The behavior of consumers while shopping or making other marketing decisions;
- Limitations in consumer knowledge or information processing abilities influence decisions and marketing outcome;
- How consumer motivation and decision strategies differ between products that differ in their level of importance or interest that they entail for the consumer; and
- How marketers can adapt and improve their marketing campaigns and marketing strategies to more effectively reach the consumer.

For marketers the term "aesthetics" relates to consumers on five senses of vision, hearing, touch, taste, and smell in response to an object. Marketers to incorporate pleasing attributes to differentiate their product and to feed into consumer's emotions when making purchasing decisions use these five elements. Vision is the most important one of these senses because marketers know a consumer's visual perception is the first introduction and this can highly influence whether a consumer will even consider the purchase of the product. This includes colour, shape, pattern, movement and scale of the product.

"Packaging is the container for a product—encompassing the physical appearance of the container and including the design, colour, shape, labeling and materials used".

Packaging has a huge role to play in the positioning of products. Package design shapes consumer perceptions and can be the determining factor in point-of-purchase decisions which characterize the majority of shopping occasions, (Nielsen, 2007).

In recent years the marketing environment has become increasingly complex and competitive. A product's packaging is something which all buyers experience and which has strong potential to engage the majority of the target market. This makes it an extremely powerful and unique tool in the modern marketing environment.

In addition to its benefits in terms of reach, some marketers believe that packaging is actually more influential than advertising in influencing consumers, as it has a more direct impact on how they perceive and experience the product.

"In most cases, the experience has been that pack designs are more likely to influence the consumer perception of the brand."

(Nielsen, 2007), For products with low advertising support, packaging takes on an even more significant role as the key vehicle for communicating the brand positioning.

Firms spend more money on packaging than on advertising, and packaging is often the most distinguished marketing effort (Dickson, 1994). Labels are one of the most important features of product packaging, and they are designed to communicate a message (Héroux, Laroche & McGown, 1988).

Product labels are sources of information designed to attract consumers´ attention, to communicate a message that will motivate consumption. Considerable effort and resources are allocated to product labeling, however, little research exists on how consumers actually process and use the information on the product label. According to Héroux *et. al.* (1988), marketers spend considerable time and money on packaging products in a manner that will attract consumer attention and promote its consumption.

Ted Mininni (2009), Why should more emphasis be placed on the colour packaging conveys now? Stand at the end of an aisle in the supermarket or Target store. Can you, while scanning hundreds of items, pick out a few that are instantly recognizable from that vantage point? Now, ask yourself what it is about specific products that make them quickly identifiable from the myriad other products in the retail environment. There has to be something unique about the packaging of those products that makes them stand outs. Colour? Brand mark? Packaging shape? Photographic imagery or graphics? All of these factors?

A question that emerges is therefore how consumers perceive product quality from the product label? To answer this question, this paper focuses on colours in label design as the symbols that convey quality signals to customers on the basis of collected various information. The emphasis of this study is on the colour compositions that are deemed most appealing to consumers, regardless of the reasons for their choices.

Why colours? Colours have meanings and, as such, they are a fundamental tool in corporate marketing strategies and communications. These underlying meanings are often used for the purpose of product and brand differentiation (Schmitt & Pan, 1994) and also on the basis of consumer perceptions (Grossman & Wisenblit, 1999).

(T. Giski, 2009), Colours as ease-of-use of the package have immediate impacts in the consumers psyche. Particular colours convey very particular messages. In a world filled with consumer materials, and an endless variety of very competitive products, packaging could be the edge that sets one product apart from another. Even if the products in comparison are virtually the same, having the same ingredients, the same benefits, or even the same manufacturer, the product packaged to look prettier, more appealing, more genuine, or perhaps more professional will often win out.

Choosing a package on design alone, while not always the best choice, is sometimes the only thing we consumers have to go on when it comes to picking a single product in a sea of similar goods. Don't believe this is true? Look around your home at the products you purchase. Compare them with other products that are of similar quality or value. What sets them apart? Is it perhaps the sub-conscious attraction to the packaging? Another experiment: Walk down the shampoo aisle at your supermarket. All of the products essentially do the same thing (clean your hair), and yet, some products readily stand out from others because the design style or the colour naturally appeal to your aesthetic sense. If you consider yourself young and hip, perhaps the brightly coloured bottles are attractive. A professional may perhaps choose a classic "clean" and thoughtfully designed bottle in a subtle colour.

Interest in how label design can be used as a marketing device stems from ever growing competition in world markets. In this setting, the assessment of quality signals that go beyond the traditional label compositions becomes increasingly important. Previous research shows that labels provide a quality cue that consumers use to assess alternative products with respect to their own values following a set of subjective rules (Hall & Winchester, 2000; Reynolds & Gutman, 1988).

First, the use of physical features (packaging, labels) as quality signals has not been studied as thoroughly as other signals, as for example brand, price, warranty and store name. Thus the importance of an research is using colours in labels to assess consumers´ quality perception. Then this paper opens up new opportunities for marketing research, especially concerning the use of colours to extract information on consumer behavior. Finally, this area of research also has direct managerial implications. A better understanding of colour compositions can be used as a tool for creating labels that are recognizable and evoke brand and corporate images, thus changing consumers´ behavior.

This study of literatures focus is on the impact of labels colours as signals from the consumer point of view of quality perception, and thus the studies involving consumers' reactions to these quality signals are emphasized in the literature review.

Previous research stresses that packages have an impact on consumers' choice. As a matter of fact, packages are suggested to have great impact as a means of direct communication (Peters, 1994). A package is acknowledged as a marketing communication tool as packages convey meanings directly to consumers when the decision to purchase is being made. As such, it is commonly accepted that packages convey meanings about the product and its features, benefits and usage (Garber *et. al.*, 2000; Rothschild, 1987).

PRODUCT'S INTRINSIC AND EXTRINSIC ATTRIBUTES

Products constitute an array of intrinsic and extrinsic attributes that consumers use to determine product quality (Miyazaki, Grewal, & Goodstein, 2005). A top priority for marketers is to find out which of the many extrinsic and intrinsic cues consumers use to signal quality (Zeithaml, 1988).

Attributes that signal quality have been categorized into intrinsic and extrinsic cues (Olson, 1977; Olson & Jacoby, 1972). Intrinsic cues involve the physical composition of the product. In one hand, intrinsic attributes cannot be changed without altering the nature of the product itself and are consumed as the product is consumed (Olson, 1977; Olson & Jacoby, 1972). On the other hand, extrinsic cues are product-related but not part of the physical product itself, by definition, they are outside the product.

Which type of cue, intrinsic or extrinsic, is more important in signaling quality to the consumer? Researchers who tackled this question (Darden & Schwinghammer, 1985; Etgar & Malhotra, 1978; Olson & Jacoby, 1972; Rigaux-Bricmont 1982; Szybillo & Jacoby, 1974) concluded that intrinsic cues have higher predictive value and were in general more important to consumers in judging quality than extrinsic cues.

However, some studies (e.g. Sawyer, Worthing & Sendak, 1979) have shown that extrinsic cues can be more important to consumers than intrinsic cues. Extrinsic cues are conceived to be used as quality indicators when consumers act without enough information about intrinsic product attributes. This is a rather common situation that occurs when consumers have little or no experience with the product, or when consumers do not have enough time or interest to evaluate the intrinsic attributes, or cannot readily evaluate the intrinsic attributes.

The consumer relies on extrinsic attributes such as price, brand, package and warranty, as substitutes for intrinsic product attributes. The most studied extrinsic cue is the relationship between price and perceived quality; almost 100 studies have been published in the past 30 years. (Brucks, Zeithaml, & Naylor, 2000).

COLOURS CONVEY MESSAGES

(Ian Roberts, Aug. 02, 2004), Colour is the most instantaneous and wonderful means for delivering and communicating messages and meanings to the intended audience. Much of the reaction to colour is subtle, triggered by tiny nerve ending and chemicals in the brain, that either excite, sadden, overwhelm or inspire the viewer, when coming in contact with various colours. Different hues and saturation levels can convey elegance, creativity and seriousness, while others convey experience, excitement, vitality and dependability. Below, you will find some general guidelines on how to go about conveying your message to the masses, while using something as simple as colour.

1. *Yellow:* Yellow is perceived as cheerful and energetic, yet mellow and soft. Just like the mid summer sunshine, it portrays hope, happy times and used as a way to grab one's attention.
   Examples: NY City Taxi Cabs, Arm & Hammer Baking Soda, Kodak Films, Dummies Books, Nestle Quick Chocolate Milk, and McDonalds. In nature yellow can be seen on bees, fish, sunflowers and of course, the sun.
2. *Orange:* Orange is a friendly, vital, inviting, energetic and playful colour. Orange is perhaps the hottest of all colours, which is why almost everyone can relate to it in some way or another, especially children.
   Examples: Sunkist (fruit and soda), KIX cereal, Cingular Wireless, Nickelodeon, Tide detergent,

Jamba Juice and Southwest Airlines. Other naturally occurring orange colours are goldfish, flowers and tangerines!

3. *Red:* Red excites, stimulates and creates arousal. People often think of the colour as daring, dynamic, bold and sexy. In print, red is an aggressive colour, whereas it commands attention and demands action. *Examples:* Coca-Cola, Staples, Red Cross, Budweiser, CNN and the Chicago Bulls. Other everyday examples are red sports cars, red dresses, red lipsticks, red ties as well as red STOP signs.
4. *Brown:* Brown is the ultimate traditional earth colour, associated with substance, durability and security. It's earthly tones lend perfectly to food and food-related items, even used in restaurants and coffee houses.
   Examples: UPS (United Parcel Service), Hersheys Chocolate, Godiva, Baltimore Orioles, aged and rich beers, coffees, cigars and chocolates. Other examples are brown leather chairs, furniture and portfolios covers.
5. *Green:* Green is the colour of nature, and everything that goes with it. It has been described as refreshing, healing, soothing and prestigious (when associated with money and banks).
   Examples: 7-Up, Sprite, First Union Bank, Apple Jacks cereal, DoubleMint gum, Scope mouth wash and GreenPeace. Other examples of soothing green can be found everywhere in nature, from vegetables to meadows and forests.
6. *Blue:* Blue is a very stable and dependable colour. As with the ocean and sky that are always constant, blue inspires confidence, commitment and a sense of serenity and peace.
   Examples: HP, IBM, BMW and Volks Wagon. Many financial institutions, mortgage brokers and large corporations that are conservative in nature, tend to use blue. Water bottling companies also use blue to portray freshness.
7. *Purple:* Purple reflects elegance, sensuality, spirituality and creativity. Purple is perhaps the most

complicated and rare colour, hence referred to as a majestic and royal, fit for kings.

Examples: This colour is representative of rare and sensual products or services, such as lingerie shops, flower shops, etc. Most businesses are hesitant to use purple because of its sensual properties.

8. *Black:* Black is strong, classic, mysterious and powerful. The most sophisticated shade of the spectrum, people associated it with style, elegance, and expensive taste.

   Examples: Many designer logos are comprised of simple black lettering or logos. They include DKNY, Calvin Klein, Rolex, Rolls Royce, Kenneth Cole and YSL.

Even though the fact that packages convey meanings is well acknowledged, it seems that there are few scholarly studies focusing on packages as a means of communication (Underwood, 2001; Garber, 1995; Gordon *et. al.*, 1994). The reason for the few studies on packages may be that marketing communication is traditionally connected with planned activities such as advertising, personal selling, sales promotion, and publicity. However, it can be postulated that the scholarly interest in packages will enhance as it appears that the role of packages as a marketplace phenomenon is changing (Kauppinen, 2001).

CONSUMERS' USE OF PRODUCT QUALITY SIGNALS

When consumers choose among competing products, they face quality and product performance uncertainty. So, they are likely to rely on heuristics to judge quality across competitive products since consumers have finite time horizons and no incentive to perform thorough comparative studies prior to purchase (Dawar & Parker, 1994).

The economics and marketing literature have both found that signals serve mostly as heuristics in assessing product quality when there is a need to reduce the perceived risk of purchase (Jacoby, Olson, & Haddock, 1971; Olson, 1977), the consumer lacks expertise and thus the ability to assess quality

(Rao & Monroe, 1988), consumer involvement is low (Celci & Olson, 1988), objective quality is too complex to assess or the consumer is not in the habit of spending time objectively assessing quality (Allison & Uhl, 1964; Hoch & Ha, 1986), or there is an information search preference and need for information (Nelson, 1970, 1974, 1978).

The signals that are more studied include brand names (Akerlof, 1970; Darby & Kari, 1973; Olson, 1977; Ross, 1988) or brand advertising (Milgrom & Roberts, 1986), product features or appearance (Nelson, 1970; Olson, 1977), price (Leavitt, 1954; Milgrom & Roberts, 1986; Olson, 1972, 1977; Rao & Monroe, 1989; Wolinsky, 1983), and product/retail reputation, store names, warranties, or guarantees (Cooper & Ross, 1985; Emons, 1988; Olson, 1977; Rao & Monroe, 1989).

Although few of the results from these studies can be generalized, brand names have been found to be more important than price, which is in turn more important than physical appearance. Retail reputation or store name has been found to be least consequential in signaling product quality (Jacoby, Szybillo, & Busato-Schach, 1977; Rao & Monroe, 1989). Nevertheless, packages are one of the main elements of the product appearance and as such are an important source of information since consumers rely heavily on labels for product information and also packaging is a significant marketing expenditure larger than advertising itself.

CONSUMER REACTIONS TO PACKAGES

Several studies have investigated issues such as packages as a means of attracting the attention of consumers (Underwood *et. al.*, 2001; Garber *et. al.*, 2000; Goldberg *et. al.*, 1999; Schoormans & Robben, 1997). Other studies researched packages as a means of communication as well as a means of communicating brand and product meaning (Underwood & Klein, 2002; Garber *et. al.*, 2000, Schoormans & Robben, 1997; Gordon *et. al.*, 1994; Homer & Gauntt, 1992; Rigaux-Bricmont, 1981; McDaniel & Baker, 1977).

Packages are found to attract attention (Underwood *et. al.*, 2001; Garber *et. al.*, 2000; Goldberg *et. al.*, 1999; Schoormans & Robben, 1997). In fact, Goldberg *et. al.* (1999) found that by dismissing such non-verbal signs as colours, the attention to verbal signs can be increased. Pictures on packages are emphasized to attract attention, particularly when consumers are not very familiar with the brands (Underwood *et. al.,* 2001).

Furthermore, packages are claimed to attract attention when their appearances are not typical within a product class (Garber *et. al.,* 2000; Schoormans & Robben 1997). In other words, past research has discovered that deviating packages attract attention. Other studies show that deviating package colours attract attention (Garber *et. al.,* 2000; Schoormans & Robben 1997). Underwood *et. al.* (2001), on the other hand, found that pictures on packages attract attention particularly in cases when consumers are less familiar with a brand.

Studies that have focused on other single signs than pictures on packages have found that such single package signs as colours (Gordon *et. al.,* 1994), brand names (Rigaux-Bricmont, 1981), and materials (McDaniel & Baker, 1977) convey brand meaning.

Thus, findings concerning past research show that preferences linked to the package appearance suggest to have an impact on the choice behavior of consumers. This implies that the appearance of the packages has an impact on the formation of the consideration set (Schoormans & Robben, 1997; Garber, 1995) and this claim is supported in a study by Garber *et. al.* (2000).

In terms of the formation of the consideration set Garber *et. al.* (2000) found, on the one hand, that novel package appearances has a positive impact on the formation of the consideration set, particularly when the consumer is looking for variety (Garber *et. al.,* 2000). On the other hand, Schoormans and Robben (1997) found that novel package appearances have a positive impact on the formation of the consideration set and on the evaluation of the brands that may be considered, if the deviation of the new packages is moderate.

The importance of communicating the right product and brand values on packages is fundamental, as well as achieving the appropriate level of aesthetics and visual standout. There is generally a need for the package to be distinctive in appearance (Nancarrow *et. al.*, 1998).

CONSUMERS' REACTIONS TO COLOURS

Colours are one of the non-verbal signs that are recognized as an important marketplace phenomenon (Garber *et. al.*, 2000; Grimes & Doole, 1998; Gorn *et. al.*, 1997; Schoormans & Robben, 1997; Evans *et. al.*, 1996; Gordon *et. al.*, 1994; Belizzi & Hite, 1992; Danger, 1987; Danger, 1987). Colours´ importance is especially recognized when it refers to advertising and packaging (Belizzi *et. al.*, 1983). The function of colours to attract attention is emphasized by arguing that colours are the most important visual sign to attract consumers´ attention, as it is the first sign that the consumers notices on a package (Danger, 1987; Danger, 1987).

However, Kojina *et. al.* (1996) also suggest that preferences regarding colours and patterns may have an impact on brand choices. This finding by Kojina *et. al.* (1996) is supported by Gordon *et. al.* (1994), who also found that such package sign as colours have an impact on brand choices.

When it comes to specific signs that attract attention, it can be found that past research suggests that such signs as colours attract attention. Garber *et. al.* (2000) and Schoormans & Robben (1997) found that colours on packages attract the attention of consumers. As a matter of fact, it is postulated that colours are the first sign that the consumer pays attention to on a package (Danger, 1987; Danger, 1987). Previous studies support the idea that colours attract attention particularly when consumers seek for variety in their brand choices (Garber *et. al.*, 2000; Schoormans & Robben, 1997).

Gordon *et. al.* (1994) focused their research on the colours of packages. Their results support the suggestion that colours do communicate. Colours were found to be related to the brand as they were found to communicate the quality of the brand. Furthermore, colours were implied to be related to the core product as the study found that colours communicated, for example, such a feature of the product as taste. Their study also implies that colours have an impact on the behavior of consumers. For example, they discovered that colours have an impact on brand evaluations and on brand choices. So as pointed out, Gordon *et. al.* (1994) support the idea that colours on packages may have an impact on brand evaluation and on brand choices.

CONSUMERS' PURCHASE INTENTION

It is well accepted that packages have an essential role in influencing the consumer purchase choices and intention at the point of purchase. These past research findings are related to the current study, their findings contribute to the understanding of the impact of packages on consumer behavior and more closely their purchase intention at the point of purchase.

Another finding is that appearances have an impact on attitudes concerning brands and packages as well as purchase intentions. The studies on behavior communication have focused on the impact of the package appearance on various phases in the choice process.

Such issues as the formation of the consideration set (Garber *et. al.*, 2000; Schoormans & Robben, 1997), product recall (Rettie & Brewer, 2000), product and brand evaluation (Underwood & Klein, 2002; Schoormans & Robben, 1997; Homer & Gauntt, 1992; Gordon *et. al.*, 1994) and choice behavior (Gordon *et. al.*, 1994; Kojina *et. al.*, 1986) have been emphasized.

COLOURS IN PRODUCT LABELS

The literature is mostly silent on how individuals respond to label colour compositions. De Mello and Pires Gonçalves (2008) found that there are strong preferences for selected of colours in the composition design of product labels.

There is nevertheless a rich body of research on reactions to colours, which can be innate/instinctive (Humphrey, 1976) or learned/associative (Langenbeck, 1913, cited in Hupka *et. al.*, 1997). If they are instinctive, colour signals trigger affective reactions in the brain. But, if they are learned, preferences over colours are learned over time as shared affective meanings or as result of past experiences and/or conscious associations in language, literature and myths (Osgood *et. al.*, 1957).

Colours can be associated with objects on different dimensions. Osgood *et. al.* (1957) shows empirically that there is an association between colour and objects at least on the basis of an evaluative scale of preferences. On an activity scale of preferences, the ordering of colours generally follows the hue dimension: "hot" colours, such as red and yellow, lean towards activity, black and white are by and large neutral and "cold" colours, such as green and blue, are closer to the passive end of the spectrum. Colours can also be ordered along a saturation dimension on potency scales: the more saturated the colour, the more potent the object being judged is perceived. It appears that the evaluative effect of colour interacts with the nature of an object, whereas the effects of colour upon judged activity and the potency of objects with which they are associated are systematic and consistent with the hue and saturation dimensions, respectively.

Because of its powerful underlying interpretations, colour is an important marketing tool, including for the creation of brand images (Madden *et. al.*, 2000). There appear to be universal patterns in reactions to colours, which makes it possible to construct international colour codes. The country-culture clusters identified by Aslam (2006) are based on language and communication similarities and indicate the meanings and associations of colours in selected clusters.

Reactions to labels are more complex. Labels provide important extrinsic cues (*i.e.*, attributes that are not part of the physical product) to be used by consumers to assess quality (Verdú Jover *et. al.*, 2004; Rocchi & Stefani, 2005).

DISCUSSION FOR FINDINGS

Economics of information theory (Nelson, 1970, 1974; Darby & Karni, 1973) classifies products into three categories according to how consumers evaluate the product. This classification was initially developed to help explain the notion that consumer information about quality often has "profound effects upon the market structure of consumer goods" (Nelson, 1970).

Nelson (1970) defined two types of qualities that had distinct characteristics in terms of consumer evaluation processes. Search qualities are those that can be fully evaluated prior to purchase. Experience qualities are those that must be first purchased and consumed before the consumer is able to evaluate, thus are products which quality can be evaluated only after purchase. Darby and Karni (1973) introduced credence goods to extend the information acquisition classification into a more precise classification. Credence qualities are those that the consumer can never evaluate completely, even after purchase and consumption, i.e. those accepted on faith.

Signaling is most useful for products which quality is unknown before purchase, such as experience goods. Thus, signaling may not be appropriate for search products, well known or mature products, or consumer markets with highly familiar buyers. Signaling may be particularly effective in markets for relatively new products or products about which consumers are relatively uninformed but are quality sensitive. Therefore, signals are unlikely to convey quality for credence products, which quality is not discernible even after purchase and use (Darby & Kami, 1973).

(Ian Roberts, Aug. 02, 2004), Whether you are designing a self-promotion piece, or one for a client, always keep in mind that colour can make or break an advertisement piece, packaging or product or service, if used incorrectly. In brief, signaling is most effective under conditions in which pre-purchase information about quality is limited, and post-purchase information about quality is not ambiguous, i.e. experience goods.

Hence for the purpose of this research, experience goods will be included in the design to assess how colours are used as signals by consumers in terms of their quality perception. A few examples for such experience goods are: education, jobs, hotels, vacations, transportation, sport clubs, newspapers, music records, ovies, restaurants, food and beverages.

Perceived quality appears to be associated consistently with high prestige stores, high prices, and physical attributes of products such as colour. Consumer income and educational level also affect perceptions of quality. These consumer demographic characteristics interact with each other and with the marketing mix in a complex manner (John J. Wheatley and John S.Y. Chiu).

CONCLUSION

When they choose among competing products consumers are faced with quality and product performance uncertainty, hence, they rely on cues as extrinsic attributes, for instance, brand, price, package and warranty, as signals of perceived quality. Little research has been done on packages as extrinsic attributes used by consumers as signs of perceived quality, thus this study is a small contribution to that lack of scholarly research on packages.

Colours are important elements of marketing strategies, and they are essential features of packages, especially in product labels. Labels are one of the most important features of product packaging, and they are designed to communicate a message. Through this literature survey, builds on consumer quality perception and signals of quality from product cues. In this research, colours combinations in labels are considered as the extrinsic attributes used as signals of quality by consumers.

Further the research can be undertaken to establish empirical validity to demonstrate that consumers' quality perception responses to the extrinsic cues, colours in product labels. In this sense, the extrinsic attributes considered, colour can be help the consumers to predict the quality perception.

In this literature survey research colours are the cues used as signals of quality perception by sellers and buyers. Some specific products, experience goods, i.e. beverages, will be traded among sellers and buyers, and the only quality signal used by all sellers and buyers are colour in product labels.

Product appearance can influence consumers in many different ways. Insights into the different ways in which appearance characteristics, such as form and colour, may influence consumer choice, and by differentiating the roles played by product appearance managers can make a better use of packaging and labels as marketing tools.

Colours are a fundamental variable in marketing decisions. Inappropriate choice of product package or label colour may lead to strategic marketing failure. Furthermore, colour is the least expensive way of changing a product. Thus marketing management has a lot to gain from acquiring a more acute knowledge about the meanings consumers give to colours and how they use this attributes to perceive product quality. It is possible to improve packaging and label design.

Additionally, being able to design by using colours to elicit consumers' perceived quality and purchase intent is a powerful tool for managers. Of especial interest would be to include experience goods in the service sector, such as hotels, restaurants, financial services, jobs, teams.

This survey of literature study above study can be shortly stated as colours do have very well communication impact on quality perception. The brand image gets boosted by a higher level because of the colours. This impact may be listed on the important elements which affect the quality perception next to Brand and Price. It can be again argued that the brand image relies upon the colour to a smaller extent. A label's colour has got its own indispensability when the customer has a choice of new type of products.

References

Agarwal, S. and Teas, R. (2000). The Effects of Extrinsic Product Cues on Consumers' Perceptions of Quality, Sacrifice, and Value. *Journal of the Academy of Marketing Science*, Vol. 28, No. 2, pp. 278-90.

Agarwal, S. and Teas, R. (2002). Cross-national Applicability of a Perceived Quality Model. *Journal of Product & Brand Management*, Vol. 11, No. 4, pp. 213-36.

Aslam, M.M. (2006). Are You Selling the Right Colour? A Cross-cultural Review of Colour as a Marketing Cue. *Journal of Marketing Communications*, Vol. 12, No. 1, pp. 15-30.

Bellizzi, J.A., Crawley, A.E. and Hasty, R.W. (1983). The effects of colour in store design. *Journal of Retailing*, 59(1), pp. 21–45.

Belizzi, J.A. and Hite, R.E. (1992). Environmental Colour, Consumer Feelings and Purchase Likelihood. *Psychology and Marketing*, 9(5), 347-63.

Brucks, M., Zeithaml, V. and Naylor, G. (2000). Price and Brand Name as Indicators of Quality Dimensions for Consumer Durables. *Journal of the Academy of Marketing Science*, Vol. 28, No.3, pp. 359-74.

Danger, E.P. (1987). *Selecting Colour for Packaging*. Vermont: Gower Publishing Company.

Danger, E.P. (1987). *The Colour Handbook. How to Use Colour in Commerce and Industry*. Vermont: Gower Publishing Company.

Darby, M.R. and Kami, E. (1973). Free competition and the optimal amount of fraud. *Journal of Law and Economics*, Vol. 16, April, pp. 66-86.

Dawar, N. and Parker, P. (1994). Marketing Universals: Consumers´ Use of Brand Name, Price, Physical Appearance, and Retailer Reputation as Signals of Product Quality. *Journal of Marketing*, Vol. 58, pp. 81-95.

De Mello, L. and Pires Gonçalves, R. (2008). Message on a Bottle: Colours and Shapes in Wine Labels. In: Proceedings of the Fourth International Conference of the Academy of Wine Business Research, *Academy of Wine Business Research*.

Dickson, P.R. (1994). *Marketing management*. Forth Worth (TX): The Dryden Press.

Evans, M.J., Moutinho, L., and Raaij, W.F.V. (1996). *Applied Consumer Behaviour*. Harlow: Addison-Wesley Publishing Company.

Garber, L.L. (1995). The Package Appearance in Choice. In: *Advances in Consumer Research*, Kardes, F.R. and M. Sujan (eds.). Provo (UT): Association for Consumer Research, 22, 653-60.

Garber, L., Burke, R., and Jones, J. (2000). The Role of Package Colour in Consumer Purchase Consideration and Choice. *Marketing Science Institute*, Working Paper, Report No. 00-104.

Garber, L., Hyatt, E., and Starr, R. (2000). The Effects of Food Colour on Perceived Flavor. *Journal of Marketing Theory and Practice*, (Fall), 59-72.

Garber, L. and Hyatt, E. (2003). Colour as a Tool for Visual Persuasion. In: *Persuasive Imagery: A Consumer Response Perspective*, Scott, L.M. and Batra, R. (eds.). Mahwah (NJ): Lawrence Erlbaum Associates..

Goldberg, M.E., Liefield, J., Madill, J. and Vredenburg, H. (1999). The Effect of Plain Packaging on Response to Health Warnings. *American Journal of Public Health*, 89(9), 1434-35.

Gordon, A., Finlay, K., and Watts, T. (1994). The Psychological Effects of Colour in Consumer Product Packaging. *Canadian Journal of Marketing Research*, 13, 3-11.

Gorn, G., Chattopadhyay, A., Yi, T. and Dahl, D.W. (1997). Effects of Colour as an Exectutional Cue in Advertising: They're in the Shade. *Management Science*, 43 (10), 1387-1400.

Grimes, A. and Doole, I. (1998). Exploring the Relationship Between Colour and International Branding: A Cross-Cultural Comparison of the UK and Taiwan. *Journal of Marketing Management*, (4), 799-817.

Grossman, R.P. and Wisenblit, J.Z. (1999). What we know about consumers' colour choices. *Journal of Marketing Practice Applied Marketing Science*, Vol. 5, No. 3, pp. 78-88(11).

Hall, J. and Winchester, M.K. (2000). What is really driving wine consumer? *Australian and New Zealand Wine Industry Journal*, Vol. 15 pp. 93-6.

Héroux, L., Laroche, M. and McGown, K.L. (1988). Consumer product label information processing: an experiment involving time pressure and distraction. *Journal of Economic Psychology*, 9, 195-214.

Homer, P.M. and Gauntt, S.G. (1992). The Role of Imagery in the Processing of Visual and Verbal Package Information. *Journal of Mental Imagery*, 16 (3 and 4), 123-44.

Humphrey, N.K. (1976). The colour currency of Nature, In: *Colour for Architecture*, T. Porter and B. Mikelides (Eds.), pp. 95–98 (London: Studio Vista).

Hupka, R.B., Zaleski, Z., Otto, J., Reidl, L. and Tarabrina, N.V. (1997). The colours of anger, envy, fear, and jealousy: a cross-cultural study, *Journal of Cross-cultural Psychology*, 28(2), pp. 156-71.

Ian Roberts, Aug. 02, 2004, Colour Convey Messages: retrieved from http://www.webdesign.org/web-design-basics/colour-theory/colours-convey-messages.1611.html.

John J. Wheatley and John S.Y. Chiu (2009), The Effects of Price, Store Image, and Product and Respondent Characteristics on Perceptions of Quality, *Journal of Marketing Research*, Vol. 14, No. 2 (May, 1977), pp. 181-86 (article consists of 6 pages) Published by: American Marketing Association retrieved from http://www.jstor.org/stable/3150467

Kauppinen, H. (2001). *Colours as Non-verbal Signs on Packages. A Semiotic Approach*. Helsingfors: Swedish School of Economics and Business Administration.

Kirmani, A. and Rao, A. (2000). No Pain, No Gain: A Critical Review of the Literature on Signaling Unobservable Product Quality. *Journal of Marketing*, Vol. 64, pp. 66-79.

Kirmani, A. (1997). Advertising Repetition as Signal of Quality: If It´s Advertised So Much, Something Must Be Wrong. *Journal of Advertising*, 26, 3, p. 77.

Kojina, M., Hoken, J., and Takahashi, K. (1986). The Role of Colour and Pattern as Mediators of Product Selection. *Journal of Human Ergology*, 15, 13-25.

Lars Perner (2008), Consumer Behavior: The Psychology of Marketing, retrieved from http://www.consumerpsychologist.com/

Madden, T.J., Hewitt, K. and Roth, M.S. (2000). Managing images in different cultures: a cross-national study of colour meanings and preferences. *Journal of International Marketing*, 8(4), pp. 90-107.

Miyazaki, A., Grewal, D. and Goodstein, R. (2005). The Effect of Multiple Extrinsic Cues on Quality Perceptions: A Matter of Consistency. *Journal of Consumer Research*, Vol. 32, pp. 146-53.

McDaniel, C. and Baker, R.C. (1977). Convenience Food Packaging and the Perception of Product Quality. *Journal of Marketing*, 41(4), 57-58.

Nancarrow, C., Wright, L.T. and Brace, I. (1998). Gaining Competitive Advantage from Packaging and Labelling in Marketing Communications. *British Food Journal*, Vol. 100/2, pp. 110-18.

Nelson, P. (1970). Information and Consumer Behavior. *Journal of Political Economy*, 78(2), 311-29.

Nelson, P. (1974). Advertising as Information. *Journal of Political Economy*, 82, 729-54.

Nielsen's global packaging survey (2007), Consumer towards packaging of FMCG products: retrieved fromhttp://www.scribd.com/doc/15463797/Consumer-Behaviour-towards-packaging-of-FMCG-products?autodown=pdf

Olson, J.C. and Jacoby, J. (1972). Cue Utilization in the Quality Perception Process. In: Proceedings of the Third Annual Conference of the Association for Consumer Research, *Association for Consumer Research*, pp. 167-179.

Olson, J.C. (1977). Price as an Informational Cue: Effects on Product Evaluations. In: *Consumer and Industrial Buying Behavior*, Arch Woodside, Jaglish N. Sheth, and Peter D. Bennett, eds. New York: Elsevier, 267-86.

Osgood, C.E., Suci, G.J. and Tannenbaum, P.H. (1957). *The Measurement of Meaning* (Urbana, IL: University of Illinois Press).

Peters, M. (1994). Good Packaging Gets Through to the Fickle Buyer. *Marketing*, (Jan. 20), 10.

Rao, A.R. and Monroe, K.B. (1989). The Effect of Price, Brand Name, and Store Name on Buyers' Perceptions of Product Quality: An Integrative Review. *Journal of Marketing Research*, Vol. 26, pp. 351-57.

Reynolds, T.J. and Gutman, J. (1984). Advertising Is Image Management. *Journal of Advertising Research*, (Feb./Mar.), 27-37.

Reynolds, T.G. and Gutman, J. (1988). Laddering theory, method, analysis and interpretation. *Journal of Advertising Research*, Vol. 19, No. 28, pp. 11-31.

Rigaux-Bricmont, B. (1981). Influences of Brand Name and Packaging on Perceived Quality. In: *Advances in Consumer Research*, Mitchell, A. (eds.). St. Louis: Association for Consumer Research, 9, 472-77.

Rocchi, B. and Stefani, G. (2005). Consumer's Perception of Wine Packaging: A Case Study. *International Journal of Wine Marketing*, Vol. 18, No. 1, pp. 33-44.

Rotschild, M.L. (1987). *Marketing Communications. From Fundamentals to Strategies*. Toronto: D.C. Heath and Company.

Sawyer, A.G., Worthing, P.M. and Sendak, P.E. (1979). The role of laboratory experiments to test marketing strategies. *Journal of Marketing Strategies*, 43, pp. 60–67.

Schoormans, J.P.L. and Robben, H.S.J. (1997). The Effect of New Package Design on Product Attention, Categorization and Evaluation. *Journal of Economic Psychology*, 18 (2-3), 271-87.

Schmitt, B.H. and Pan, Y. (1994). Managing corporate and brand identities in the Asia-Pacific Region. *California Management Review*, 36(4), 32-48.

Ted Mininni (2009), Maximizing Brand Image through Package Design, retrieved from http://www.thedieline.com/blog/article-maximizing-brand-image-through-package-design.html.

T. Giski (2009), Does product packaging significantly influence consumer buying behavior? retrieved from http://www.t.giski.2009./doest.product.significantly./influence/consumer.buying.behaviour.

Underwood, R.L. and Ozanne, J.L. (1998). Is Your Package an Effective Communicator? A Normative Framework for Increasing the Competence of Packaging. *Journal of Marketing Communication*, 4, 207-20.

Underwood, R.L. (1999). Construction of Brand Identity Through Packaging: A Qualitative Inquiry. In: *Marketing Theory and Applications*, Menon, A. and A. Sharma (eds.). Illinois: American Marketing Association, 10 (Winter), 147-48.

Underwood, R.L., Klein, N.M., and Burke, R.B. (2001). Packaging Communication: Attentional Effects of Product Imagery. *The Journal of Product and Brand Management*, 10(7), 1-19.

Underwood, R.L. and Klein, N.M. (2002). Packaging as Brand Communication: Effects of Product Pictures on Consumer Responses to the Package and Brand. *The Journal of Marketing*, 10(4), 58-68.

Verdú Jover, A.J., Lloréns Montes, F.J. and Fuentes Fuentes, M.M. (2004). Measuring Perceptions of Quality in Food Products: The Case of Red Wine. *Food Quality and Preference*, Vol. 15, pp. 453-69.

Zeithaml, V. (1988). Consumer Perceptions of Price, Quality, and Value: A Means-end Model and Synthesis of Evidence. *Journal of Marketing*, Vol. 52, 2-22.

16

Gender Bias in the Entrepreneurial Leadership Style

Some Reflections on its Evidence and Reasoning

A. SURYANARAYANA

ABSTRACT

Entrepreneurs drive themselves and others relentlessly, yet their personalities inspire others. This entrepreneurial leadership style often incorporates certain behaviors stemming from the leader's personal characteristics and the circumstances of self-employment. Controversy over whether men and women have different leadership styles continues. Several researchers and observers argue that women entrepreneurs have certain acquired traits and behaviors that suit them for relations-oriented leadership.

A more important issue here is how to capitalize on both male and female leadership tendencies. Connie Glaser believes that the best approach to leadership takes the entrepreneurial style.

We have to recognize, however, that authorities disagree about whether an entrepreneurial personality exists. For example, Howard, H. Stevenson of Harvard Business School says, "You can't build a single psychological profile of the entrepreneur because there are too many examples that break the rules". Based on a literature review, Jim Grant concluded that there are apparently few, if any, personality or behavioral differences between men and women entrepreneurs. Studies reviewed by Bass indicate no consistent pattern of male-female differences in leadership style. This Paper looks briefly at some of the evidence and reasoning that shows that gender differences do and do not exist between the leadership styles of today's entrepreneurs. *(200 Words)*

INTRODUCTION

Effective entrepreneurship requires the right behaviors, skills, and attitudes. Two such major dimensions of entrepreneurship are: (a) initiating structure, and (b) consideration.[1] Initiating structure is the degree to which the entrepreneur organizes and defines relationships in the group by such activities as assigning tasks and specifying procedures. Consideration is the degree to which he creates an environment of emotional support, warmth, friendliness, and trust. The most entrepreneurs emphasize both these dimensions. The situation, however, often influences which leadership dimension should be emphasized. Many task-related attitudes and behaviors of effective entrepreneurs have been identified. Among them are: (1) adaptability to the situation, (2) direction-setting, (3) high performance standards, (4) risk taking and a bias for action, (5) ability to interpret environmental conditions, (6) frequent feedback, (7) stability of performance, and (8) strong customer orientation.

Many relationship-oriented attitudes and behaviors of entrepreneurs have also been identified. Among them are: (1) alignment of people, (2) mobilization, (3) concert building, (4) inspiration, (5) satisfaction of human needs, (6) making work meaningful for people, (7) emotional support and encouragement, and (8) promotion of principles and values. Understanding entrepreneurship through behaviors and attitudes has its limitations. The specific behaviors under the task and relationship dimensions need to be highlighted to provide useful guidelines for the practice of entrepreneurship. It would also be helpful to understand which combination of behaviors and attitudes is likely to be the most effective in a given enterprise.

Entrepreneurs drive themselves and others relentlessly, yet their personalities inspire others. This entrepreneurial leadership style often incorporates certain behaviors stemming from the leader's personal characteristics and the circumstances of self-employment. Controversy over whether men and women have different leadership styles continues. Several researchers and observers argue that women entrepreneurs have certain acquired traits and behaviors that suit them for relations-oriented leadership.

THE ENTREPRENEURIAL LEADERSHIP STYLE

Many entrepreneurs use a similar leadership style that stems from their key personality traits and characteristics. (The same is true to a lesser extent for intrapreneurs, company employees who take on entrepreneurial projects for the firm, such as a business start-up.) The general picture that emerges is of a task-oriented and charismatic leader. Entrepreneurs drive themselves and others relentlessly, yet their personalities inspire others.

One of the important styles of a leader is the entrepreneurial style. It stems from the leader's personal characteristics and the circumstances of self-employment. We have to recognize, however, that authorities disagree about whether an entrepreneurial personality exists. For example, Howard H. Stevenson of Harvard Business School says, "You can't build a single psychological profile of the entrepreneur because there are too many examples that break the rules". Instead, Stevenson regards entrepreneurship as a behavior focusing on the pursuit of opportunity without regard to the resources currently under control.[2]

This entrepreneurial leadership style often incorporates certain behaviors that are described below more in detail:[3]

Strong Achievement Motive and Sensible Risk Taking

Entrepreneurs have stronger achievement motives than do most leaders. Building a business is an excellent vehicle for accomplishment and risk taking. The theory surrounding achievement motivation indicates that the entrepreneur would take sensible risks or pursue realistic goals. Because they take sensible risks, many entrepreneurs do not perceive themselves as being risk takers—just as many tightrope walkers believe they are not taking risks they are in control. Wilson L. Harrell, a consultant to entrepreneurs expresses it this way: "When we ask entrepreneurs if they are risk takers, they say no! Entrepreneurs are so sure they'll succeed that, to them, there's no risk." By solving problems creatively they reduce risk.[4]

High Degree of Enthusiasm and Creativity

Related to the need for achievement are enthusiasm and creativity. Entrepreneurs' enthusiasm, in turn, makes them persuasive. As a result, they are often perceived as charismatic. Some entrepreneurs are often so emotional that they are regarded as eccentric.

Tendency to Act Quickly when Opportunity Arises

Entrepreneurs are noted for seizing upon opportunity. When a deal is on the horizon, they push themselves and those around them extra hard. As the founder of an information system firm told his staff after receiving an important inquiry, "Cancel all your weekend plans. We work until this proposal is completed to my satisfaction and that of our prospect".

Constant Hurry

Entrepreneurs are always in a hurry. When engaged in one meeting, their minds typically begin to focus on the next meeting. Their flurry of activity rubs off on group members and those around them. Entrepreneurs often adopt a simple dress style in order to save time, and they repeatedly allow very little slack time between appointments.

Visionary Perspective

Entrepreneurs and intrapreneurs, at their best are visionaries. They see opportunities others fail to observe.

Specifically, they have the ability to identify a problem and arrive at a solution.

Dislike of Hierarchy and Bureaucracy

Entrepreneurs are not ideally suited by temperament to working within the mainstream of bureaucracy. Many successful entrepreneurs are people who were frustrated by the constraints of a bureaucratic system. Intrapreneurs, by definition, fit reasonably well into a bureaucracy, yet they do not like to be restrained by tight regulations. The implication for leadership style is that entrepreneurs and intrapreneurs deemphasize rules and regulations when managing people.

Preferences for Dealing with External Customers

One of the reasons why entrepreneurs and intrapreneurs have difficulty with bureaucracy is that they focus their energies on products, services, and customers, rather than on employees. Some entrepreneurs are gracious to customers and money lenders but brusque with company insiders.

GENDER DIFFERENCES IN ENTREPRENEURIAL LEADERSHIP STYLE

Controversy over whether men and women entrepreneurs have different leadership styles continues. Several researchers and observers argue that women have certain acquired traits and behaviors that suit them for relations-oriented leadership. Consequently, women leaders frequently exhibit a cooperative, empowering style that includes nurturing team members. According to this same perspective, men are inclined toward a command-and-control., militaristic leadership style. Women find participative management more natural than do men because they feel more comfortable interacting with people. Furthermore, it is argued that women's natural sensitivity to people gives them an edge over men in encouraging group members to participate in decision-making.

Let us look briefly at some of the evidence and reasoning that shows that gender differences do and do not exist between the leadership styles of today's entrepreneurs as organizational leaders. We emphasize this because more and more women hold formal leadership positions especially as entrepreneurs today than in previous decades. Also, sex roles are less rigid today. A significant side issue here is that the terms sex and gender arouse controversy for both scientific and political reasons. As the term is used by many researchers, gender refers to perceptions about the differences among males and females.[5]

An example would be to believe that women entrepreneurs tend to be better listeners than their male peers. Sex differences, however, refer to actual (objective and quantitative) differences, such as the fact that the mean height of men exceeds that of women. Despite these observations, the terms gender and sex are still used interchangeably in gender usage and to some extent in scholarly writings. In this era of celebrating diversity, we hope nobody would be offended by either term.

Argument for Gender differences in Entrepreneurial Style

In an article that stimulated considerable debate, Judy Rosener concluded that men and women do tend toward opposite styles. Based on self-reports, she found that men tended toward a command-and-control style. In contrast, women tended toward a transformational style, relying heavily on interpersonal skills.[6] Cary Cooper of Britain contends that men tend to manage by punishment and women by rewards. He observes that women are socialized to manage people and relationships in the home, and have taken their skills from the home and transformed them to the workplace. Relying more on data, Cooper reports:

> Our studies have shown that women tend to be more participatory in their management style and they are seen by both male and female subordinates to be much more caring than male counterparts. In practical terms, this means that men's style of management contributes to stress, by putting much pressure on people and stopping them from producing their best.[7]

Based on some of his more recent research, Bass has found some specific male-female differences in entrepreneurial leadership style. Data collected from subordinates suggests that women are less likely to practice management-by-exception (intervening only when something goes wrong). Yet women and men appear to use contingent recognition with equal frequency. Even when the women entrepreneurs studied do practice management-by-exception, they typically temper criticism with positive feedback. Bass also found that women entrepreneurs are slightly more likely to be described as charismatic. In a survey of sixty-nine world-class leaders (nine-women included), women scored higher on the transformation factor than did men.[8]

Based on his experiences in conducting workshops on caring leadership, James Autry thinks that women get the idea of caring more quickly than men. He contends that women are more willing to reach out, to reveal their feelings, to connect, and to bond. From Autry's perspective, men fear such approaches. The differences in caring can surface in such ways as women managers giving more reassurance to group members.[9]

A related perspective is that women entrepreneurs are more likely than their male counterparts to perceive their business as a family. As corporate managers, women tend to place a major emphasis on forming caring, nurturing relationships with employees. Women are also more likely than men to praise group members. And when an employee falls short of expectations, women are more likely to buffer criticism by finding something praiseworthy.[10]

Argument Against Gender Differences in Leadership Style

Based on a literature review, Jim Grant concluded that there are apparently few, if any, personality or behavioral differences between men and women managers. Also, as women move up the corporate ladder, their identification with the male model of managerial success becomes apparent; they consequently reject even the few managerial feminine traits they may have earlier endorsed. Studies reviewed by Bass (other than his own research) indicate no consistent pattern of male-female differences in leadership style.[11]

To what extent these stereotypes of men and women entrepreneur-leaders are true is difficult to judge. Even if male and female differences in leadership style do exist, they must be placed in proper perspective. Both men and women leaders differ among themselves in leadership style. Plenty of male leaders are relations-oriented, and plenty of women practice command and control (the extreme task orientation). Many women believe that women entrepreneurs can be more hostile and vindictive than their men counterparts.

Male-female differences have been observed in leadership style. Women have a tendency toward relationship-oriented leadership, whereas men tend toward command and control. Some people argue, however, that male-female differences in leadership are inconsistent and not significant. Rather than searching for the one best style of leadership, managers are advised to diagnose the situation and then choose an appropriate leadership style to match. To be effective, a leader must be able to adapt his or her style to the circumstances.

A more important issue is how to capitalize on both male and female leadership tendencies. Connie Glaser believes that the best approach to leadership takes advantage of the positive traits of both men and women. She sees a new management style that blends the male and female sides:

> While the female may impart that sense of nurturing, the sensitivity to individual and family roles, that's offset by certain traits that the male brings to the table. The ability to make decisions quickly, the sense of humor, the risk taking—those are qualities that traditionally have been associated with the male style of management.[12]

CONCLUDING REMARKS

Entrepreneurial leadership style includes these elements: strong achievement motivation and sensible risk-taking, high degree of enthusiasm and creativity, rapid response to opportunity, hurriedness, visionary perspective, dislike of hierarchy and bureaucracy, and preference for dealing with external customers. Regardless of the gender differences, there is no one best or most effective entrepreneurial leadership style. Paul Hersey, Kenneth, H. Blanchard, and Dewey, E. Johnson explain that there is no one best way to lead an enterprise because entrepreneurial leadership is situational.[13]

Over thirty five years ago Ralph Stogdill made a statement about selecting a leadership style that still holds today: *The most effective leaders appear to exhibit a degree of versatility and flexibility that enables them to adapt their behavior to the changing and contradictory demands made on them.*[14] More recently, Thomas, R. Horton (1992) has observed that CEOs practice many different styles to achieve their objectives. Among these styles is 'public person or private', 'loose cannons or reflective thinkers', and 'autocrats or participative leaders'.[15] All these observations, the author believes, also hold good in the case of entrepreneurs, male or female.

Notes and References

1. Ralph, M. Stogdill and Alvin, E. Coons (eds.), Leader Behavior: Its Description and Measurement (Columbus: The Ohio State University Bureau of Business Research, 1957); Carrololl L. Shartle, Executive Performance and Leadership (Englewood Cliffs, N.J.: Prentice-Hall, 1956).
2. Cited in Warshaw, "The Mind-Style of the Entrepreneur", p. 30.
3. Based in part on Michael Warshaw, "The Mind-Style of the Entrepreneur", *Success,* April 1993, pp. 28-33; Frank A. deChambeau and Fredericka Machenzie, "Intrapreneurship", *Personnel Journal,* July 1986, p. 40.
4. Wilson, L. Harrell, "Aggression: It's the Entrepreneur's Insurance", *Success,* April 1993, p. 8.
5. Gary, N. Powell, "The Effects of Sex and Gender on Recruitment", *Academy of Management Review,* October 1987, pp. 731-43.
6. Judy Rosener, "Ways Women Lead", *Harvard Business Review,* November-December, 1990, pp. 119-25.
7. Quoted in Roz Morris, "Management: Why Women are Leading the Way", in Michel Syrett and Clare Hogg (eds.) *Frontiers of Leadership* (Oxford, England: Blackwell Publishers, 1992), p. 271.
8. Cited in "Debate: Ways Men and Women Lead", *Harvard Business Review,* January-February, 1991, p. 151.
9. James, A. Autry, *Life and Work: A Manager's Search for Meaning* (New York: William Morrow, 1994).

10. Debra Phillips, "The Gender Gap", *Entrepreneur,* May 1995, pp. 110-11.
11. Bernard M. Bass, *Bass & Stogdill's Handbook of Leadership: Theory, Research, & Managerial Applications*, 3rd ed. (New York: The Free Press, 1990), p. 725.
12. Cited in Phillips, "The Gender Gap", p. 112.
13. Paul Hersey, Kenneth, H. Blanchard, and Dewey, E. Johnson, *Management of Organizational Behavior: Utilizing Human Resources,* 7th ed. (Upper Saddle River, N.J.: Prentice-Hall, 1996), p. 91.
14. Ralph, M. Stogdill, "Historical Trends in Leadership Theory and Research", *Journal of Contemporary Business,* Autumn 1974, p. 7.
15. Thomas, R. Horton, The CEO Paradox: *The Privilege and Accountability of Leadership* (New York: AMACOM, 1992), p. 115.

17

HRD Interventions for an Inclusive and Faster Growth in a Global Economy

A. SURYANARAYANA

INTRODUCTION

In the past two decades or so, most societies around the world have experienced changes, unparalleled in scale and scope to those encountered in preceding centuries. These include the globalization of industries; regional economic integration; the formation of international strategic alliances across firms in different industries and countries; the lowering of immigration and emigration barriers to the movement of people, thus contributing to growing diversity in the workforce; and quantum advances in telecommunication that enable almost instantaneous access to information and communication at the click of a mouse.[1]

To cope with these dynamics, organizations have to develop and retain a cadre of globally minded executives who can move with chameleon-like ease from one country to another. The development and retention of this cadre of executives who have perfected the art of acting local worldwide—referred to by some as "*corporate diplomats*"—are not easy.[2] Some companies lose market share and prospective business because their executives are unable to perform effectively in their countries. Thus, companies have to recruit and develop such talent. However, even after a company has successfully hired and nurtured this talent, with the emergence of "boundaryless" careers, organizations have to work hard to retain these people.[3] Increasingly, highly skilled and qualified employees are willing to leave their country of origin to relocate elsewhere, for career, personal, and/or financial reasons.

In order for a company to survive and thrive in this new calculus of global competition, they have to effectively manage their human resources, including their selection, training and development, compensation, and retention. Thus, Human Resource Management (HRM) has become pivotal to a firm's global competitiveness because capital and technology cannot be effectively allocated nor transferred across international boundaries in the absence of people. Increasingly, highly skilled and qualified employees are willing to leave their country of origin to relocate elsewhere, for career, personal, and/or financial reasons. These important interventions involved in global workforce management are greatly influenced by several factors both in the external environment and within the internal environment of the firm.

This paper seeks to address many of the challenges and opportunities that arise in the context of global economic turbulence. Drawing upon research findings, the paper examines how environmental and institutional constraints, including culture, impact Human Resource Development (HRD) interventions such as Global HR Planning, Global Staffing, Global Workforce Training and Development, Global Workforce Performance Management, Compensation for Global Workforce, etc. In the context of global economic turbulence, we need to emphasize the critical role of the HR function in dealing with global workforce issues effectively in achieving organizational objectives. Managers and leaders have a central responsibility in recrafting HR strategies for supporting and implementing these HR functions with professional assistance of HR specialists. Recrafting HR strategies is pertinent to firms of all sizes and kinds everywhere and is critical for the successful operation of global business.

CHALLENGES AND OPPORTUNITIES IN GLOBAL HRM

For those managers and business decision-makers throughout the world who are interested and engaged in doing business beyond their own country's borders, exciting opportunities and significant challenges are arising rapidly with the growing influence of globalization.[4] We are witnessing extraordinary changes, pressures, and challenges confronting profit and non-profit organizations throughout the world. Organizations struggle to prosper and even survive under the continually developing influence of globalization, with its increasing market accessibility and openness, technological advancements, cross-border direct and virtual exchanges and interactions, common cultural convergence, often unpredictable and adversarial socio-political environments, and especially unrelenting competition. Within this global context, we note many difficult and vexing workforce-related challenges, such as those faced in Europe driven by pressures for greater economic flexibility, and forcefully illustrated by recent demonstrations, and even violence, in France in protest against new employment laws that favor business staffing needs and promote long-term increased employment at the short-term expense of younger workers.

In Asia, with multinationals' ongoing experience and technological advancements, we find India's low cost but labor force supporting the country's continuing development as a major leader in cost-saving offshore foreign direct investment arrangements (both in-house and outsourced) in many forms of more mundane back office business processes, as well as competitive high-tech research and development.

The People's Republic of China, following nearly two decades of remarkable economic growth accompanied by unfathomable societal sacrifice, displacement, and pain, is experiencing increasingly frequent and uncharacteristically vocal protests from its citizenry, now met by a major official shift by the Central Government epitomized in its "People First" policy. Companies planning for business development in China should consider possible implications for their internal operations and practices of this newly espoused priority in China involving the present and future labor force. Indeed, in China and beyond, many business leaders consider the internal and external environments in which they must operate to be in a state of crisis. However, as a Chinese word for crisis (*weiji*) carries with it the double meanings of both "threat" and "opportunity", organizations large and small throughout the world may find that their effective management of their workforce can serve to seize opportunities to propel them ahead within the globally competitive arena.

Recrafting HR strategies is pertinent to both large Multinational Corporations (MNCs) and to small and medium-size firms everywhere and is critical for the successful operation of global business. Key activities within HRD interventions include HR Planning, staffing, training, compensation, performance management, and managing employee relations, all of which are made more challenging on a global scale due to the myriad cultural and national differences in foreign operations. These important interventions involved in global workforce management are greatly influenced by several factors both in the external environment and within the internal environment of the firm.

GLOBAL MARKET CONTEXT

Company leaders endeavor to manage their organizations within our global market context, with its associated rapidly changing social, political, economic, and technological forces. Within this global context, leaders face the need to carry out their work activities through the efforts of their own home country employees as well as their foreign employees, agents, organization partners, and suppliers. As organizational boundaries become more permeable and less distinct with new work relationships and collaborative agreements (such as strategic alliances, international joint ventures, and outsourced services), and with corresponding new, more flexible workforce arrangements (for example, part-time and temporary employees and contracted labor services), the perception of what constitutes an organization's workforce must also be adjusted. Thus, this changing workforce that is essential for achieving organizational goals and objectives is becoming more global, diverse, flexible, multi-sourced, and complex in nature, presenting vastly different opportunities and demands and increasingly difficult challenges than were even faced at the end of the twentieth century.

With this global context in mind, we must emphasize the importance of balancing attention on the local context in global workforce management, because key factors influencing the effective management of human resources can differ dramatically from one local context to another.[5] One has to examine each of the important external factors (such as the economy, social preferences, competition, demographics, innovation, technology, management practice, and governments) and internal factors (such as the company culture, its climate, company strategy, and organizational structure), which often interact and are closely interrelated, to gain a clearer picture of the broad context for managing a global workforce.[6]

CULTURAL FOUNDATIONS OF GLOBAL HRM

Culture is central to the study and preparation for managing a global workforce effectively. Understanding cultural differences is critical to success in global business, because there are roles played by culture in global workforce management. We have to examine and take into account all the important and relevant dimensions for gaining insights and understanding about the cultures of employees that staff our organizations domestically and abroad. However, views differ about how global and regional economic integration affected and will affect the different dimensions of culture, including convergence, divergence, and *cross-vergence*. Convergence and divergence perspectives may represent polar extremes. As most firms struggle to find the optimum trade-off between globalization and localization, that is, "*glocalization*", perhaps the reality is closer to a more balanced or middle grow view called "crossvergence", or the intermixing of cultural systems between different countries.[7] Notwithstanding the importance of recognizing cultural differences, we have to be cautious about developing inflexible cultural stereotypes and exaggerating the influence of cultural differences.

CHANGES AND CHALLENGES IN THE GLOBAL LABOUR MARKET

For recrafting HR strategies, one has to examine major trends in the global labor market along their implications for governments and firms. These trends include changes in world demographics, impacts of immigration on developed countries, the emergence and influence of contingent workers as a significant component of the labor force, and the positive and negative impact of the increased use of offshore sourcing as an alternative to domestic production and operations. Finally, we have to accommodate the implications of these trends while designing the HR strategies.[8]

THE KEY ROLE OF GLOBAL HRM IN SUCCESSFUL MNC STRATEGY

International HR can have several forms of strategic influence on an organization's ability to compete in the global marketplace. In turn, particular strategies and structures that MNCs choose to use tend to have an impact on international HRM practices. Designing and operating a contingency model to understand how different types of international HRM practices may be selected to support the effective implementation of distinctive competitive strategies and organizational structures alone is an imperative in this context.[9]

GLOBAL HR PLANNING

Global HR Planning provides a vital link between MNC strategy and the implementation of strategy through the human factor. Global HR Planning should scan the environment for both immediate and longer-term threats and opportunities as they influence the supply of labor and human talent to meet immediate and anticipated long-term work demand. This critical function also should carefully examine appropriate approaches for organizing and designing work and working arrangements to meet company objectives as well as carefully consider sources of talent—both internal and external—for filling work demand. Finally, HR Planning should look internally to design and coordinate various HR activities that build long-range capability to ensure MNC survival and competitiveness.[10]

GLOBAL STAFFING

Important general factors that influence Global Staffing at all employee levels include company business strategy, company stage of international development, specific foreign market experience, host government restrictions, host government restrictions, and incentives, socio-cultural considerations, plans for individual and organization development, and situational factors. Important areas of consideration for global recruitment include the geographic scope of recruitment and whether interr al *versus* external candidates should be sought. Managers should consider several alternative recruitment methods to ensure that they are able to attract an optimal number of qualified candidates at a reasonable cost.[11]

GLOBAL SELECTION

General guiding principles and practices for Global Selection should include triangulation, maintaining a focus on job relevance, investing in building interviewing skills among supervisors, and being aware and controlling for the potentially distorting influence of cross-cultural differences.

When selecting employees for foreign assignments, MNCs might consider psychometric, experiential, and clinical risk assessment approaches. Finally, to increase the likelihood of foreign assignment success, MNCs should more broadly consider other candidate characteristics besides technical competence, including interpersonal skills, personal intent and motivation for obtaining international work experience, cross-cultural sensitivity, adaptability, tolerance for ambiguity, overall inquisitiveness, and the viability of a positive experience for accompanying family members.[12]

GLOBAL TRAINING AND WORKFORCE DEVELOPMENT

We need to examine the strategic role and key contributions of Global Workforce Training and Development as well as the fundamental concepts and principles for guiding them. Critical imperatives in this regard include building global competencies and workforce alignment. Particular considerations should be made to ensure the effective training of Host Country Nationals at all levels and expatriates as well as female expatriates who face unique challenges.[13]

GLOBAL PERFORMANCE MANAGEMENT

Performance Management at home and abroad is not just an annual or semiannual performance appraisal event but should be considered an ongoing process, beginning with a careful design of work and clear sharing of performance expectations followed by regular feedback. Effective performance management on a global scale involves linking individual employee performance to company priorities and strategies as well as being sensitive to cross-cultural differences and local conditions. It is important to be aware of general principles and practices of effective performance management and appraisal and to adapt these to unique needs of Parent Country Nation (PCN) expatriates, local workforce Host Country Nations (HCNs), Third Country Nations (TCNs), and inpatriates to provide optimal support in their differing assignments.[14]

COMPENSATION FOR A GLOBAL WORKFORCE

Compensation, including the overall system of rewards—formal and informal—provides the driving force for effectively attracting, retaining, and encouraging human talent at home and abroad. Important and fundamental practices for managing compensation on a global scale include managing global compensation strategically, considering performance-based pay where appropriate, anticipating the influence of local culture, using a total rewards systems perspective, and addressing the duality challenge of global integration and localization. Careful consideration should be made to effectively address the unique needs, goals, and circumstances of major employee categories within the global workforce, including PCN expatriates, HCNs, and TCNs.[15]

MANAGING GLOBAL ASSIGNMENTS

Rapidly changing global conditions and interests in reducing traditional expatriate costs are leading to a considerable increase in various forms of more flexible, short-term international assignments, including work as a "virtual" expatriate with international teams at foreign sites as well as working with global virtual teams where all members are separated by country location and culture. These short-term international assignments present new advantages for conducting business on a global scale as well as new challenges for managing these foreign assignments, including more frequent travel.[16]

Important issues and practices are associated with successfully managing various assignments for working abroad, including pre-departure planning and preparation, on-site management for effective adjustment and on-going support, and repatriation. Besides these considerations for the traditional PCN expatriate assignment, there are additional issues that may be unique to women expatriates and third-country nationals in their expatriate assignments as well as HCN *inpatriates* who are assigned to work at MNC headquarters.[17]

GLOBAL EMPLOYEE RELATIONS

The primary focus of employee relations in global workforce management is on the nature in which employees' personal interests, rights, and needs are protected and served by MNCs, which also are influenced by other external factors such as unions and government legislation. Critical challenges for human and worker rights in today's global workplace include forced labor, harmful child labor, workplace discrimination, health and safety hazards, and job insecurity and displacement. As part of their corporate responsibility, organizations should work hard to address and resolve these serious challenges, including cooperating and working closely with government and other non-profit organizations. MNCs also can do much to optimize the effectiveness of their ER policies and practices, open communications, employee involvement and development, effective management of discipline, and, where necessary, termination.[18]

CONCLUDING REMARKS

We are unashamed supporters of globalization. In this Paper, we specifically refer to global strategy and HRD interventions as those operating with one global market in mind, emphasizing standardization across countries and centralized control from headquarters in managing the business. We believe that the worldwide sharing of ideas through open global trade and other forms of cooperative interaction leads to greater advancement in innovation in all areas of human endeavor, which ultimately can benefit humanity. On an individual level we frequently note and experience firsthand how involvement in international business and education generally results in new insights leading to business process and productivity improvements as well as personal growth and development. We are witnessing a significant convergence of economic, technological, political, and social practices around the world, from instant communications facilitated by the Internet and global cell phones to cigarette-free workplaces, restaurants, and even entire countries.[19]

More specifically in international management and human resources we are seeing an increased sharing and adoption worldwide of recognized best practices that contribute to global competitive advantage. Where possible, we have to advocate the adoption and use of best practices and general principles of effective HRM where such convergence is warranted, such as in the systematic processes of training design and performance management. However, we have to be mindful of the limitation of "universal" perspectives in management and of the pervasive impact of cultural differences, particularly involving the implementation of company plans and objectives, which require local customization and adjustment from a divergence perspective.[20] Greater access to markets in both developed and emerging developing country markets, as well as reform to their own trade regimes, would be a powerful contribution to economic recovery in the region.[21] Furthermore, it is in the long-term economic interest of MNCs, individually and collectively, to invest in the ongoing care and development of the labor force of the countries where operations are located.[22] In addition, the human resource function is increasingly placed in the role of the "conscience" of the organization and has an important responsibility of creating and monitoring an organizational culture and overall environment that supports and encourages ethical behavior, including the moral responsibilities.[23]

Notes and References

1. Tung, R.L., 1998. "A Contingency Framework of Selection and Training of Expatriates Revisited". *Human Resource Management Review*, Vol. 8, No. 1, pp. 23-27.
2. Samer, R., Yiu, L., and Sondergaard, M., 2000. "Business Diplomacy Management: A Core Competency for Global Companies". *Academy of Management Executive*, Vol. 14, No. 1, pp. 80-92.
3. Tung, R.L., 1998. "American Expatriates Abroad: From Neophytes to Cosmopolitans". *Journal of World Business*, Vol. 33, No. 2, pp. 125-44.
4. M. Steers and L. Nardon, *Managing in the Global Economy* (Armonk, NY: M.E. Sharpe, 2006).
5. R.S. Schuler and S.E. Jackson, "A Quarter-Century Review of Human Resource Management in the U.S.: The Growth in Importance of the International Perspective", *Management Review*, 16(1) (2005): pp. 11-35.

6. T. Kell and G.T. Carrott, "Culture Matters Most", *Harvard Business Review,* 83(5) (2005): 22-23.
7. D. Ralston, D. Holt, R.H. Tersptra, and Kai-Cheng Yu, "The Impact of National Culture and Economic Ideology on Managerial Work Values: A Study of the United States, Russia, Japan, and China", *Journal of International Business Studies,* 28(1) (1997): 177-207.
8. Martin and Widgren, "International Migration: Facing the Challenge", (2002).
9. H.Conn and G. Yip, "Global Transfer of Critical Capabilities", *Business Horizon* (January/February 1997): 22-31.
10. C.R. Greer, *Strategic Human Resource Management: A General Managerial Approach,* 2d ed. (Upper Saddle River, NJ: Prentice-Hall, 2001.
11. D. Wiechmann, A.M. Ryan, and M. Hemingway, "Designing and Implement Global Staffing Systems: Part I—Leaders in Global Staffing", *Human Resource Management,* 42(1) (2003): 71-83.
12. P.R. Sparrow, "International Recruitment, Selection, and Assessment", in the *Global Manager: Creating the Seamless Organization,* ed. P. Joynt and B. Morton (London: IPD House, 1999).
13. M.R. Carell, N.F. Elbert, and R.D. Hatfield, *Human Resource Management: Strategies for Managing a Diverse and Global Workforce,* 6th ed. (Fort Worth, TX: Dryden Press, 2000): 1254-55.
14. R. Bacal, Performance Management (New York: McGraw-Hill, 1999).
15. S.J. Perkins and C. Hendry, "International Compensation", in the *Global Manager: Creating the Seamless Organization,* ed. P. Joynt and R. Morton (London: IPD, 1999): 115-43.
16. M. Harvey and M. Buckley, "Managing inpatriates: Building Global Core Competency", *Journal of World Business,* 32(1) (1997): 35-52.
17. T. Cavusgil, U. Yavas, and S. Bykowicz, "Preparing Executives for Overseas Assignments", *Management Decision,* 30(1) (1992): 54-58
18. P. Lewis, A. Thornhill, and M. Saunders, *Employee Relations: Understanding the Employment Relationship,* (New York: Prentice-Hall, *Financial Times,* 2003).
19. C. Prahalad and Y. Doz, *The Multinatioinal Mission* (New York: Free Press, 1988).
20. C. Bartlett and S. Ghoshal, "Organizing for Worldwide Effectiveness: The Transnational Solution", *California Management Review,* 31(1) (1989): 54-74.
21. S. Panitchpakdi, "Aid is Good; Trade is Better", *Wall Street Journal,* 17 January 2005, A14.
22. M. Marquardt and N.O. Berger, "The Future: Globalization and New Roles for HRD", *Advances in Developing Resources,* 5(3) (2003): 283-95.
23. M.R. Vickers, "Business Ethics and the HR Role: Past, Present, and Future", *HR Planning,* 28(1) (2005): 26-32.

18

New Product Launching
A Strategy during Recession

K. Jawahar Rani and Mrs. J. Srilekha

ABSTRACT

Everyone is talking about recession. The talk alone may be enough to trigger one, whether the underlying economics dictate it or not. From observations of recessions past, we know that consumers are quick to rein in spending when hard times are predicted. Many business leaders behave the same way. Anticipating reduced sales, they are inclined to cut back on variable costs, including marketing, in order to deliver on the expectations of the financial market.

However, a great deal of evidence suggests that it's not a good idea to reduce marketing spend during recession in order to hit financial targets. Doing so may leave your brand in a less competitive position when the economy recovers. Over the years, research studies have confirmed that the best strategy in terms of long-term ROI is to increase marketing expenditure during an economic slowdown. An analysis of the Profit Impact of Marketing Strategies (PIMS) database, presented at a March 2008 IPA conference, provides the latest evidence.

This study emphasis a new product launch has greater impact during a recession than at other times. A product that is unique or demonstrably better than others should be able to command a higher price, even among price-conscious shoppers. Competitors who are running scared may be late in countering a new product with their "me-too" offerings.

EXECUTIVE SUMMARY

"It was the best of times, it was the worst of times".
—Charles Dickens (1859): A Tale of Two Cities

Every change in the marketplace, every disruption in the economy, every shift in technology, and every change in consumer attitudes and outlook create opportunities for successful new products. Since these changes are greater than before during tough times, new product opportunities are actually more numerous during economic turbulence. The companies that develop and install new products during downturns in the economy tend to outperform their more timid rivals during the recession and come roaring out of the starting gates when the economy begins to expand.

Many might think that during times of economic recession consumers are in no mood to experiment with, or purchase inventive products. Counter-intuitively, starting a business or launching an invention during a recession can be one of the smartest moves to make-depending of course, on if you take certain factors into account. Looking at past recessions and consumer psychology can give us ideas on the types of inventions that can succeed during an economic downturn. Let's walk through some of these themes that appear on the psychological landscape during a recession.

All around, people are watching others suffer economic hardship, losing their jobs and homes. A result of this is a mindful gratitude that they are not that person they see struggling on the nightly news or in their neighborhood. An appreciation of what one already has, as opposed to what one can attain becomes paramount. People are looking to improve themselves to compete in a tougher job market.

During boom times companies rush to get to market as quickly as possible in order not to miss opportunities. A downturn, therefore, could be a perfect time to develop and introduce radical and unproven new technology that can take years to get right.

There are other advantages of expanding during a recession; it is easier to negotiate better deals with suppliers and partners as they become dependent on the revenue your business brings. Tax incentives for R&D, starting new businesses, and hiring people are often introduced during recessions to revive the economy. It is also well known that teams become more focused and work harder in the face of a powerful enemy. Recession can be such an enemy. Boom times have the excitement of the overall activity in the field as well as easy sales. But excitement is fleeting while the resolve to outlast a recession stays.

Biographical Notes

Dr. K. Jawahar Rani is a Professor in the Department of Management Studies in St. Joseph Engineering College. She has 20 years of academic experiences and specialized in Marketing. Her research areas of interest are Marketing, HR and Production and she is a life member of ISTD and MMA.

Mrs. J. Srilekha is a lecturer in the Department of Management Studies in Velammal College of Management and Computer Studies. She has 9 years of industrial and teaching experience in field of management studies. Her research area of interest is marketing. She is currently involved with teaching Postgraduate Management courses and research activities.

Key words: Financial Targets, Competitive position, Economic slowdown.

REVIEW OF LITERATURE

HOW TO MARKET DURING RECESSION

By

Harvard Business Online, Published on March 3, 2008, Author : John Quelch

1. Research the Customer

Instead of cutting the market research budget, you need to know more than ever how consumers are redefining value and responding to the recession. Price elasticity curves are changing. Consumers take more time searching for durable goods and negotiate harder at the point of sale. They are more willing to postpone purchases, trade down, or buy less. Must have features of yesterday are today's can-live-without. Trusted brands are especially valued and they can still launch new products successfully, but interest in new brands and new categories fades. Conspicuous consumption becomes less prevalent.

2. Focus on Family Values

When economic hard times loom, we tend to retreat to our village. Look for cozy hearth-and-home family scenes in advertising to replace images of extreme sports, adventure, and rugged individualism. Zany humor and appeals on the basis of fear are out. Greeting card sales, telephone use, and discretionary spending on home furnishings and home entertainment will hold up well, as uncertainty prompts us to stay at home but also stay connected with family and friends.

Now may be the time to drop your weaker distributors and upgrade your sales force.

3. Maintain Marketing Spending

This is not the time to cut advertising. It is well documented that brands that increase advertising during a recession, when competitors are cutting back, can improve market share and return on investment at lower cost than during good economic times. Uncertain consumers need the reassurance of known brands, and more consumers at home watching television can deliver higher than expected audiences at lower cost-per-thousand impressions. Brands with deep pockets may be able to negotiate favorable advertising rates and lock them in for several years. If you have to cut marketing spending, try to maintain the frequency of advertisements by shifting from 30-second to 15-second advertisements, substituting radio for television advertising, or increasing the use of direct marketing, which gives more immediate sales impact.

4. Adjust Product Portfolios

Marketers must reforecast demand for each item in their product lines as consumer's trade down to models that stress good value, such as cars with fewer options. Tough times favor multi-purpose goods over specialized products, and weaker items in product lines should be pruned. In grocery-products categories, good-quality own-brands gain at the expense of national brands. Industrial customers prefer to see products and services unbundled and priced separately. Gimmicks are out; reliability, durability, safety, and performance are in. New products, especially those that address the new consumer reality and thereby put pressure on competitors, should still be introduced, but advertising should stress superior price performance, not corporate image.

When economic hard times loom, we tend to retreat to our village.

5. Support Distributors

In uncertain times, no one wants to tie up working capital in excess inventories. Early-buy allowances, extended financing and generous return policies motivate distributors to stock your full product line. This is particularly true with unproven new products. Be careful about expanding distribution to lower-priced channels; doing so can jeopardize existing relationships and your brand image. However, now may be the time to drop your weaker distributors and upgrade your sales force by recruiting those sacked by other companies.

6. Adjust Pricing Tactics

Customers will be shopping around for the best deals. You do not necessarily have to cut list prices, but you may need to offer more temporary price promotions, reduce thresholds for quantity discounts, extend credit to long-standing customers, and price smaller pack sizes more aggressively. In tough times, price cuts attract more consumer support than promotions such as sweepstakes and mail-in offers.

7. Stress Market Share

In all but a few technology categories where growth prospects are strong, companies are in a battle for market share and, in some cases, survival. Knowing your cost structure can ensure that any cuts or consolidation initiatives will save the most money with minimum customer impact. Companies such as Wal-Mart and Southwest Airlines, with strong positions and the most productive cost structures in their industries, can expect to gain market share. Other companies with healthy balance sheets can do so by acquiring weak competitors.

8. Emphasize core values

Although most companies are making employees redundant, chief executives can cement the loyalty of those who remain by assuring employees that the company has survived difficult times before, maintaining quality rather than cutting corners, and servicing existing customers rather than trying to be all things to all people. CEOs must spend more time with customers and employees. Economic recession can elevate the importance of the finance director's balance sheet over the marketing manager's income statement. Managing working capital can easily dominate managing customer relationships. CEOs must counter this. Successful companies do not abandon their marketing strategies in a recession; they adapt them.

OBJECTIVE OF THE STUDY

1. To determine the buying strategy of customers during recession.
2. To determine the expectation of customers from a marketer during recession period.
3. To determine the expectation among customers for new product.

SCOPE OF THE STUDY

The study is aimed at finding out the preferences for the new product. The study also aims at finding out the expectation of the customers for the new product during recession period, determining the interpretation, the top of mind awareness among the customers and the way that stimulate the customers to purchase the product. The data collection is taken only within the Chennai city.

Limitations

- The study was restricted to the Chennai city, which could be hardly considered as the representative of entire country.
- The error, known as response error could arise due to the information given by respondents because of bias.
- The conclusion drawn from the research may not represent the entire population.
- The survey was conducted only with the customers who purchased 'Actimind'.

Research Methodology

Research design	-	Descriptive research
Research instrument	-	Questionnaire with closed-ended questions
Research method	-	Survey method

Sampling data

Sample design	-	Convenience
Data type	-	Primary data
Sampling unit	-	'Actimind' Users
Sampling area	-	Chennai city

Data Collection

The research data has been collected through survey method, they are the primary data. Secondary data consist of the data about the company and its other details.

Research Design

The research design is the specification of methods and procedures for acquiring the information needed to structure or solve the problem. It is the overall operational pattern or framework of the research study that stipulates what information to be collected from which sources and by what procedures. If it is good design it will ensure that the information obtained is relevant to the research problem.

Type of Research

Descriptive

Descriptive research is the one that simply describes something such as demographic characteristics of consumer who use the product. The descriptive study is typically concerned with the determining frequency with which something occurs or how two variables vary together.

Research Instruments

In market research two instruments are used to collect primary data they are questionnaire method and mechanical devices, however, this research has been done by using questionnaire method. The questionnaire consists of closed ended questions. Both dichotomous and multiple choice questions were also used

Sample Design

Sample represents the population. It refers to the technique or the procedure the researcher should adopt in selecting items for sample. Sample design has been determined before data is collected. It contains sample size, sample unit, etc.

Sample Size

Sample size used for this research is 50.

Sample Unit

Sample unit is "Actimind" users of Chennai city.

ANALYSIS AND INTERPRETATION

Preference for New Product

Need	*Percentage*	*Number of persons*
Less cost	30	15
Quality	30	15
Brand	40	20

Preference for the Product

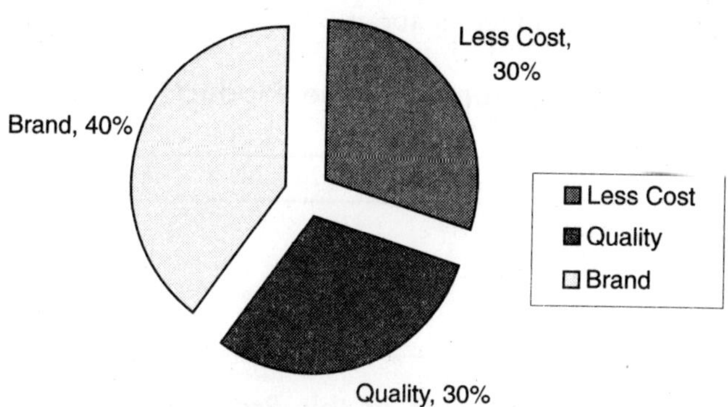

Inference

High amount of the people are prefer brand, its percentage is about 40%. Next goes to cost and quality.

Type of Offer During Recession

Type of offer during Recession	*Percentage*
Cash discount	30
Buy one get one	22
Pack in premium	28
Extra quantity	20

Type of Offer During Recession

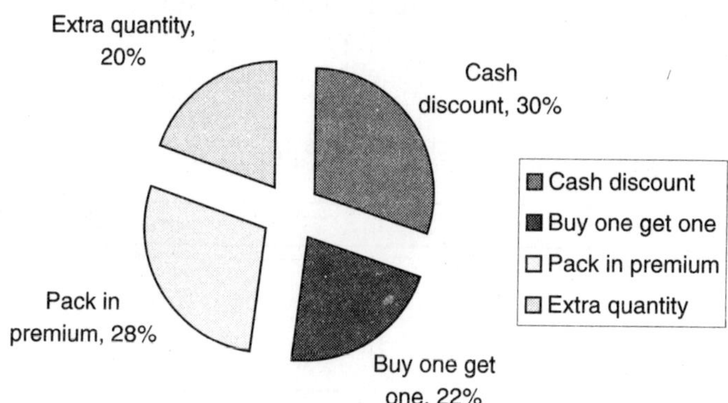

Inference

High amount of the people expect cash discount during recession, its percentage is about 30%.

Awareness of the Product

Awareness of the product	*Percentage*
Television	30
Radio	4
Newspaper	50
Friends	20

Awareness of this Product

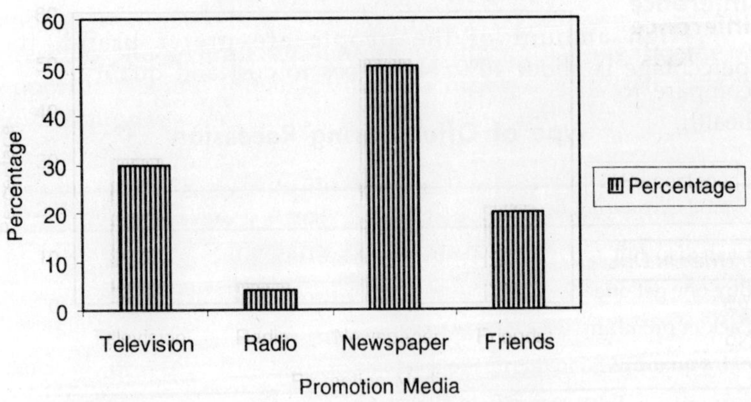

Inference

Many customers came to know about the product through Newspaper, the amount of percentage is 50% and the rest came to know through television and friends.

Focused Group

Focused group	*Percentage*
Kids	50
Teenagers	25
Middle-age	20
Old people	5

Focused Group

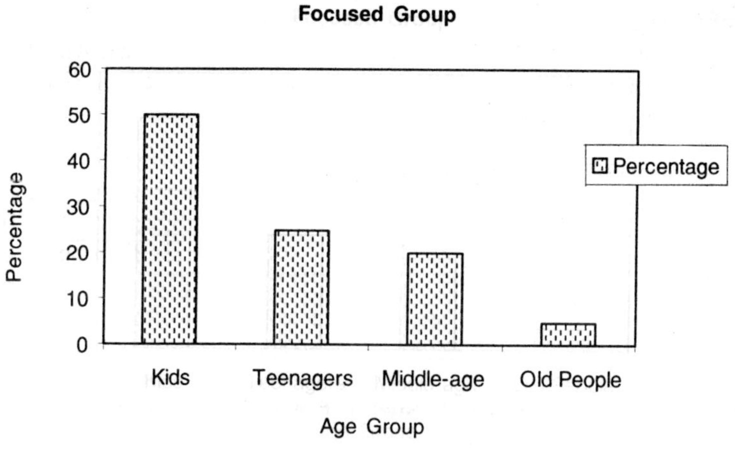

Inference

Kids are more interested in buying this products when compare to adults as this product is mainly focused for kids health.

Increase in Demand after Recession

Increase in Demand after Recession	*Percentage*
Yes	62
No	38

Increase in Demand after Recession

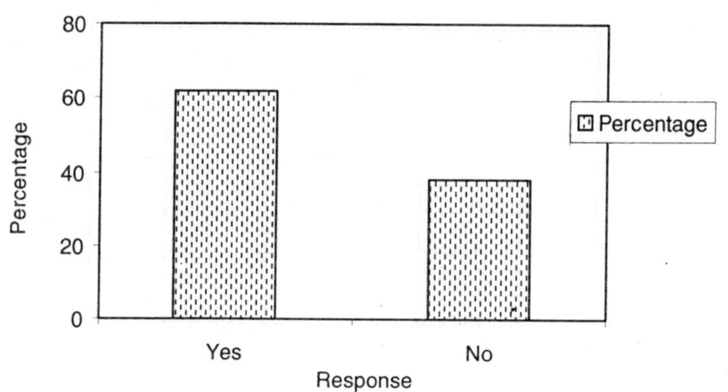

Inference

Many customers feel that there will be great demand for this product after recession. Their amount of percentage is 62%.

Cost Under Budget

Cost Under Budget	*Percentage*
Yes	56.3
No	43.7

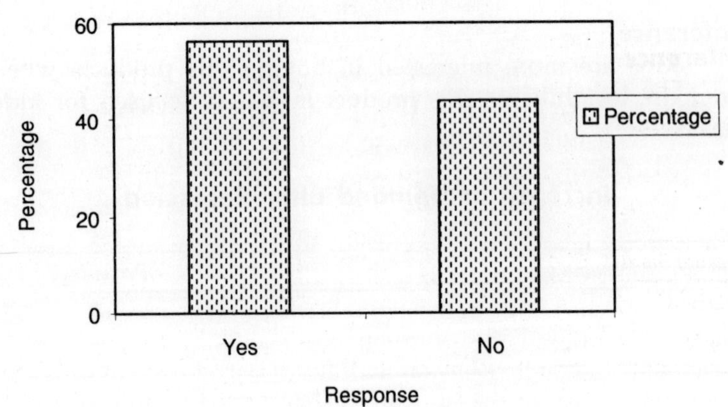

Inference

Many customers feel that the cost of the product is under their budget. Their amount of percentage is 56.3%.

Gender

Gender	*Percentage*
Male	47.5
Female	52.1

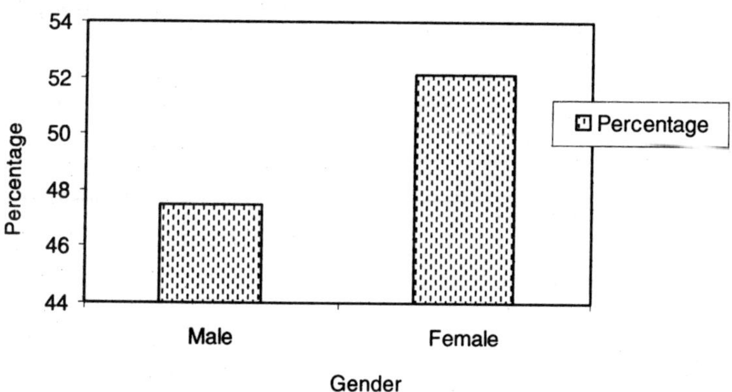

Inference

The female respondents is more when compare to male respondents.

Marital Status

Marital Status	*Percentage*
Married	87
Single	13

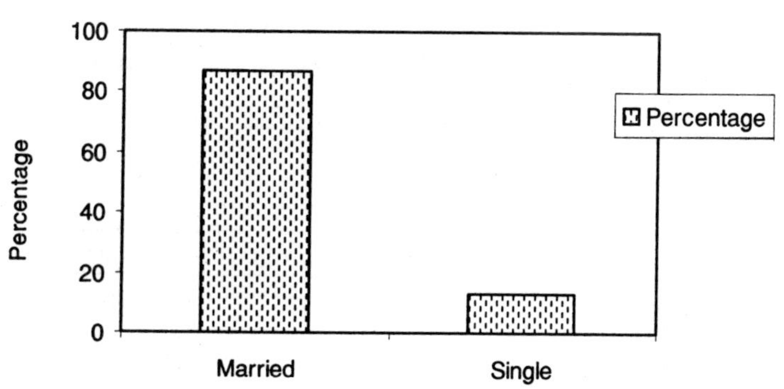

Inference

Almost all the respondents are married. The amount of percentage is 87%.

Work Status

Work status	*Percentage*
Business	30.1
Employee	14.6
Student	23.7
Home-maker	22.2
Others	9.4

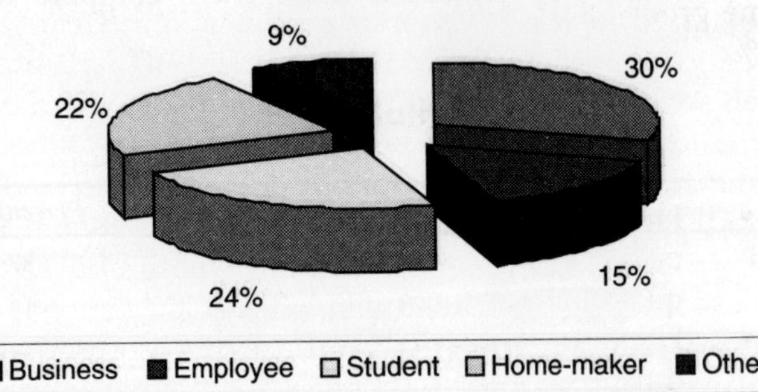

Inference

Many customers who buy this product are housewife and business people.

Income Status

Income Status	*Percentage*
Below Rs. 10000	10.2
Rs. 10000-25000	16.7
Rs. 25000-35000	14.6
Above Rs. 35000	58.5

Income Status

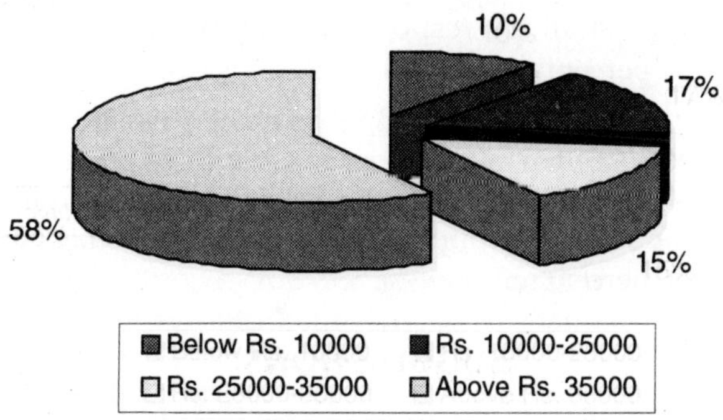

Inference

Many respondents who buy this product belong to the income group of above Rs. 35,000; their amount of percentage is 58%.

RESEARCH FINDINGS

- High amount of the people are prefer brand its percentage is about 40%. Next goes to cost and quality.
- High amount of the people expect cash discount during recession, its percentage is about 30%.
- Many customers came to know about the product through Newspaper, the amount of percentage is 50% and the rest came to know through television and friends.
- Kids are more interested in buying this products when compare to adults as this product is mainly focused for kids health.
- Many customers feel that there will be great demand for this product after recession. Their amount of percentage is 62%.
- Many customers feel that the cost of the product is under their budget. Their amount of percentage is 56.3%.

- The female respondents is more when compare to male respondents.
- Almost all the respondents are married. The amount of percentage is 87%.
- Many customers who buy this product are housewife and business people.
- Many respondents who buy this product belong to the income group of above Rs. 35,000; their amount of percentage is 58%.

SUGGESSTIONS

Majority of the people's purchasing behavior is based on watching advertisements. The people get stimulated to purchase the product by seeing attractive advertisements. So the company should spend some money for advertisements when they introduce some new product.

CONCLUSION

I would like to suggest that the company could introduce the new product with full faith of obtaining good results. The customers are expecting a high quality product from the company. Also while introducing the product the company should concentrate more on advertisements because peoples' purchasing behavior is highly based on watching Ads. The company should advertise their product in regular intervals to create proper awareness among people. I would like to conclude that the company can get a market in recession by introducing a new product.

Note : The new product I have taken for this research is "Actimind" a health drink which comes from Britannia. The new drink for children is fortified with nutrients, including vitamins, choline, to help improve memory and Iodine to increase mental development.

References

Alam, I. and C. Perry (2002), 'A customer-oriented new service development process', *Journal of Services Marketing*, Vol. 16, No. 6, pp. 515-34.

News of Warren Buffett's investment in General Electric was also reported widely. This information was published by MSNBC.com and can be explored further at http://www.msnbc.msn.com/id/26976416/.

McKinsey & Company's research on "Learning to Love Recessions" can be found at http://www.mckinseyquarterly.com/Strategy/Strategic_Thinking/Learning_to_love_recessions_1197_abstract.

APPENDIX

QUESTIONNAIRE

1. Why do you go for this new product?
   (a) Less cost (b) Quality (c) brand
2. What type of offer do you expect during recession?
   (a) Cash Discount (b) buy one get one
   (c) pack in premium (d) Extra quantity
3. How do you come to know about this product?
   (a) Television (b) radio (c) News paper (d) friends
4. Who is being more attracted towards this product in your family?
   (a) Kids (b) Teenager (c) Middle age people
   (d) Old people
5. Do you think the demand for the product increase after recession?
   (a) Yes (b) No
6. Does this product cost come under your budget?
   (a) Yes (b) No
7. Genders: (a) Male (b) Female
8. Marital Status: (a) Married (b) Single
9. Work status:

   ☐ Business ☐ Employee ☐ Student ☐ Home-maker ☐ Others

10. Income:

   ☐ Below Rs. 10,000 ☐ Rs. 10,000-25,000

   ☐ Rs. 25,000-35,000 ☐ Above Rs. 35,000

Information Needs of SMEs' Stakeholders on Financial Reporting

Preliminary Views from European Emerging Countries' Perspective

JIRI STROUHAL AND ADELA DEACONU

ABSTRACT

In the context of the international drive to simplify the SMEs' financial reporting, one may identify a stringent call for the identification and serious analysis of the SMEs' specific users of information and their needs. It appears that these needs are not sufficiently developed at present, through market research and accounting literature, so that they can play a useful part in the accounting regulators current actions. Hence, the main objective of this paper is to identify and rank the users and their needs, within the European area and for emergent economies, taken into consideration the fact that especially in these areas, there are few such analyses. Having this purpose, we start from theories regarding accounting systems differentiation in accordance with their influential factors, which we will particularize to the SMEs' environment. The framework which we are going to develop for analyzing the influential factors, adapted to small entities and emerging economies, in correlation with the taxonomies for users' identification established by some theories, will represent our project's theoretical support. There will be made an analysis of current documents regarding SMEs' financial reporting (IFRS for SMEs and the updated version of the 4th Directive of EU) and we will engage in ample sectional analyses through survey-inquiries with the aim to establish an identification and raking scheme for users and their needs.

Keywords: Financial Reporting, SMEs, Stakeholders, Czech Republic, Romania, European Union JEL Code: M41.

1. INTRODUCTION

This study is related to the European context starting from the assumption of adapting the accounting to the environmental conditions. Calling upon the literature that approached the influential factors of accounting systems, it submits a framework for analysis through which it may identify and determine the influence of environmental factors (cultural, institutional and accounting related) upon SMEs' financial reporting.[1] The study is different from the above mentioned papers as it aims to differentiate the accounting systems less dominant within a certain space and time context from the central focus of the respective papers which was large companies.

Hereinafter, this research aims to determine and rank the major SMEs' stakeholders' groups[2] and their specific needs,[3] based on economic theories adjustable to this type of entities. It starts from the idea that financial reporting must be aimed at stakeholders; it must suit their demands and meet their needs. The study follows the approach from the SMEs' stakeholders' point of view (including the manager), but also the producers of information.

Through this, study covers a gap in the literature that focused on such analysis from the perspective of the accounting profession and regulators rather than the perspective of the users and producers of information. Moreover, even if there are studies on identifying the SMEs' specific stakeholders there are not enough papers regarding their needs. Also, the studies mentioned above are not differentiated on clusters, and some are not empirically sustained.

The fourth objective in this research represents the quantification and determination of the SMEs' financial reporting cost's influence.[4] It arises from the lack of research on this subject and it covers the professional organizations' need to underline the SMEs standards they propose. For example, the European Commission indicates in its survey applied to member-states, which was the first step in the accounting simplification process it undertakes (EU, 2006), the necessity to reduce the administrative burden on companies by 25% (including the financial reporting field) without justifying the estimation method.

The literature we analyzed concerning stakeholders and their needs highlights the importance of identifying them in order to develop specific SMEs accounting regulations, but it does not determine their direct influence upon SMEs' financial reporting. There will be correlated the objectives of this research in order to be able to finally propose an accounting model dedicated to SMEs that would cover the specific conceptual framework, recognition criteria, measurement and disclosure.[5]

2. LITERATURE REVIEW

Firstly, there has to be mentioned the literature behind this research theme from the conceptual point of view, i.e. the factors that influence different accounting systems, respectively theories/schemes for stakeholders' identification. In both cases, the literature is full of studies which are used within this research. Thus, the influential factors and the classification of accounting systems are approached by Nair and Frank (1980), Doupnik and Salter (1993), Nobes (1998), Gernon and Meek (2001) or Hung and Subramanyam (2007). The general criteria for stakeholders' identification, considered either from the manager's or from the stakeholders' point of view are approached, for example, by: Carroll (1989) quoted by Collier (2008), Clarkson (1995) quoted by Frooman (1999), Donaldson and Preston (1995), Mitchell *et. al.* (1997), Frooman (1999), Itnner and Larcker (2002) and Carroll and Buchholtz (2003) quoted by Clulow (2005) or Collier (2008).

Secondly, we have to name studies that would help us in achieving all research objectives: SMEs' specific stakeholders, their needs, administrative burden of financial reporting for SMEs, respectively the possibilities for developing an accounting system for SMEs.

The identification of SMEs' specific stakeholders is rarely a subject in the literature. In the case of transitional economies is quoted Dang *et. al.* (2006) and for the European context there are Collis and Jarvis (2002) and Kajüter *et. al.* (2007) quoted by Evans *et. al.* (2005).

The stakeholders' needs regarding SMEs' financial reporting are approached at the European level by Collis and Jarvis (2002), Paoloni *et. al.* (2003), Riistama and Vehmanen (2004), Haller and Eierle (2004) quoted by Evans *et. al.* (2005), Evans *et. al.* (2005), Evans *et. al.* (2007). Along with the academic literature there could be mentioned certain empirical studies undertaken by accounting regulation or consultancy organizations that outlined the most important stakeholders in SMEs, studies like: KfW Bankengruppe, 2004; Bundesverband der Deutschen Industrie e.V. and Ernst and Young, 2005; DRSC *et. al.*, 2007 quoted by Evans *et. al.* (2007). Other research projects or professional demarches on SME reporting are in progress, but not yet published.

As regards to the administrative burden of financial reporting for SMEs, although all the papers sustain its significance and the need for accounting regulation to decrease it, very few papers have approached its scale and its direct influence, for example Keasey and Short (1990) and Collis and Jarvis (2002) quoted by Evans *et. al.* (2007) or Haller and Eierle (2007).

The solutions for simplifying the SMEs' accounting are approached firstly by professional organizations. The most remarkable steps were taken by the IASB through its standard for SMEs (IASB, 2009), respectively, the simplifications proposed by the European Commission (EU, 2007). The literature did not develop concrete technical solutions regarding a standard for SMEs as it commented on these two actions taken by the professional/accounting regulating organizations. Thus, both in the stages of DP and ED, the IASB standard received much criticism and/or recommendations. One of the main observations was that the IASB did not really take into account the SMEs specific stakeholders and their needs. From this point of view there was also criticism brought to the European Commission's latest publications which address further simplifications of accounting rules and propose a differentiation of entities from an accounting point of view, according to sub-criteria regarding size and types of users. The importance of undertaking field studies in Europe is outlined as these studies would clarify the above aspects and their results would be taken into account in future SMEs accounting simplifications. Finally, Sian and Roberts (2007) quoted by Evans (2007) show that the usefulness of an IFRS for SMEs [or other standards in general] may differ significantly between countries (developed and developing).

3. METHODOLOGY AND RESEARCH DESIGN

For achieving the research's first objective—*establishing a framework analysis of the SME's financial reporting influential factors*—it is used a theoretical approach, starting from the proposed taxonomy for the influential factors (e.g., Nobes 1998), adapting it to the characteristics of the SMEs. For this purpose there are identified and assessed the SMEs environment's specific factors thus building an analysis framework. This will allow shaping different clusters to be considered when processing empirical data within the project.

The *identification of the stakeholders and their needs* will be done based on the stakeholders' theory, adapted to SMEs. These characteristics bring about typical stakeholders and their needs adapted to the SMEs' working environment. There is combined the regulatory and instrumental approach of the stakeholders' theory. The first one will lead to outlining some normative assumptions regarding the variables that define the stakeholders' domain (Mitchell *et. al.*, 1997). The second one will reflect the manner in which the company is taking into account the impact of the stakeholder to which it links its performance-aimed actions (see Donaldson and Preston, 1995; Polonsky and Scott, 2005). We also have to refer to the property rights theory and to the classical theory of the shareholder-manager, endorsed by Jensen and Meckling (1976) quoted by Foss *et. al.* (1999), respectively by Alchian (1991). This last group of theories is helpful in distinguishing between the shareholder-manager—present in the majority of SMEs—and the other stakeholders of SMEs. Within the stakeholders' theory, we share the ideas of Mitchell *et. al.* (1997) that offer a flexible, adaptable scheme to any environment framework for the attributes needed to identify the stakeholders (power, legitimacy and urgency).

There is necessary also to add an empirical approach to these conceptual analyses, backed up by taxonomic and similitude techniques based on field studies. Data gathering will be done through interviews and survey inquiry. Believing it is possible to extract a shared view of the different managers and stakeholders by using a representative of SMEs from each CRP partner's country, everything in the context of a transition or stable economy. In order to ensure that the validity the study will not be affected by the virtual rather than objective reality basis due to its focus on the human unpredictable behavior (Clarkson *et. al.*, 1994 quoted by Clulow, 2005) there will be complemented the manager's perception and the other stakeholders' perception with different analyses. These could include content analysis of the documents reflecting the European forums' opinion regarding the SMEs' stakeholders, comment letters to IASB's standard IFRS for SMEs or other documents.

Data gathered through interview and survey, double checked through content analysis of the documents, will be then processed using statistical techniques. There is considered two-way analysis of models: a matrix analysis to link the stakeholders, their needs and the ranking of these two groups (also considering the testing of the 3 hypothesis for stakeholders salience belonging to Mitchell *et. al.*, 1997); a multi-criteria decision modeling approach using the analytical hierarchy process (AHP method) (Saaty, 2004) to estimate stakeholder value matrix.

4. FUTURE STEPS OF ONGOING RESEARCH

Furthermore, there will be studied the impact of users needs upon the financial reporting regulations' methods of elaboration. The assessments in the literature and our own investigations, including the determination of SMEs' overheads, are going to justify the opportunity of developing a stand-alone accounting standard, which will contain a conceptual framework, and adequate recognition, valuation and disclosure criteria. There will be proposed such a model, which represents a normative and practical instrument, useful both to producers and users of accounting information, having in mind an optimum cost-benefit rate.

The outcome of the study will serve to observing significant elements of recognition, measurement and disclosure and the cost of obtaining them in terms of time, money and effort, from the SME stakeholders' point of view.

Finally, there will be suggested *conceptual and technical solutions for simplifying the SMEs' financial reporting*, differentiated by selected clusters.

Notes and References

1. Alchian, A.A. (1991), Development of economic theory and antitrust: a view from the theory of the firm, *Journal of Institutional and Theoretical Economics*, No. 147.
2. Clulow, V. (2005), Futures dilemmas for marketers: can stakeholder analysis add value?, *European Journal of Marketing*, Vol. 39, No. 9/10, pp. 978-97.
3. Collier, P.M. (2008), Stakeholder Accountability, *Accounting, Auditing & Accountability Journal*, Vol. 21, No. 7, pp. 933-54.
4. Collis, J., Jarvis, R. (2002), Financial information and the management of small private companies, *Journal of Small Business and Enterprise Development*, Vol. 9, No. 2, pp. 100-10.
5. Dang, D.S., Marriott, N. and Marriott, P. (2006), Users' perceptions and uses of financial reports of small and medium companies (SMEs) in transitional economies: Qualitative evidence from Vietnam, *Qualitative Research in Accounting & Management*, Vol. 3, No. 3, pp. 218-35.

References

Donaldson, T., Preston, L.E. (1995), The stakeholder theory of the corporation: concepts, evidence, and implications, *Academy of Management Review*, Jan. 1995, Vol. 20, No. 1.

Doupnik, T.S., Salter, S.B. (1993), An empirical test of judgemental international classification of financial reporting practice, *Journal of International Business Studies*, Vol. 24, No 1, http://web.ebscohost.com

European Commission (2007), *Communication de la Comission des Communautes Europeennes relative a la simplification de l environnement des societes en matiere juridique, comptable et de controle des comptes*, 10.07.2007, Bruxelles.

European Commission, Internal Market and Services DG, Free movement of capital, company law and corporate governance, Accounting (2006), *Agenda paper for the meeting of the accounting regulatory committee, 24 November 2006: Simplification of accounting rules for small and medium-sized companies – Discussion of possible amendaments to the Fourth and Seventh Company Law Directives (ARC/18/2006)*(Brussels, 14.11.2006)

Evans, L. *et. al.* (2005), Problems and Opportunities of an International Financial Reporting Standard for Small and Medium-sized Entities. The EEAEAA-FRSC FRSC's Comment on the IASB's Discussion Paper, *Accounting in Europe*, Vol. 2, published for the European Accounting Association by Taylor and Francis.

Frooman, J. (1999), Stakeholder influence strategies, *Academy of Management Review*, Vol. 24, No. 2, http://web.ebscohost.com, Database: Business Source Premier

Gernon, H., Meek, G.K. (2001), *Accounting: an international perspective*, Irwin McGraw-Hill Publications, Fifth Edition, Singapore.

Haller, A. and Eierle, B. (2007), German Accounting Standards Board (GASB) Comment on the Exposure Draft of an IFRS for SMEs, IASB website: http://www.iasb.org*.

Hung, M., Subramanyam, K.R. (2007), Financial statement effects of adopting international accounting standards: the case of Germany, *Rev Accounting Stud*, Vol. 12, published online, pp. 623-57.

International Accounting Standards Board (IASB) (2007), *Exposure Draft of a Proposed IFRS for Small and Medium-sized Entities*, IASB website: http://www.iasb.org*.

Evans, L., Di Pietra, R., Chevy, J., Cisi, M., Eierle, B. and Jarvis, R., European Accounting Association Financial Reporting Standards Committee Comment on the Exposure Draft of an IFRS for SMEs (2007), IASB website: http://www.iasb.org*.

Mitchell, R.K., Agle, B.R., Wood, D.J., Towards theory of stakeholders' identification and salience: defining the principle of who and what really counts, *Academy of Management Review*, 1997, Vol. 22, No. 4, pp. 853-86.

Nair, R.D., Frank, W.G. (1980), The Impact of disclosure and Measurement Practices on International Accounting Classifications, *The Accounting Review*, Vol. LV, No. 3, pp. 426-50.

Nobes, C. (1998), Towards a General Model of the Reasons for International differences in Financial Reporting, *Abacus*, Vol. 34, No. 2, http://web.ebscohost.com

Polonsky, M.J., Scott, D. (2005), An Empirical Examination of the Stakeholders' Strategy Matrix, *European Journal of Marketing*, Vol. 39, No. 9/10, pp. 1199-1215.

Saaty, T.L. (1994), How to make a decision: The Analytic Hierarchy Process, *Interfaces*, Vol. 24, No. 6, pp. 19-43.

20

Soft Computing Intelligent Decision Support Systems Model for Health Management

TARUN DHAR DIWAN, SHRIDHAR DIWAN, NILMANI VERMA AND BHOOPENDRA DHAR

ABSTRACT

Machine Learning is relatively a new field of research whose major objective is to acquire knowledge from large amounts of data. In medical and health care areas, due to regulations and due to the availability of computers, a large amount of data is becoming available. On one hand, practitioners are expected to use all this data in their work but, at the same time, such a large amount of data cannot be processed by humans in a short time to make diagnosis, prognosis and treatment schedules.

The main objective of this research is to evolve a Soft computing based IDSS for Health Care Management so that novel and hidden knowledge patterns can be generated to automate and quicken the process of decision making in clinical diagnosis as well as other domains of health care management. In order to reach the main goal of the research, applications of clustering techniques are to be explored on medical databases to discover knowledge patterns. We have used 5 databases namely health disease, Breast Cancer, Immunization Program (Polio Database), and Medical Dataset of Patients collected from free Internet repository, Public health care sector and from renowned private nursing homes.

In the research work an experiment have been conducted covering different sphere of health care to achieve the main objectives of this research work. Before conducting these experiments a comprehensive literature review has been done. The results of these experiments successfully provide answers to the research questions raised in the beginning of this research work. These experiments can work synergistically which can produce single knowledge pattern or different pieces of knowledge patterns so that health care planners can take advantage of this knowledge discovery to lower healthcare costs while improving healthcare quality. This simulates the main concept of Soft computing Intelligent Decision Support Systems Model for Health Management.

The results of these experiments accumulatively simulate the answer of the main research question, i.e. *Can we evolve* Soft computing based *an intelligent decision support system model based on* applications of clustering techniques *for health care planners so that novel & hidden knowledge patterns can be generated to automate & quicken the process of decision-making in clinical diagnosis as well as other domains of health care management?*

APPLICATIONS OF CLUSTERING TECHNIQUES USING HEALTH CARE MANAGEMENT

The main objective of this experiment is to establish a system to find out the patients those are the most likely to have a similar disease. The results of the experiment have shown that clustering techniques can help to identify the pair of patients suffering from same disease. Identifying patients suffering from same diseases is a main aspect of medical diagnosis. The dataset used for this experiment is made available from private sector and in order to perform experiment it is converted to Excel Format. This dataset is about the patients and their symptoms of possible disease with their respective results of different tests. The patient records data set contains the attributes *name, gender, fever, cough, abdominal pain, CBC (Complete Blood Test), LFT (Lever Functioning Test) and S. Widal (Serum Widal).*

In order to conduct this experiment a dataset of 175 records of patients with 8 attributes (both symmetric and asymmetric) has been used. Among all the attributes, *name (an object-id)* and *gender* are symmetric binary attributes, and the remaining attributes are asymmetric binary attributes. To perform the experiment the following three records (record no. 15, 16, and 17) have been selected randomly (refer Figure 1) from the given dataset of patients as shown in Figure 2.

FIG. 1
Randomly Selected Three Records from Patient Database

15	JAGADEESH TS	M	Y	N	N	P	N	N
16	VIBHA MISHRA	F	Y	N	N	P	P	N
17	RAMACHANDRAN T	M	Y	Y	N	N	N	N

FIG. 1.2
A Snapshot of Patient Database

Microsoft Excel - Hospital Data- formatted

A15 JAGADEESH TS

	A	B	C	D	E	F	G	H
1	Name	Gender	Fever	Cough	Abdomi-1al Pai-1	CBC	LFT	S.Widal
2	UMA KANT DUTT	M	1	1	-1	1	-1	-1
3	DIGVIJAY SINGH RAWAT	M	1	-1	-1	1	1	-1
4	RITESH KUMAR AGRAWAL	M	-1	1	1	-1	1	-1
5	PRASHANT MOHAN AGARWAL	M	1	1	-1	1	-1	-1
6	SAMEER GOYAL	M	-1	1	-1	1	1	-1
7	KAREPAGOL BASAVARAJ	M	1	-1	-1	-1	-1	1
8	RAKSHITA	F	-1	1	-1	-1	-1	-1
9	SATINDER PAL SINGH BAINS	M	-1	-1	1	1	1	-1
10	SUTHAR JITENDRA AIDANRAM	M	-1	-1	-1	-1	-1	-1
11	KRISHNA BHARDWAJ	F	1	1	-1	1	1	-1
12	NEHETE GIRISH PITAMBAR	M	1	-1	-1	-1	1	-1
13	SHASHI KUMAR H B	M	-1	1	1	-1	-1	-1
14	NIKHITHA M S	F	-1	1	1	-1	1	-1
15	JAGADEESH TS	M	1	-1	-1	1	-1	-1
16	VIBHA MISHRA	F	1	-1	-1	1	1	-1
17	RAMACHANDRAN T	M	1	1	-1	-1	-1	-1
18	VIVEK CHANDRA	M	1	1	-1	1	1	-1
19	CHAUHAN DAKSHA DHIRAJLAL	M	-1	1	-1	1	1	-1
20	CHINGJEI KONYAK	M	1	-1	-1	-1	-1	-1
21	TESSY AUGUSTINE	F	-1	1	-1	-1	-1	-1
22	CHITRA R	F	1	-1	1	-1	1	-1
23	BIMAL V J	M	1	-1	-1	-1	1	-1
24	JAWADE SUGAT AMBADAS	M	-1	1	-1	-1	-1	-1
25	MISS LOPAMUDRA	F	1	-1	-1	-1	-1	-1
26	SIMON PHILIPOSE	M	-1	1	1	1	-1	1
27	RUPALI ARORA	F	1	1	-1	-1	1	-1
28	RAJSHREE MISHRA	F	-1	-1	-1	1	-1	-1
29	M SRIDEVI	F	-1	1	-1	-1	1	-1
30	AMIT KUMAR RANJAN	M	-1	1	1	-1	-1	-1
31	SWASTIKA SWARO	F	1	-1	-1	-1	-1	-1
32	BHAT ANEESH SHANKARNARAYAN	M	1	-1	-1	1	-1	-1
33	JYOTI BABU C	F	-1	1	-1	1	1	-1
34	JEYALAKSHMI V	F	-1	1	-1	-1	1	-1
35	ANIL KUMAR SINGH	M	1	1	-1	1	-1	1
36	VEENA PRABHU	F	[illegible]	[illegible]	[illegible]	[illegible]	[illegible]	[illegible]

Sheet1 / Sheet2 / Sheet3

Ready

For asymmetric attribute values, let the value Y (yes) and P (positive) be set to 1, and the value N (no or negative) be set to 0. Suppose that the distance between two objects (patients) pair-wise is computed based only on the asymmetric variables as shown in Figure 3 and Figure 4.

FIG. 3
Randomly Selected Three Records with Attribute Values Represented as 0's and 1's

7		Fever	Cough	Abdominal Pain	CBC	LFT	S.Widal
8	JAGADEESH TS	1	0	0	1	0	0
9	VIBHA MISHRA	1	0	0	1	1	0
10	RAMACHANDRAN T	1	1	0	0	0	0
11							

FIG. 4
Values of Symptom Attributes and Test Results of Sample Three Patients

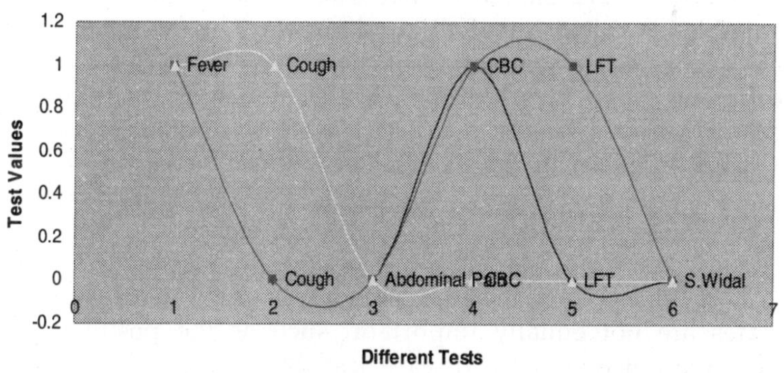

One approach involves computing a dissimilarity matrix from the given binary data. If all binary variables are thought of as having the same weight, we have a 2-by-2 contingency table, as shown in Table 1, where q is the number of variables that equal 1 for both the objects i and j, r is the number of variables that equal 1 for object i but are 0 for object j, s is the number of variables that equal 0 for object i but equal 1 for object j, and t is the number of variables that equal 0 for both the objects i and j. The total number of variables is p, where $p = q + r + s + t$.

TABLE 1

A Contingency Table for Binary Variables

		object j		
object i		1	0	Sum
	1	q	r	$q + r$
	0	s	t	$s + t$
	Sum	$q + s$	$r + t$	p

A binary variable is 'symmetric' if both of its states are equally valuable and carry the same weight, that is, there is no preference on which outcome should be coded as 0 or 1. One such example could be the attribute gender having the states male and female. Similarity that is based on symmetric binary variables is called invariant similarity in that the result does not change when some or all of the binary variables are coded differently. For invariant similarities, the most well-known coefficient for assessing the dissimilarity between objects i and j is the simple matching coefficient, defined in Equation 1.1:

$$d(i,j) = \frac{r+s}{q+r+s+t} \qquad \text{(Eq 1.1)}$$

A binary variable is 'asymmetric' if the outcomes of the states are not equally important, such as the positive and negative outcomes of a disease test. By convention, we shall code the most important outcome, which is usually the rarest one, by 1 (e.g., HIV positive), and the other by 0 (e.g., HIV negative). Given two asymmetric binary variables, the agreement of two 1's (a positive match) is then considered more significant than that of two zeros (a negative match). The similarity based on such variables is called non-invariant similarity. For non invariant similarities, the most well-known coefficient is the Jaccard coefficient *Equation 1.2*, where the number of negative matches, d, is considered unimportant and thus is ignored in the computation.

$$d(i,j) = \frac{r+s}{q+r+s} \qquad \text{(Eq. 1.2)}$$

According to the Jaccard Coefficient formula *(From Equation 1.2)*, the distance between each pair of the three patients, Jagdeesh, T.S. (*jagdeesh*), Vibha Mishra (*vibha*), and Ramachandran, T. (*rama*) should be,

$$d(jagdeesh, vibha) = \frac{0+1}{2+0+1} = 0.33 \qquad \text{(Eq. 1.3)}$$

$$d(jagdeesh, rama) = \frac{1+1}{1+1+1} = 0.67 \qquad \text{(Eq. 1.4)}$$

$$d(rama, vibha) = \frac{1+2}{1+1+2} = 0.75 \qquad \text{(Eq. 1.5)}$$

These measurements suggest that *Rama and Vibha* (*refer Equation 1.5*) are unlikely to have a similar disease they have the highest dissimilarity value among the three pairs. Of the three patients, *Jagdeesh and Vibha* (refer *Equation 1.3*) are the most likely to have a similar disease as shown in Figure 5.

FIG. 5
Measurements of Dissimilarity Value among the Three Pairs

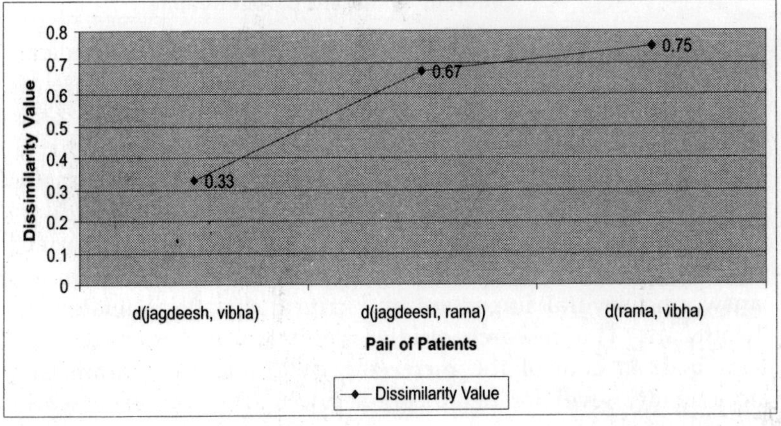

While analyzing the dataset of 175 patients we observed that various groups of patients shown different symptoms and test results as shown in Figure 6. The same method can be applied to all the records of the dataset and can be find a cluster of patients most likely to suffer from the same disease.

FIG. 6
Various Groups of Patients Showing Different Symptoms and Test Results

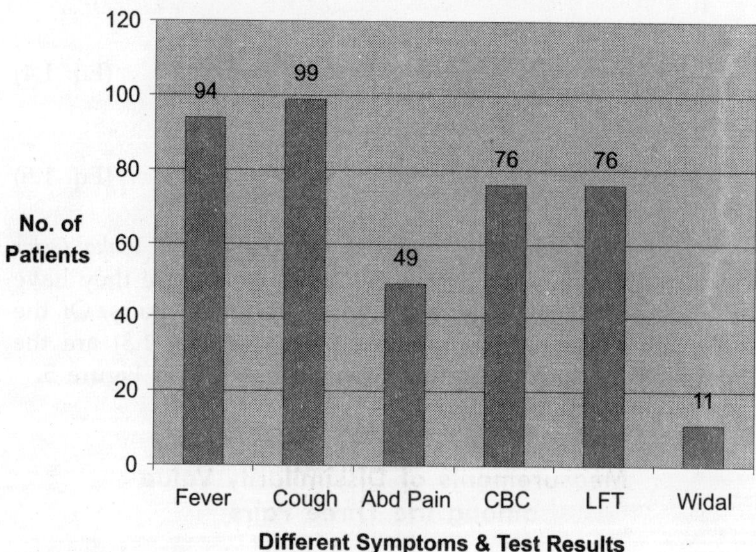

Medical diagnosis is one of major problem in medical application. This includes the limitation of human expertise in diagnose disease manually. This experiment has found that clustering techniques can help them to improve this domain. Identifying patients suffering from same diseases is a main aspect of medical diagnosis.

Treatment records of millions of patients can be stored and computerized and data mining techniques may help in answering several important and critical questions related to healthcare. The research studies on healthcare management aim both to control the increasing costs and to increase the accessibility level for healthcare services. The proposed work shows the great potential to discover knowledge pattern from massive healthcare data. A new problem we faced when trying to test out new idea dealing with finding the group of patients suffering from similar disease was in inherent limitation of the available data, because we only have access to limited sources, our results and experiments no doubt reflect some bias. Much of the work published in this domain also suffers from the fact that it tries to reach general conclusion using very small data sets collected on a local scale.

Treatment records of millions of patients can be stored and computerized and data mining techniques may help in answering several important and critical questions related to healthcare. The research studies on healthcare management aim both to control the increasing costs and to increase the accessibility level for healthcare services. The proposed work shows the great potential to discover knowledge pattern from massive healthcare data. A new problem we faced when trying to test out new idea dealing with finding the group of patients suffering from similar disease was in inherent limitation of the available data, because we only have access to limited sources, our results and experiments no doubt reflect some bias. Much of the work published in this domain also suffers from the fact that it tries to reach general conclusion using very small data sets collected on a local scale.

CONCLUSION

Classification using Clustering, clustering technique has been used to find out the patients those are the most likely to have a similar disease. In order to conduct this experiment a dataset of 175 records of patients with 8 attributes (both symmetric and asymmetric) has been used. Among all the attributes, *name (an object-id)* and *gender* are symmetric binary attributes, and the remaining attributes are asymmetric binary attributes.

To perform the experiment the three records have been selected randomly. According to the Jaccard Coefficient formula the distance between each pair of the three patients, *Jagdeesh T.S. (jagdeesh), Vibha Mishra (vibha), and Ramachandran T. (rama)* has been measured. These measurements suggest that

Rama and Vibha (Equation 1.5) are unlikely to have a similar disease they have the highest dissimilarity value among the three pairs. Of the three patients, *Jagdeesh and Vibha (Equation 1.3)* are the most likely to have a similar disease.

The same method can be applied to all the records of the dataset and can be find a cluster of patients most likely to suffer from the same disease. Medical diagnosis is one of major problem in medical application. This includes the limitation of human expertise in diagnose disease manually. The results of the experiment have shown that clustering techniques can help to identify the pair of patients suffering from same disease. Identifying patients suffering from same diseases is a main aspect of medical diagnosis. These results also simulate the answer of the research question stated.

Can we find the clusters of patients suffering from same disease?

21

A Study on Time Management among Various Types of Employees at Chennai City

P.T. Vijayshree and K.A.A. Atthiya Beevi

INTRODUCTION

People are the most important and valuable resources for every organisations or institutions. Effective employees can contribute to the effectiveness of the organisation. Competent and motivated people can make things happen and enable an organisation to achieve its goals. These kind of motivated people will follow discipline in the office premises like reaching on time, following all rules and regulations, etc. But for some time say for a year or so some of the offices is facing problems of lots of late comers just because of various reasons. So the researcher thought of doing a project on late coming of employees to the job and foreseeing that there is any other possible reason for this late coming, etc. and this will be analysed by using research methodology and statistical tools.

STATEMENT OF THE PROBLEM

1. The problem of employees reporting late to the job.
2. To know whether it affects the daily job requirements.
3. There is no proper mode of transport.
4. Increase in lateness rate subsequently affects the office's daily job requirements.

SCOPE OF THE STUDY

1. This study would enable employers to recognise the employees' various problems
2. This will help further to take various strategic decisions regarding lateness like grace time, bus facilities, etc.
3. The study helps in getting suggestions from the employees and to make further improvements that benefit the employees.

OBJECTIVE

1. To know whether employees could complete job requirements if they come late also.
2. To know the remedial measures taken by the management regarding lateness.
3. To study the factors like economical and psychological factors that determines lateness.
4. To know the satisfaction level of employees on disciplinary action taken by the management.
5. To know the employees' perception and to suggest remedial measures to reduce the lateness rate prevailing in the company.

PROCEDURE—METHODOLOGY

Research is a careful investigation or enquiry especially

through search for new facts in any branch of knowledge, research comprises defining and redefining problems, formulating hypothesis or suggested solutions, collecting and organising and evaluating data, making deduction and reaching conclusion, and at last carefully testing the conclusion to determine whether they fit the formulating hypothesis.

RESEARCH DESIGN

For descriptive study, a proper procedure should be prepared keeping in mind the objectives of the study and the resources available. The descriptive design is also called the survey design since it takes into account all the steps involved in a survey and hence the design was found to be the most suited design.

DATA SOURCE

There are two types of data that are available to the researcher.

PRIMARY DATA

All those, which are collected a fresh, for the first time and happens to be original in character. Primary data generated through personal interviews, surveys, observations, through questionnaires, depth interviews and content analysis. Primary data was collected by means of administering a questionnaire to the supervisors in the factory.

SECONDARY DATA

All those, which have already been collected by someone else and which have been passed through statistical process. Secondary data either may be published or unpublished data. This type of data is used because of its availability and because of economy, ease with which information can be obtained.

SAMPLE DESIGN

The sample design used here is convenience sampling. Under the convenience sampling the samples are selected on the convenience of the researcher, thus the research study may include the study objects which are conveniently located.

SAMPLE SIZE

Due to time and resources constraint available the sample size is taken as 100 employees of different organisations within Chennai city.

LIMITATIONS OF THE STUDY

1. Respondents were reactant in giving correct answers.
2. The work is a continuous and was very conscious. Filling up the questionnaire was difficult as the researcher had to interrupt the workers of different organisations.
3. Time was a major constraint and detailed information was not collected from the employees
4. Employees in different shifts were not accessible as such ideal opinion could not be collected.

FINDINGS OF THE STUDY

1. Most of the employees (65%) are in the age of 45-58 and 18% of the employees are in the age of 18-25.
2. 69% of the employees are married, therefore there may be some personal problems in reaching the premises on time.
3. 75% of the employees are permanent in their job, and 25% of the employees are not permanent in their job, they are temporarily employed.
4. 89% of the respondents were satisfied with their present job.
5. It is inferred that half of the respondents were living 20 kms away from the premises. Therefore, it is

clearly noted that employees facing difficulty in reaching the office premises.

6. Most of the employees (43%) are using two-wheelers.
7. Half of the employees are not feeling any difficulty in reaching the office premises, may be because of their mode of travel and the distance they live.
8. It is inferred that 45% of the employees were partially aware of the lateness and 40% of the respondents were fully aware.
9. Day shifts seems to be comfortable to major chunk of the employees.
10. 91% of the respondents known that the late comings is misconduct of standing orders.
11. It is clearly said that most of the late comings will fall on day shifts.
12. It is clear that 85% of the respondents come late to the office premises for 15 minutes.
13. More or less it is shocking to know that 24% of the respondents report late more than 4 times in a month.
14. 98% of the respondents said that company is giving grace time for the employees.
15. It is good to know that most of the respondents (73%) said that time management is the best measure to reduce late comings.
16. .It is good to know that company is conducting training program on time management in order to reduce late coming.
17. It is inferred that maximum no. of respondents could complete the job requirements if they come late also.
18. Most of the respondents were facing difficulty in reaching factory premises because of traffic jam.
19. It is clearly understandable that supervision in the company is normal and relationship between the co-workers and the supervisors are satisfied.
20. More than half of the respondents said that lateness affect their earnings, since three late are allowed in a month.

21. 70% of the respondents said that their lateness rate was low and they didn't receive any memo for such lateness.
22. Most of the people said that warning is the foremost remedial measures taken by the management and then follows memo and counselling.
23. Most of the employees said that disciplinary actions taken by the management are satisfied.
24. 36% of the respondents suggested to provide staff bus, 21% counselling and 17% suggested for motivation.

SUGGESTIONS

1. Creating full awareness among employees about lateness.
2. Staff bus can be arranged to the employees to reduce late coming from far away places.
3. Self-development classes can be arranged for time management, discipline, etc.
4. Counselling should be arranged for chronic late comers to know their problems and guide them in a better way to reduce late coming.
5. Awarding the employee who is not coming late for the job for a year or appreciating him by his immediate superiors will encourage other to do so.

CONCLUSION

The lateness rate will be automatically reduce to certain percentage after the bridge construction got over. Because traffic jam among Chennai city roads was a major constraint told by most of the respondents in spite of that we can reduce certain percentage of lateness by implementing self-development classes and activities on a regular bases and conducting the counselling sessions especially to chronic late comers and others which will help to reduce the lateness rate.

A Study on Business Process Analysis in Controlling (Sap Implementation)

M. GANESAN

INDUSTRY PROFILE

Radiators are heat exchangers used to transfer thermal energy from one medium to another for the purpose of cooling and heating. The majority of radiators are constructed to function in automobiles, buildings, and electronics. The radiator is always a source of heat to its environment, although this may be for either the purpose of heating this environment, or for cooling the fluid or coolant supplied to it, as for engine cooling.

RADIATION AND CONVECTION

One might expect the term "radiator" to apply to devices that transfer heat primarily by thermal radiation. While a device which relied primarily on natural or forced convection would be called a "convector". In practice, the term "radiator" refers to any of a number of devices in which a liquid circulates through exposed pipes (often with fins or other means of increasing surface area), notwithstanding that such devices tend to transfer heat mainly by convection and might logically be called convectors. The term "convector" refers to a class of devices in which the source of heat is not directly exposed.

ENGINE COOLING : RADIATOR

Radiators are used for cooling internal combustion engines, chiefly in automobiles but also in piston-engined aircraft, railway locomotives, motorcycles, stationary generating plants or any similar use of such an engine. They operate by passing a liquid coolant through the engine block, where it is heated, then through the radiator itself where it loses this heat to the atmosphere. This coolant is usually water-based, but may also be oil. It is usual for the coolant flow to be pumped, also for a fan to blow air through the radiator.

Electronics

As electronic devices become smaller yet more capable the problem of dispersing waste heat becomes more difficult. Tiny radiators known as heat sinks are used to convey heat from the electronic components into a cooling air stream.

Heat sinks, which dissipate thermal energy, should not be confused either with electric radiators or electromagnetic radiator elements, a sub-division of antenna in electronics which transmit or receive electromagnetic energy.

COMPANY PROFILE (MANUFACTURING INDUSTRY)

The Company Name is Undisclosed to Maintain Confidentiality

Manufacturing Company, is a worldwide leader in thermal management for almost 90 years. Manufacturing Company specializes in design, engineering, testing, and manufacture of heat transfer products for a wide range of applications, the company has 35 plants spread over 15 countries and employs nearly 8000 personnel. The company has an annual turnover of approximately used 1.8 billion.

As a part of its plan to expand its global presence, Manufacturing Company started facility in December 2006. The state of the art manufacturing facility spread over an area of 8000 square feet in Industrial park in Chennai is engaged in providing thermal management solutions to that nation's domestic engine, commercial vehicle and off-highways markets. Manufacturing Company in India has a design centre, which caters to the design and product development needs of Manufacturing Company in India as well as globally. We're at work in practically every corner of the world; inside the things you see every day.

Manufacturing Company has been a worldwide leader in thermal management for almost 90 years. They design, engineer, test, and manufacture heat transfer products for a wide range of applications and markets. We're at work in practically every corner of the world; inside the things you see every day.

Innovation—It's what started the company and keeps them going today. Their heat transfer innovations have set industry standards for efficiency, economy and durability. With more than 2,000 patents, they remain the leading innovator in the field.

Problem Solving—Today's heat transfer challenges grow more complex and sophisticated by the day. That's why they have hundreds of skilled engineers with a thorough background in heat transfer and most importantly, a willingness to look at problems from a variety of perspectives.

Manufacturing Expertise—They specialize in solving thermal management problems. Through their award winning just in time and just in sequence manufacturing processes, they can supply heat transfer solutions that are not only feasible, but also reliable and economical to incorporate manufacturing process.

Research and Testing—Manufacturing Company products have a reputation for reliability, as they are dedicated to researching and testing every product that bears their name.

Their multiple technical centers and wind tunnels-located in three continents—support this mission.

Commitment to Customer Satisfaction—Their number one priority is to focus on the needs and requirements of the customers. They have the resources, the staff, and the environment to make customer satisfaction flourish. They have for close to a investor's relation.

NATURE OF ASSIGNMENT

Manufacturing Company India has implemented SAP R/3 Enterprise-wide Resource Planning (ERP) System for its business transaction processing in the month of December 2008. The implementation covers core modules of SAP viz., Sales and Distribution (SD), Materials Management (MM), Production Planning (PP), Quality Management (QM), Finance (FI) and Controlling (CO). The company is interested in re-visiting its business processes implemented in SAP to identify areas of improvement and process optimizations.

The Project, thus, envisages the following activities by the trainees/apprentices:

1. Understand the business processes as implemented in SAP.
2. Document 'As-implemented' Business Process Procedure.
3. Obtain Feedback from users on Process Gaps/Weaknesses.
4. Identify Critical Process modifications/enhancements.

The Project would involve study of documents such as 'Business Blueprint', 'Process Configuration' and extensive interaction with SAP users.

OBJECTIVES

Primary Objective

Understand the business processes as implemented by SAP.

Document As-implemented business process procedure.

Secondary Objectives

Evaluate Modine India's Processes *vis-a-vis* Modine Global Processes.

Identify critical process modifications.

Recommend business process improvements.

History of Sap

Headquartered in Waldorf, Germany.

Founded in 1972 by four ex-IBM executives.

Is the largest business application vendor in the world.

Largest market-share in the ERP segment - larger than three of the closest competitors combined.

SAP IMPLEMENTATION—OBJECTIVES

Provide a Key Enabler for achievement of Business Goals.

Establish Benchmark processes leading to competitive advantages.

Create knowledge-driven organization.

Align to processes with the group.

WHAT IS SAP R/3

The third generation set of highly integrated software modules.

Perform common business functions based on best business practices.

SAP R/3 SAMPLE OF MODULES

1. Financial Accounting
2. Controlling (Costing)
3. Sales and Distribution
4. Logistics Execution
5. Materials Management
6. Production Planning
7. Quality Management

8. Plant Maintenance
9. Customer Service
10. Project Systems

CONTROLLING IN SAP

The CO application module represents the company's flow of cost and revenue.

CO is a management instrument for organizational decisions.

Components in CO

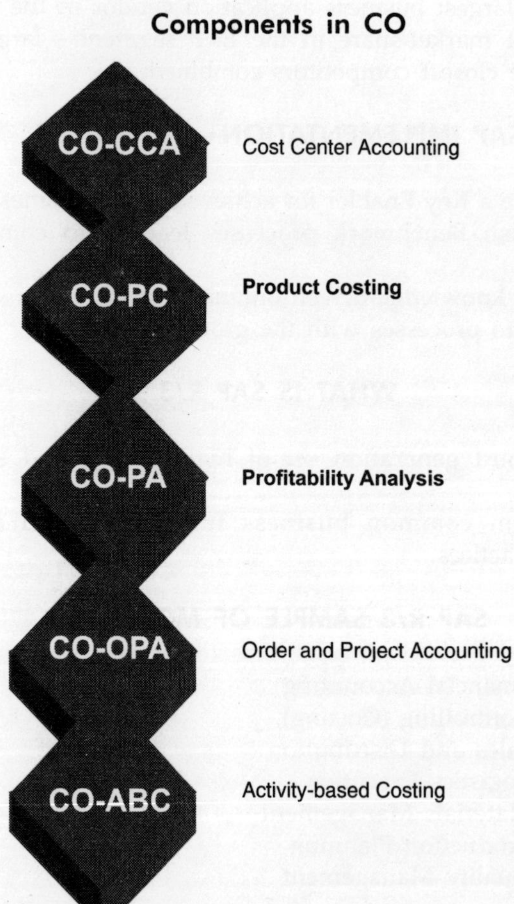

LIST OF MASTER DATA IN CONTROLLING (CO)

Cost Element

Cost Element is the part of accounting where costs are entered and organized during a settlement period. It is thus not an accounting system as such, but rather a detailed recording of data that forms the basis for business analysis. Each business transaction relevant for cost accounting provides the CO component with detailed information for the Cost Element. Cost Elements are created as Primary Cost Elements and as Secondary Cost Elements for alternative calculations and reporting purposes.

Cost Elements with similar characteristics are collected in one cost element group. Cost Element groups can be used whenever several cost elements have to be processed in one transaction like information system, planning, allocations.

For MTSI, the Primary cost elements will have the same number as the GL account. Secondary cost elements will be created in 5XXYYY series. XX represents the cost element category and YYY will be a sequential number for the cost elements created in that category.

Cost Center

A Cost Center is an organizational unit within a controlling area that represents a clearly delimited location where costs are incurred. The definition can be based on functional requirements, allocation criteria, physical location, and/or responsibility for costs. Cost Centers can be collected according to various criteria into groups. Cost Center Hierarchy is a tree structure representing all cost centers belonging to a controlling area from a controlling perspective. It comprises all cost centers for a given period and therefore represents the whole enterprise. Each cost center can be assigned to only one group in the standard hierarchy but to as many alternative groups as you require.

The Cost Center standard hierarchy for MICA will be CCTR_HIERI – Cost Center Hierarchy Modine India. The cost centers will be numbered 3XXYY where XX is the grouping code and YY will be a sequential number assigned to cost centers created in the group.

Activity Type

Activity Types classify the activities produced in the cost centers within a Controlling area. The prices of the activity types of a cost center can be either entered manually or calculated by the system based on the costs allocated to the activities. Prices can be calculated either using plan costs or actual costs. To plan and allocate quantities the system records quantities that are measured in activity units. Activity units are valuated using allocated price. Activity types with similar characteristics can be grouped into activity type groups.

Profit Center

A profit center is a management oriented organization unit used for internal controlling purposes. Profit center allows to analyze the areas of responsibility and to delegate responsibility to decentralized units, thus treating them as "companies within the company". It aims at determining the profit for internal areas of responsibility using period end accounting or cost of sales approach.

Profit centers can be grouped together according to company-specific criteria for use in reporting, allocations or planning functions. Profit Center Hierarchy is a special type of profit center group that contains all profit centers belonging to the controlling area and reflect the organizational structure of Profit Center Accounting.

The Profit Center Standard Hierarchy for MICA will be PCTR_HIERI-Profit Center Hierarchy Modine India. The structure of the Profit Center Accounting will be product-oriented and the below profit centers will be used:

EPG - Engine Product Group
PTC - Power Train Cooling
PTM - Passenger Thermal Management
DSCUS - Design Center US
DSCEU - Design Center EU

The below profit centers will be used to capture the costs and allocate to the product profit centers.

CORPS - Corp. Sales
CORPA - Corp. Admin
CORPM - Corp. Management
PRODS - Production Support

Internal Orders

Internal orders are normally used to plan, collect and settle the costs of internal jobs and tasks. SAP system enables to monitor the internal orders throughout their entire life cycle from initial creation through the planning and posting of all the actual costs, to the final settlement and archiving. Internal orders are categorized as either orders used only for monitoring objects in Cost Accounting or Productive orders that are value added and can be capitalized.

An enterprise's Internal Orders can be used for different controlling purposes like time restricted jobs, long-term cost monitoring and statistical orders.

Budget is the approved cost structure for an internal order or order group. In contrast to planning, budget management is binding. The original budget can be updated with supplements and returns. Budgeting requires a budget profile which defines the period during budgeting is maintained and if it is allowed for total annual values.

Statistical Internal Orders to be used in MICA for the following two purposes:

1. Budget monitoring of Greenfield projects with AFE.
2. Capturing material and activity costs of prototypes statistically. Real CO assignment to be posted to Prototype Cost Center.

Statistical Key Figure

Statistical Key Figures are used as the basis for internal allocations. They can be defined as Fixed values or total values. Fixed values are valid for the posting period and for all the subsequent posting periods. Total values are valid only for the posting period in which they were entered. Statistical key Figures can be gathered into groups.

Two Statistical Key Figures HC—Head Count and SQFT—Square Foot will be used. Additional Statistical Key Figures can be created if needed for allocations.

Product Cost Collector

Product Cost Collector collects the periodic actual costs incurred in the production of a material. It can be created for a material, plant and production process. The production process is defined in accordance with a controlling level. The controlling level contains the characteristics that are used to determine the quantity structure. In Repetitive manufacturing, collective entry transaction enables creation of product cost collectors for all production versions. It contains costing variant for plan and actual, costing sheet, overhead key, results analysis key and variance key.

LIST OF PROCESS IN CONTROLLING (CO)

Process Description

Material Overhead

Costs for acquiring and handling material for production and production support constitute material overheads. These expenses are applied to the product based on material cost using a costing sheet. They are not applied through activity prices and material overhead cast centers are not part of allocation process.

A costing sheet contains costing sheet rows to determine the values to be posted. It comprises calculation base, overhead and credit. Calculation base defines the primary cost elements to which overhead is to be applied. Overhead specifies the percentage of overhead to be applied. Credit specifies the cost object to be credit and the cost element. Overhead is calculated on the base by applying the specified percentage and then credited to the object defined.

Period End Processing

Overhead calculation enables to apply overheads to cost objects. The percentage of overhead is taken from the overhead key in the costing sheet.

For productions orders, the system defaults the costing sheet from the valuation variant specified in the planned costing variant and actual costing variant determined through the default values in the order type.

Work in process function valuates the unfinished product at actual rates. This is the differences between the debit and credit of an order that has not been fully delivered. The difference between the WIP of the current period and the WIP of the previous period corresponds to the inventory change of unfinished products. The inventory change can be transferred to FI and PCA when settled.

Variance calculation determined the difference between the actual costs debited to the object and the credit from goods receipt. It shows the causes of the variances and assigns the variances to different variance categories depending on the cause. This process determines the production variances and planning variances for informational purposes.

The actual costs debited to an order can be more or less than the credit posted to the order for goods receipt. Settlement transfers to FI and other CO components the differences between the debit and credit of an order. The order balance can be reduced to zero by transferring the differences to FI and also to PCA. Variances are transferred to CO-PA enabling to see additional contribution margins. During settlement. Work in process can be transferred to FI and PCA.

Variance Calculation Process

Variance calculation is designed to display variances in target and actual costs. It explains the balance of a cost object, or to be more precise, the balance of actual debits and actual credits by putting this balance into different variance categories.

The balance between actual debit and actual credit (total variances) is settled to Financial Accounting (FI) during period-end closing, and the variances that have been categorized can be settled to Profitability Analysis (CO-PA) if required.

Possible variance categories are as follows:

- Scrap variance (difference between planned and unplanned scrap).
- Price variance (arises from price changes to the material components or activities).
- Resource-usage variance (arises from the use of other materials or activities, etc.).
- Quantity variance (arises from changed consumption quantities).
- Input variance (miscellaneous, usually changes to overhead rates).
- Output price variance (arises if the finished material is delivered to the warehouse at a different price than the standard price).
- Mixed-price variance (variance between a standard price that was calculated in a mixed calculation for more than one procurement alternative and the costing of a procurement alternative).

Variance Settlement Process

If variances are to be settled to Profitability Analysis, you need to enter a PA transfer structure in Customizing. Variances can only be settled to Profitability Analysis with standard price control, but not using the moving average price control for the material.

The cost object balance is always settled to FI. For the recommended method using standard price control, this is a price difference account for the material.

Cost Center Assessment Process

Assessment is an activity that you perform periodically, during the period-end closing in Overhead Cost Controlling (CO-OM), in which primary and secondary overhead costs are assessed from one or more sender objects to one or more receiver objects.

Assessment means that the sending cost center is credited and the receiving cost center is charged under a freely definable secondary cost element. The original cost elements that were charged by the sender cost center are lost, and are converted to one or more assessment cost elements (secondary cost elements).

Assessment groups together the posted primary and secondary costs and allocates them to the receiving cost center(s) in an assessment cost element.

For example, you could assess the cost from the reception cost center to the other cost centers based on the head count managed in those cost centers.

PA Cycle Assessment Process

In this step, the costs from the cost centers Management, Accounting, Finished Goods Warehouse, Inventory Differences, Research and Development, Marketing, Sales and FSE are transferred to CO-PA. This enables taking those costs into account when the contribution margin (margin after corporate overhead costs) is determined.

Budgetary Control Process

A control technique where by actual results are compared with budgets.

Any differences (variances) are made the responsibility of key individuals who can either exercise control action or revise the original budgets.

Internal Order Creation Process

If this is the first transaction of an R/3 session, a SET CONTROLLING AREA box will appear. UT is the controlling area to be entered. Controlling area can be set in a user's defaults".

From the Easy Access menu bar: System > User profile > Own data > Parameters tab,

Parameter = CAC
Value = UT, Click the SAVE icon.

IO's must have the same business area as the cost center or WBS element being posted to. So if you want to combine transactions of cost centers and WBS elements, an Order group can be created to combine the IO's.

AFE Monitoring Process

The Budget Monitoring Reports play an important role in insuring that units operate within the limits of their budgets and take appropriate action when budget deficits appear imminent. They show a fund's overall performance and allow management to get involved in resolving outstanding issues.

The Office of Budget and Financial Planning centrally coordinates reviews and supports the Budget Monitoring Process. We work directly with the department head or responsible budget manager to correct the deficit situations.

Profitability Analysis Process

Profitability Analysis (CO-PA) enables you to evaluate market segments, which can be classified according to products, customers, orders or any combination of these, or strategic business units, such as sales organizations or business areas, with respect to your company's profit or contribution margin.

The aim of the system is to provide your sales, marketing, product management and corporate planning departments with information to support internal accounting and decision-making.

Master T Codes

Sap T Code	*Description*
KS01	Cost Center Creation
KS02	Cost Center Change
KS03	Cost Center Display
KA01	Cost Element Creation
KA02	Cost Element Change
KA03	Cost Elemant Display
KP26	Activity Price Creation and Change
KP27	Activity Price Display
KE51	Profit Center Creation
KE52	Profit Center Change
KE53	Profit Center Display
KO01	Internal Order Creation
KO02	Internal Order Change
KO03	Internal Order Display

Process T Codes

Sap T Code	*Description*
CO43	Actual Overhead Calculation: Product Process Orders
CO42	Actual Overhead Calculation: Product Cost Collector
CO44	Mass Processing Orders
KEU5	Execute Actual Assessment
KEU6	Actual Assessment Overview
KEU7	Pa Create Plan Asessment Cycle
KEU8	Pa Change Plan Assessment Cycle
KEU9	Pa Display Plan Assessment Cycle
CK40N	Edit Costing Run
KE30	Run Profitability Report
KE31	Create Profitablitiy Report
KE32	Change Profitability Report
KE33	Display Profitability Report
KKS5	Variance Calculation
KKS7	Scrap Calculation
KSU5	Cost Center Assessment Creation
KSU6	Actual Assessment Overview
KO02	View and Alter Interl. Order
KO03	Proto Costs Tracking
CO88	Variance Settlement Process
S_ALR_87013019	AFE Monitoring Process

Report T Codes

Sap T Code	*Description*
KSB5	Co Document Actual Costs
KABP	Co Plan Document
S_ALR_87013611	Cost Centers Actual/Plan/Variance
KSBT	Activity Type Price Report
KSBT	Cost Center Actual Line Items
KSBP	Cost Center Plan Line Items

KS13	Cost Centers Master Data Report
KA23	Cost Elements Master Data Report
KL13	Activity Types Master Data Report
KK04	Statistical Key Figures Master Data Report
KOB1	Product Cost Collector Actual Costs
KOB8	Product Cost Collector Wip/Results Analysis
KOB3	Product Cost Collector Variance Analysis
9KE9	Profit Center Document Display
KE5Z	Profit Center Actual Line Items
KE5Y	Profit Center Plan Line Items
S_ALR_87013326	Profit Center Plan/Actual/Variance
KE24	PA: Actual Line Item List
KE25	PA: Plan Line Item List

PERIOD CLOSING PROCESS

Overview

The year-end closing in asset accounting must be carried out before the year-end closing in General Ledger Accounting. Once the fiscal year is closed, you can no longer post or change posted values in Asset Accounting.

Change History

Date	*Name*	*Description*
04.06.2009	HELEN, A.	Period Closing Process

TRIGGER

Period Closing Process

Overhead calculation enables to apply overheads to cost objects. The percentage of overhead is taken from the overhead key in the costing sheet.

For productions orders, the system defaults the costing sheet from the valuation variant specified in the planned costing variant and actual costing variant determined through the default values in the order type.

Work in process function valuates the unfinished product at actual rates. This is the differences between the debit and credit of an order that has not been fully delivered. The difference between the WIP of the current period and the WIP of the previous period corresponds to the inventory change of unfinished products. The inventory change can be transferred to FI and PCA when settled.

Variance calculation determined the difference between the actual costs debited to the object and the credit from goods receipt. It shows the causes of the variances and assigns the variances to different variance categories depending on the cause. This process determines the production variances and planning variances for informational purposes.

The actual costs debited to an order can be more or less than the credit posted to the order for goods receipt. Settlement transfers to FI and other CO components the differences between the debit and credit of an order. The order balance can be reduced to zero by transferring the differences to FI and also to PCA. Variances are transferred to CO-PA enabling to see additional contribution margins. During settlement Work in process can be transferred to FI and PCA.

Input—Required Fields	*Field Value/Comments*
Controlling area	MICA

PROCEDURAL STEPS

1.1. Access Transaction by

Via Menus	(a)	Logistics → Production→ Product Cost Planning → Material Costing → Costing Run → Edit Costing Run
Via Transaction Code		CK40N

1.2. On screen "Edit Costing Run", Enter information in the fields as specified in the table below, then click CREATE COSTING RUN tab.

Field Name	*Description*	*R/O/C*	*User Action and Values*	*Comments*
Costing run	Name under which the costing run is carried out.	R	The name is assigned by the user—RT1	AVIA-AL – Cooling Module-AVIA CUMMINS RT1 – Oil cooler TESTRUN – Test run......
Costing run date	Date from which a costing run is valid.	R	Current date 04/06/2009	Enter the date from which a costing run is valid.

Note : On above table, in column "R/O/C"; "R" = Required, "O" = Optional, "C" = Conditional, "D" = Display.

1.3. On screen "Create Costing Run", Enter information in the fields as specified in the table below, and then click SAVE button.

Field Name	*Description*	*R/O/C*	*User Action and Values*	*Comments*
Description	Description of the costing run	R	Oil cooler	The description of the costing run, which is entered by the user, is designed to identify the run
Costing data				
Costing variant	Key that determines how a cost estimate is performed	R	Costing variant - MIC1	Use the drop down to get a list of costing variant

	and valuated			MIC1 - Modine (legal valuation) PPC1 - Modine (legal valuation) MIC2 - Mod.std cost est. (mat.) MIRM - Repetitive Mfg. Versions......
Costing version	Number that serves to differentiate between cost estimates for the same material	R	Costing version-01	Use the drop down to get a list of costing version 01-Version w/o Customizing 02- Version w/o Customizing 03-Version w/o Customizing 04-Version w/o Customizing...
Controlling area	Uniquely identifies a controlling area	R	The controlling area is the highest organizational unit in Controlling	Controlling area MICA Use the drop down to get a list of controlling area. 0001 – Controlling area 0001 0010 – Pre-Configured US Company MICA – Modine India CO Area MOCO – Modine Manufacturing
Company code	The company code is an organizational unit within financial accounting	R	Company code-M670	Use the drop down to get a list of company code

Note : On above table, in column "R/O/C"; "R" = Required, "O" = Optional, "C" = Conditional, "D" = Display.

1.4. On screen "Edit Costing Run", click SELECTION – CHANGE PARAMETERS option.

Field Name	*Description*	*R/O/C*	*User Action and Values*	*Comments*
Dates				
Costing date from	Date from which the cost estimate is valid	D	Current date - 06/04/2009	Costing date is already displayed
Costing date to	Date to which the cost estimate is valid	D	03/31/2010	Costing date is already displayed
Qty. structure date	Date with which the quantity structure is selected for the cost estimate with quantity structure	D	06/04/2009	It is already displayed
Valuation date	Date on which the materials and activities in a cost estimate are valuated	D	06/04/2009	It is already displayed
Create cost estimate				

Note : On above table, in column "R/O/C"; "R" = Required, "O" = Optional, "C" = Conditional, "D" = Display.

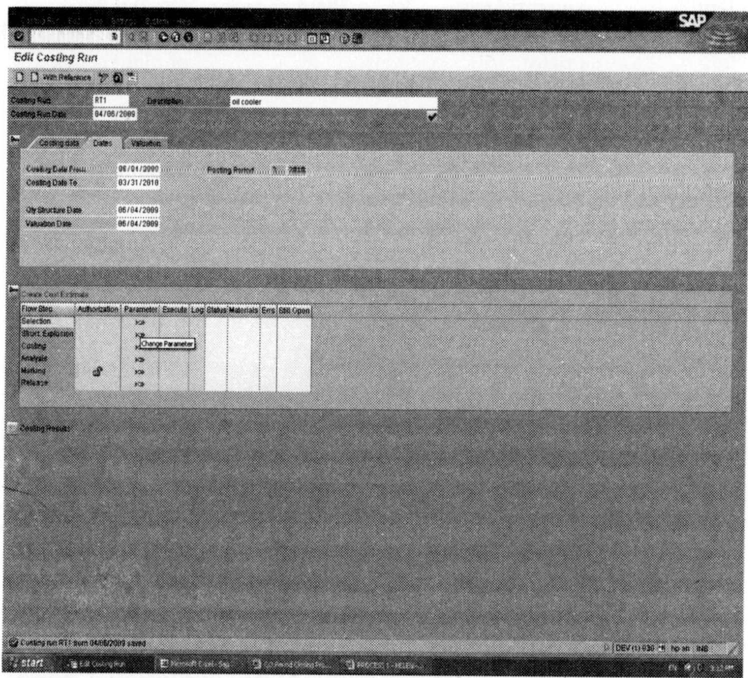

1.5. On screen "Costing Run: Selection—Change Parameters". Enter information in the fields as specified in the table below, and then click SAVE button.

Field Name	*Description*	*R/O/C*	*User Action and Values*	*Comments*
Selection using material master				
Material number	Alphanumeric key uniquely identifying the material	R	Material number - ICA00025	Use the drop down to get a list of material numbers ICA00025 – CAC assembly ICD00004 – Fin IEC00018 – Dust Cup IRC00016 – Tube IRE00018 – Header………..

Plant	Key uniquely identifying a plant	R	Plant code is typed - 0702	Use the drop down to get a list of plant codes 0701 – Bonded Warehouse 0702 – Manufacturing plant 0703 – Trading plant
Processing opts				
Background processing	Specifies background processing	O		It is selected if needed

Note : On above table, in column "R/O/C"; "R" = Required, "O" = Optional, "C" = Conditional, "D" = Display.

1.6. After saving the data the BACK option is clicked.

1.7. On screen "Edit Costing Run", the Selection Execute option is clicked and the result is obtained.

1.8. On screen "Edit Costing Run", click Struct.explosion – Change Parameters option.

1.9. On screen "Costing Run: BOM Explosion Change Parameters". Enter information in the fields as specified in the table below, and then click SAVE button.

Field Name	*Description*	*R/O/C*	*User Action and Values*	*Comments*
Processing opts				
Background processing	Specifies background processing	O		Select the option if needed
Print log	This indicator determines whether logs are printed for the costing run	O		Select the option if needed

Note : On above table, in column "R/O/C"; "R" = Required, "O" = Optional, "C" = Conditional, "D" = Display.

1.10. On screen "Edit Costing Run", the Struct.explosion – Execute option is clicked and the result is obtained.

1.11. On screen "Edit Costing Run", click Costing – Change Parameters option.

1.12. On screen "Costing Run: Cost Estimate Change Parameters". Enter information in the fields as specified in the table below, and then click SAVE button.

Field Name	*Description*	*R/O/C*	*User Action and Values*	*Comments*
Processing opts				
Background processing	Specifies background processing	O		Select the option if needed
Print log	This indicator determines whether logs are printed for the costing run	O		Select the option if needed

Note : On above table, in column "R/O/C"; "R" = Required, "O" = Optional, "C" = Conditional, "D" = Display.

1.13. After the data is saved the BACK option is clicked.

1.14. On screen "Edit Costing Run", the Costing-Execute option is clicked and the result is obtained.

1.15. On screen "Edit Costing Run", click Analysis-Change Parameters option.

1.16. On screen "Edit Costing Run", Choose Reference For Selection Parameter table appears, Select SAPand11 from the options available.

1.17. On screen "Costing Run: Analysis-Change Parameters". Enter information in the fields as specified in the table below, and then click SAVE button.

Field Name	*Description*	*R/O/C*	*User Action and Values*	*Comments*
Selection				
Costing run	Name under which the costing run is carried out	R	The name is assigned by the user - RT1	Use the drop down to get a list of costing run AVIA-AL – Cooling Module-AVIA CUMMINS RT1 – Oil cooler TESTRUN – Test run………
Costing date	Date from which a costing run is valid	R	04/06/2009	This date is maintained by the user
Output				
Cost component view	The cost component view indicates which cost components are displayed and passed on to other areas of the SAP System	D	1	The cost component is displayed already
Processing opts				
Background processing	Specifies background processing	O		Select the option if needed

Note : On above table, in column "R/O/C"; "*R*" = Required, "*O*" = Optional, "*C*" = Conditional, "*D*" = Display.

1.18. After the data is saved the BACK option is clicked.

1.19. On screen "Edit Costing Run", the Analysis – Execute option is clicked and the result is obtained.

1.20. On screen "Edit Costing Run", click Marking – Change Parameters option.

1.21. On screen "Price Update: Mark Standard Price". Enter information in the fields as specified in the table below, and then click SAVE button.

Field Name	Description	R/O/C	User Action and Values	Comments
Processing options				
Test run	This option controls whether or not a test run takes place	O		Conduct the test run if needed
With list output	Indicator specifying whether an overview of the materials is given after price update	O		Set this indicator to receive an overview screen of the updated materials after price update
Parallel processing	Indicator that controls whether prices are updated using parallel processing	O		Set this indicator to carry out price update simultaneously on multiple servers
Background processing	Specifies background processing	O		Select the option if needed

Note : On above table, in column "R/O/C"; "R" = Required, "O" = Optional, "C" = Conditional, "D" = Display.

1.22. After the data is saved the BACK option is clicked.

1.23. On screen "Edit Costing Run", the Marking – Execute option is clicked and the result is obtained.

1.24. On screen "Edit Costing Run", click Release – Change Parameters option.

1.25. On screen "Price Update: Mark Standard Price". Enter information in the fields as specified in the table below, and then click SAVE button.

Field Name	*Description*	*R/O/C*	*User Action and Values*	*Comments*
Processing options				
Test run	This option controls whether or not a test run takes place	O		Conduct the test run if needed
With list output	Indicator specifying whether an overview of the materials is given after price update	O		Set this indicator to receive an overview screen of the updated materials after price update
Parallel processing	Indicator that controls whether prices are updated using parallel processing	O		Set this indicator to carry out price update simultaneously on multiple servers
Background processing	Specifies background processing	O		Select the option if needed

Note : On above table, in column "R/O/C"; "R" = Required, "O" = Optional, "C" = Conditional, "D" = Display.

1.26. After the data is saved the BACK option is clicked.

1.27. On screen "Edit Costing Run", the Release – Execute option is clicked and the result is obtained.

1.28. Cost estimates are updated successfully.

Unit Testing Conditions and Variations

Setup Data

Data Object	*Value/Code*	*Description*	*Comments and Notes*

Conditions/Steps

Conditions and Variations	*Expected Results*	*Actual Results*	*Ok/Error*

Comments:

Tested and Approved BPP in ASIA DEV– Created Period Closing Process.

Approval: ______________ Date: ___________

LIMITATIONS OF THE STUDY

Time constraint due to which we were not able to interact much with the users of SAP process in the company.

Since we dealt in the actual process followed in the concern we were not allowed to record the entire data.

We could just learn the basics of SAP and not in detail.

FINDINGS

The main objective of our project is to find whether there exists any gap between the actual implementation SAP and the existing process that is carried on in the organization and we found there is no much gap in the process followed.

SUGGESTION

As we worked in SAP for nearly 45 days and knew the

exact functioning of it, we were able to make out the actual requirements that are to be filled, so we suggested the concern for "*Optimization of fields*" which would be of much help and time saving to the concern.

References

Business blue print.
Websites Manufacturing unit.
SAP Library Documents.

23

Personal and Psychological Factor Analysis of Investors in Mutual Funds

MRS. R. PRIYA AND K. SHYAMASUNDAR

INTRODUCTION

Most individuals lack substantial wealth or enough wealth to investment their personal funds directly into stock and shares, a practical and low risk endeavor. Equally most people lack the professional expertise and knowledge of economic business markets and individual companies to identify the sheep from the goats or the wheat from the chaff as it were. The mutual fund offers a solution, which are form of collective investments. They allow any number of investors to pool their individual investments and thereby participate in a larger and more diversified portfolio investments.

Mutual fund is a mechanism for pooling the resources by issuing units to the public and investing funds in securities in accordance with objectives as disclosed in the offer document.

The concept of mutual funds was introduced in India with the formation of Unit Trust of India in 1963, by the government of India by an act on parliament. UTI functioned under regulatory and administrative control of the Reserve Bank of India till 1978. The first scheme launched by UTI was the now infamous Unit Scheme 64 in 1964. UTI continued to be the sole mutual fund until 1987, when some public sector banks and Life Insurance Corporation of India and General Insurance Corporation of India set-up mutual funds. It was only in 1993 that private players were allowed to open shops in the country. Today, 32 mutual fund companies collectively manage Rs. 6713575.19 crore under hundreds of schemes.

In 1995, the RBI permitted private sector institutions to set-up Money Market Mutual Funds (MMMFs). Private institutions can invest in treasury bills, call and notice money, commercial paper, commercial bills accepted/co-accepted by banks, having unexposed maturity up to one year.

The industry has steadily grown over the decade. The mutual fund collects money directly or through brokers from investors. The money is invested in various instruments depending on the objective of the scheme.

The study of consumers help firms and organizations in improving their marketing strategies by understanding issues such as how the consumers are making their decisions. Because the failure or success in any business depends upon the behavior of the end-user or consumer who finally uses the product or any services.

It is the behavior of consumer, which impacts their decisions to purchase or not to purchase the product. Depending on their decision and their usage, an organization decides which products to manufacture and to continue. The positioning of the product depends on the consumption of the product and this behavior of consumers may be related to any kind of products or services.

This study attempts to analyze the personal and psychological factors which influence on the decision-making part of the consumers, especially in their investment decision in mutual funds.

OBJECTIVES

- To identify the personal and psychological factors which influence the customer decision.
- To choose out the target audience and to extend the market in different segment.
- To know the consumer attitude.
- To help in preparing the schedule of events.
- To define the basic P's of marketing.

RESEARCH METHODOLOGY

Research Methodology is a blue print for the research. A Research design is the arrangement of conditions for the collection and analysis of data in a manner that aims to combine relevance to the research purpose with economy in procedure.

This study is based on both primary and secondary data. The primary data was collected directly from the rural area by means of convenient sampling, and secondary data were collected from various journals and the articles in websites.

A questionnaire was prepared by the researchers, for collecting the necessary data. Before preparing the questionnaire the researcher made a comprehensive review of the literature and a pilot stud.

DATA ANALYSIS

In order to find out the results for the settled objectives, the following tools were applied:

- Percentage analysis.
- Chi-square analysis.
- Weighted average analysis.
- Ranking method.

Association Between the Personal and Psychological Factors and the Type of Mutual Fund of the Investors

It is expected that Personal and Psychological factors of the investors would influence the Type of Mutual Fund owned by the investors. In this regard a hypothesis has been framed and the same has been statistically tested with the chi-square test and co-efficient of contingency is computed in the following formula:

$$C = \sqrt{\chi^2/\chi^2+n}$$

When the value 'C' is equal to or nearest one, it means there is a high degree of association between two attributes.

TABLE 1

Personal and Psychological factors and the Type of Mutual Fund : Chi-Square and Co-efficient of Contingency

Sl. No.	Factors	χ^2	Table Value	Result	'C' of χ^2	Result of 'C'
1.	Age	26.41	40.1	Insignificant	0.98	High degree
2.	Income	34.15	28.9	Significant	0.99	High degree
3.	Occupation	132.69	40.1	Significant	0.99	High degree
4.	Education	34.6	40.1	Insignificant	0.99	High degree
6.	Lifestyle	49.61	40.1	Significant	0.99	High degree
7.	Perception	34.46	40.1	Insignificant	0.99	High degree

On the basis of Table 1, it can be easily inferred that there is an association between the Type of Mutual Fund Owned and income, occupation and the Lifestyle of investors.

- 50% of conservative respondents are preferring short term investment, 50% Speculative investors are preferring medium-term investment and 30% of Aggressive investors are preferring short-term investment.
- Nearly 66% of stable income group people are expecting normal return on investment, 30 percent of uncertain income group people are expecting very high retrun on investment and 45 percent of highly uncertain income group people are expecting normal return on their investment.

FIG. 1

Investors' Personality and their Term of Investment

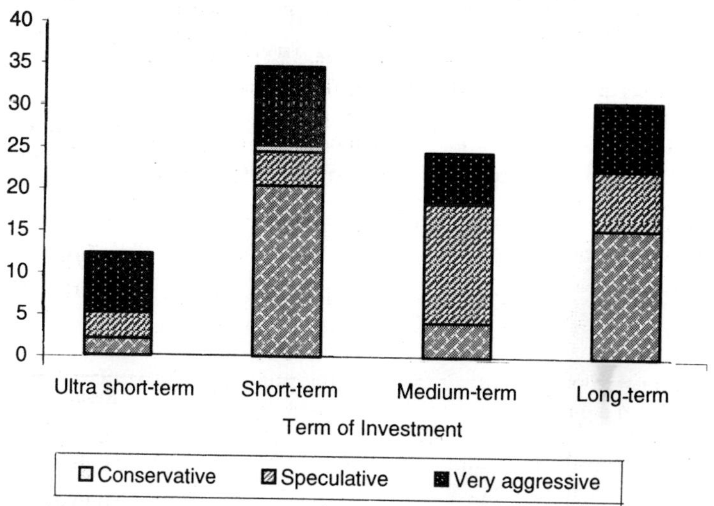

FIG. 2

Income and the Return Expectation

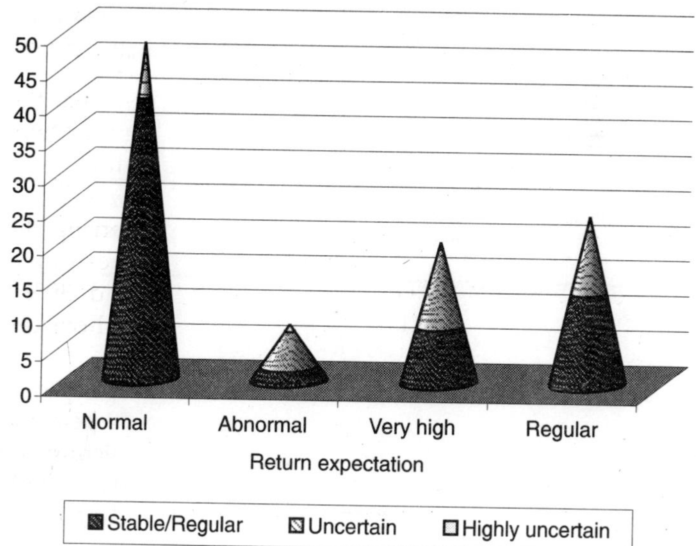

➤ More than 95 percent of stable income group people are investing below rupees five lakhs, 80 percent of uncertain income group investors are investing less than five lakh rupees and 70 percent of highly uncertain income group investors are investing rupees five lakh to ten lakh.

FIG. 3
Income and Size of Investment

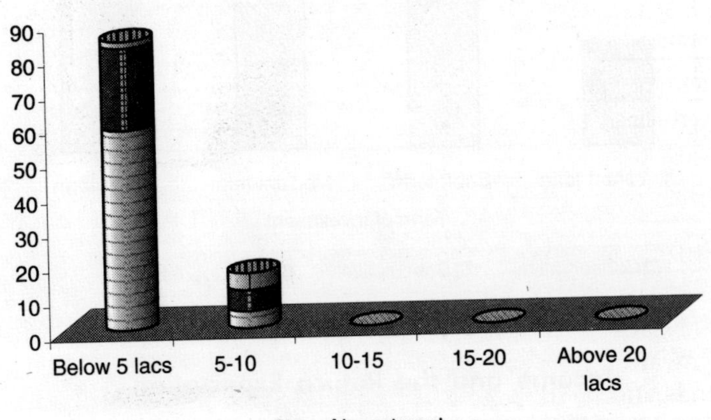

TABLE 2

Education/Analysis	*Pattern Past*	*Trend Scientific analysis*	*Word of mouth*	*Matter of luck*	*Total*
Graduates	2	3	7	2	14
Post-Graduates	47	6	23	2	78
Professional	2	1	1	4	8
Others	—	—	—	—	—
Total	51	14	27	8	100

60 percent of postgraduates are analyzing the investment choices based on the past trend, 50 percent of graduates are choose their choice based on the word of mouth of the references and 50 percent of professional people are opines that the choice as matter of luck.

TABLE 3

Source of Awareness/ Motivational factor	*Agents*	*Advertise-ments*	*Friends/ Relatives*	*Family Members*	*Total*
Agents	9	5	15	8	35
Advertisements	13	4	8	3	28
Friends/Relative	8	5	12	6	31
Others	2	2	1	1	6
Total	32	16	34	18	100

Nearly 50 percent of the respondents even though they are aware by their Agents they are motivated only by their friends and relatives to make their choice, and the respondents nearly 50% who got awareness through the advertisement they

TABLE 4

Showing Ranking of Bases for Selecting the Investment Scheme

Particulars	*I*	*II*	*III*	*IV*	*V*	*VI*	*VII*	*Weighted average score*	*Rank*
Affordability	16	20	14	18	7	17	8	972.36	V
Convenience	7	17	9	28	10	18	11	493.79	VII
Cost effectiveness	24	26	8	12	21	4	5	1410.67	III
Professional Management	24	11	6	8	6	13	32	1298.86	IV
Diversification	27	23	16	13	8	6	7	1549.39	II
Liquidity	38	16	14	7	10	6	9	2049.69	I
Transparency	13	17	21	7	8	18	16	805.48	VI

are motivated by the agents and nearly 50 percent aware by their relatives and friends they are motivated by the same references.

Investors are choosing their schemes based on the liquidity condition followed by the service provider's diversification of services and the cost effectiveness.

FINDINGS

- There is an association between the Type of Mutual Fund Owned and income, occupation and the Life-style of investors
- 50% of conservative respondents are preferring short term investment, 50% Speculative investors are preferring medium-term investment and 30% of Aggressive investors are preferring short-term investment.
- Nearly 66% of stable income group people are expecting normal return on investment, 30 percent of uncertain income group people are expecting very high retrun on investment and 45 percent of highly uncertain income group people are expecting normal return on their investment.
- More than 95 percent of stable income group people are investing below rupees five lakh, 80 percent of uncertain income group investors are investing less than five lakh rupees and 70 percent of highly uncertain income group investors are investing rupees five lakh to ten lakh.
- 60 percent of postgraduates are analyzing the investment choices based on the past trend, 50 percent of graduates are choose their choice based on the word of mouth of the references and 50 percent of professional people are opines that the choice as matter of luck.
- Nearly 50 percent of the respondents even though they are aware by their agents they are motivated only by their friends and relatives to make their choice, and the respondents nearly 50% who got

awareness through the advertisement they are motivated by the agents and nearly 50 percent aware by their relatives and friends they are motivated by the same references.

- Investors are choosing their schemes based on the liquidity condition followed by the service provider's diversification of services and the cost effectiveness.
- Urban area investors are getting awareness from the advertisement and the rural investors are aware through the agents.
- The investors who choose the Tax saving schemes, Growth fund schemes and the open-ended schemes they are satisfied with their schemes
- Generally the people are perceive that 'High risk – high return and the Low risk – Low return'

CONCLUSION

Today the Mutual fund market has blooming, with the increase of Favorable attitude of people towards saving. By nature people are interested in future savings and getting exemption from Tax payment so they go for investments, but there are some factorial influence on their decision-making. Here we identified that the income, occupation and the life-style pattern influence the people to make their investment choice in mutual fund. They are interested in short-term funds as well as short funds schemes. Conservative, speculative and the uncertain income people may target in the future period and the service providers should concentrate on liquidity schemes rather than other schemes.

References

Websites

http://www.mutualfundsindia.com/

http://finance.indiamart.co

www.indianmba.com

www.Wikipedia.com

www.icici.com

www.axisbank.com

Books

C. Bhattacharji, 'Service Sector Management'—An Indian Perspective, 2005.

C.R. Kothari, Research Methods and Techniques, Wishwa Prakasan, New Delhi.

Journals

Indian Journal of Marketing, April 2007.

Business Today, January 2005.

APPENDIX

QUESTIONNAIRE

Name

Gender (a) Malc (b) Female

1. State your age group
   (a) 20-30 (b) 30-40 (c) 40-50 (d) 50-60
2. State your Educational Qualification
   (a) Graduate (b) Post-graduate
   (c) Professional (d) Others
3. Occupation
   (a) Self-employed b) Govt. employed
   (c) Private employed (d) Retired
   (e) Others
4. State your income pattern
   (a) Stable/regular (b) Uncertain
   (c) Highly uncertain
5. ON which environment you belong to?
   (a) Rural (b) Urban
   (c) Semi-urban (d) Slum
6. Which type of person you are?
   (a) Conservative (b) Speculative
   (c) Very aggressive
7. On which Type of mutual fund you invested?
   (a) Open-Ended (b) Close-Ended
   (c) Interval fund (d) Balanced fund
   (e) Growth fund (f) Income fund
   (g) Money Market fund (h) Tax saving Schemes
   (i) Special Schemes (j) Index Schemes
   (k) Sector Specific Schemes
8. On what basis you select the scheme for your investment?
   (a) Affordability
   (b) Convenience
   (c) Cost effectiveness
   (d) Professional management
   (e) Diversification
   (f) Liquidity
   (g) Transparency

9. How did you came to know about the scheme
   (a) Agents (b) Advertisement
   (c) Friends/relatives (d) Others
10. How much return you are expecting from your investment?
   (a) Normal (b) Abnormal
   (c) Very high (d) Regular
11. What is your Term of investment?
   (a) Ultra short-term (b) Short-term
   (c) Medium-term (d) Long-term
12. Why you prefer mutual fund investment?
   (a) Tax benefit (b) Investment
   (c) Future saving (d) High return
   (e) Easy saving
13. Which type of analysis did you use before selecting the schemes for investment?
   (a) Past trend (b) Scientific analysis
   (c) Word of mouth (d) Matter of luck
14. Mention your investment size
   (a) Below 5 lacs (b) 5-10
   (c) 10-15 (d) 15-20 (e) Above 20
15. Mention your life style
   (a) Believers (b) Makers
   (c) Strivers (d) Strugglers
16. Where you got motivation to invest in mutual funds?
   (a) Agents (b). Advertisement
   (c) Friends/relatives (d) Family members
17. What is your perception about your scheme?
   (a) Less risky (b) Safety
   (c) Confirmed future return
   (d) Easy investment
18. Are you satisfied with your current scheme?
   (a) Yes (b) No
19. Whether you agree this statement?
   "High Risk-High return
   Low Risk-Low return"
   (a) Strongly agree (b) Agree
   (c) Neither agree nor disagree d) Disagree
   e) Strongly disagree
20. Your suggestion for the mutual fund improvement
   ____

24

Women Entrepreneurship in India
Issues and Policies

ILA CHATURVEDI

ABSTRACT

Entrepreneurship has been the indispensable factor contributing for the development of many countries. It is the dearth of entrepreneurship, which has been the foremost factor for backwardness of developing countries like India. Today's world is changing at startling pace, political and economic transformations seem to be occurring everywhere. These changes have created economic opportunities for women who want to own and operate business. Women of today are in several ways different from the women of yester years. During the present times, they seek social and economic independence and are prepared to take risk for the same. The main objective of this research paper is to know the co-relation between percentage of female population, female literacy and women entrepreneurship in India. The research is based on extensive use of different websites providing information related to these three variables. Statistical tools like Karl Pearson method of Co relation, t-test were applied. The findings show that there is a low degree positive co-relation between these variables It can also be inferred that the co-relation between percentage of female population, female literacy and women entrepreneurship in India is not statistically significant.

Keywords: *Women entrepreneurship, Small Scale Industry, Female population.*

Once upon a time the large part of the world was designed such that men could only set-up enterprises. Then, there were women who by compulsions of circumstances took up income generating activities to sustain themselves and their family. The men of these women were either not there or if they were; they would not or could not take the responsibilities of sustaining the family.

Succession planning, leaving an heir, an inheritor and a continuity of the lineage is for men and their sons and their sons. It is rare for a man to plan for handing over to the daughter or daughter's daughter. The reality of women entrepreneur and passing the enterprise to a daughter will be the new reality and phenomenon of Indian business.

The role of Indian women has ranged from that of a deity to that of a devdasi, from being pure to being vulgar, from being supreme to being downtrodden. The role of Indian women has undergone dramatic and drastic changes from era to era. What a woman growing up in Indian society interjects in perhaps a collage and a flux of attitudes, perceptions, roles and locations of their identity. It seems to be difficult to take a logical look at all this. To every "yes" there is a "no" and to every "no" there is a "yes". The interjected collage does not, therefore, make it easy for women to define their role and take leadership roles and to enunciate directions and goals for themselves.

WOMEN ENTREPRENEURS

Women Entrepreneurs are the women or a group of women who initiate, organize and operate a business enterprise. The government of India notes women entrepreneurs as *"an enterprise owned and controlled by women saving a minimum financial interest of 51 per cent of the capital and giving at least 51 per cent of the employment generated in the enterprise to women"*.

In fine, women entrepreneurs are house women who generate business ideas or select the best opportunity, mobilize resources, combine the factors of production, undertake risks and operate the enterprise in the most effective manner with a view to earn profit

OBJECTIVES

The *objective* of this paper is :

- ➢ To know the current literature on definition of the term "Entrepreneurship".
- ➢ To Analyze the data related with women entrepreneurship.
- ➢ To know the co-relation between percentage of female population, female literacy and women entrepreneurship in India.
- ➢ To know the push and pull factors affecting women entrepreneurship in india.
- ➢ What are all the government support schemes available to develop and improve the women entrepreneurship in India?
- ➢ What are the problems and constraints they face?
- ➢ To give and suggest to the policy measurement of the development of Women Entrepreneurship in India?

RESEARCH METHODOLOGY

The Research design chosen for this research is exploratory and experimental research design. Websites, Journals, books, reports and other published materials have been utilized to collect the secondary data and conduct review of previous researches. Karl Pearson methods of Co-relation, student's t-test were applied to analyze the collected data.

LIMITATIONS

The major limitation of this study is that the study is based upon the data of Indian states only. The Union territories were not taken into account. Secondly, while approximating the data; we were forced to omit some details because of its negligible figure.

BACKGROUND OF STUDY

Women's entrepreneurship needs to be studied separately for two main reasons. The first reason is that women's entrepreneurship has been recognized during the last decade as an important untapped source of economic growth. Women entrepreneurs create new jobs for themselves and others and by being different also provide society with different solutions to management, organization and business problems as well as to the exploitation of entrepreneurial opportunities. However, they still represent a minority of all entrepreneurs. Thus there exists a market failure discriminating against women's possibility to become entrepreneurs and their possibility to become successful entrepreneurs. This market failure needs to be addressed by policy-makers so that the economic potential of this group can be fully utilized. While without a doubt the economic impact of women is substantial, we still lack a reliable picture describing in detail that specific impact. Recent efforts initiated by the OECD (1997, 2000) are responses to this lack of knowledge and have focused the attention of policy-makers and researchers on this important topic.

The second reason is that the topic of women in entrepreneurship has been largely neglected both in society in general and in the social sciences. Not only have women lower participation rates in entrepreneurship than men but they also generally choose to start and manage firms in different industries than men tend to do. The industries (primarily retail, education and other service industries) chosen by women are often perceived as being less important to economic development and growth than high-technology and manufacturing. Furthermore, mainstream research, policies and programmes tend to be "men streamed" and too often do not take into account the specific needs of women entrepreneurs and would-be women entrepreneurs. As a consequence, equal opportunity between men and women from the perspective of entrepreneurship is still not a reality.

WOMEN ENTREPRENEURS ARE DIVIDED INTO THREE CATEGORIES

1. The first group consists of women with educational and professional qualification who takes the initiative and manages the business as well as man do. Women entrepreneurs who have the basic managerial training and educational qualification go for the medium and large scale units.
2. The second group consists of those women entrepreneurs who do not have education or any formal training in management but have developed practical skills required for the small scale sector choose, that product with which they are familiar. For example garments, dolls, handicraft items, etc.
3. The third group of women entrepreneurs works in cities and slums to help women with lower means of livelihood. They need Government support in marketing as well as in getting finance at concessional rates.

INTERNATIONAL COMPARISON

In the 1990's across North America, women increasingly have been entering ventures in self-employment. In the USA, by 1992 women already owned 27 percent of small businesses (National Women Business Owners (NFWBO), 1992). In Canada, this figure in 1996 was 40 percent (Industry Canada, 1999). Statistics collected in 1997-98 found that women were starting businesses in North America at two to five times the rate of men (National Foundation, 1999; Industry Canada, 1999) and that increasing numbers of these were home-based. There is also evidence of a trend of women in senior management leaving or wanting to leave their corporate positions to try business ownership (Catalyst, 1998; Sharp and

Sharp, 1999). In the U.S. from 1987-99, women's businesses increased 103%, their sales grew 436% and their employee ranks swelled 320% (NFWBO, 1999a). Various estimates claim that by the year 2000, almost 50 percent of all new businesses in North America will have been started by women (Business Development Bank, 1999; Industry Canada, 1999; NFWBO, 1999a). World-wide, similar patterns are becoming evident. Women-owned businesses are increasing to comprise one-quarter to one-third of businesses in the formal economies of Brazil, Equador, Mexico, Australia, Ireland, Italy, England, Germany, France, and certain African countries, and women business owners of these countries share similar concerns, according to surveys conducted 1997-98 at international conferences by the National Foundation of Women Business Owners (1998).

SSI UNITS IN INDIA

The small-scale industrial units are functioning in all the states in India. According to Third All India Census of Small Scale Industries, there are 10.52 million units functioning in India. The total employment contribution of the sector is 24.93 million, with a per unit contribution of 2.37. Table 1 presents the complete picture of SSI units in India.

TABLE 1

Name of State/UT	*No. of SSI units*	*Percentage to Total*	*Women SSI Percentage to Total*	*Female Literacy*	*Female Population*
(1)	*(2)*	*(3)*	*(4)*	*(5)*	*(6)*
Jammu & Kashmir	73125	.70	.54	47.4	41.82
Himachal Pradesh	76198	.72	.35	49.2	68.08
Punjab	376826	3.58	2.73	46.6	63.55
Uttaranchal	106484	1.01	.83	49.1	60.26
Haryana	223294	2.12	1.35	46.3	56.31

(Contd.)

TABLE 1 (*Contd.*)

(1)	(2)	(3)	(4)	(5)	(6)
Delhi	177080	1.68	.9	45.1	75
Rajasthan	441572	4.20	3.42	48	44.34
Uttar Pradesh	1707977	16.23	6.83	47.3	42.98
Bihar	519351	4.94	4.65	47.9	33.57
Sikkim	368	.01	.01	46.7	61.46
Arunachal Pradesh	1252	.01	.01	47.4	44.24
Nagaland	13861	.13	.02	47.6	61.92
Manipur	47999	.46	1.01	49.5	59.70
Mizoram	11116	.11	.35	48.4	86.13
Tripura	24352	.23	.08	48.7	65.41
Meghalaya	22520	.21	.34	49.4	60.41
Assam	194379	1.85	1.11	48.2	56.03
West Bengal	771388	7.33	6.55	48.3	60.22
Jharkhand	132446	1.26	.74	48.5	39.38
Orissa	388227	3.69	3.59	49.3	50.97
Chhattisgarh	263990	2.51	.94	49.3	52.4
Madhya Pradesh	793552	7.54	6.47	47.9	50.28
Gujarat	530314	5.04	5.05	47.9	58.6
Maharashtra	803568	7.64	9.46	48	67.51
Andhra Pradesh	875430	8:32	7.25	49.4	51.17
Karnataka	658821	6.26	9.7	49.1	57.45
Goa	7097	.07	.08	49	75.51
Kerala	452826	4.30	13.09	51.4	87.86
Tamil Nadu	787965	7.49	12.20	49.7	64.55

Sources : **http://www.smallindustryindia.com.ssiindia/census.htm
* Census of India 2001.

Inferences

The foregoing table has following inferences:

- It is inferred from Table 1 that the state of Uttar Pradesh tops the list with more than 17 lakh SSI units followed by Andhra Pradesh, Maharashtra, Madhya Pradesh and Tamil Nadu. Sikkim has the lowest number of Small Scale units (368 units.)
- It also reveals that among the small scale industrial units owned by women entrepreneurs in India, Kerala tops the list with 13.09 percent of units, followed by Tamil Nadu with 12.20 percent of units. Tamil Nadu ranks second in the total number of small-scale units owned by women entrepreneurs in India. The Census Survey also shows that most of these enterprises are concentrated in few states including Kerala, Tamil Nadu, Karnataka, West Bengal and Uttar Pradesh.
- Table 1 reveals that the sex ratio is also highest in Kerala (87.86) followed by Tamil Nadu (49.7) and Andhra Pradesh (49.4) and Meghalaya.
- Table 1 also reveals that the literacy rate among states is highest in Kerala (51.4) followed by Mizoram (86.13) and Himachal Pradesh.

TABLE 2
Classification of SSI Units Owned by Men and Women on the Basis of Registration

Characteristic	*Registered Units (in lakhs)*	*Unregistered Units (in lakhs)*	*Total*
Men	12.37(13.08)	82.2(86.92)	94.57(100)
Women	1.38(12.93)	9.26(87.07)	10.64(100)
Total	13.75(13.07)	9.26(86.93)	105.21(100)

Note : Figures in brackets represent percentages to total.

Inferences

The Table 2 has following inferences :

- It reveals that among the 94.57 lakh SSI units owned by men functioning in India, 86.92 per cent are unregistered and registered units amount to 13.08 per cent.
- In the total number of SSI units owned by men functioning in India more than fourth-fifths of the units (86.92%) are unregistered.
- In 10.64 lakh SSI units owned by women, 87.07 per cent units are unregistered and 12.93 per cent units are registered.
- More than four-fifths of SSI units (87.07%) owned by women are unregistered.

TABLE 3

Co-relation between Women Entrepreneurship, Female Population and Female Literacy in India

Sl. No.	*Particulars*	*Results*
1	Karl Person Co-Relation between Female Population in India and Women entrepreneurship in SSI	.386 Low Degree Positive Co-relation
2	Karl Person Co-Relation between Female Population in India and Female literacy in India	.218 Low Degree Positive Co-relation
3	Karl Person Co-Relation between Female literacy in India and Women entrepreneurship in SSI	.106 Low Degree Positive Co-relation

To test it further statistically, **student's t-test** has been used. The following hypotheses were developed. Value of t has been calculated by applying the following formula:

$$t = r\sqrt{\frac{n-2}{1-r^2}}$$

H_0: There is no co-relation between and female

population in India and women entrepreneurship in SSI (r=0).

H_1: There is significant correlation between and female population in India and women entrepreneurship in SSI (r#0).

The table value of t at 5% level of significance for 27 degree of freedom is 2.05. The calculated value of t is .386. Since the calculated value of t is less than the table value of t, we accept H_0. Thus, it can be inferred that the co-relation between women entrepreneurship in SSI and female population in India is *statistically insignificant*.

AND

H_0: There is no correlation between and female population in India and female literacy in India (r=0).

H_1: There is significant correlation between and female population in India and female literacy in India (r#0).

The table value of t at 5% level of significance for 27 degree of freedom is 2.05. The calculated value of t is .218. Since the calculated value of t is less than the table value of t, we accept H_0. Thus, it can be inferred that the co relation between female population in India and female literacy in India is *statistically insignificant*.

AND

H_0: There is no correlation between women entrepreneurship in SSI and female literacy in India (r=0).

H_1: There is significant correlation between women entrepreneurship in SSI and female literacy in India (r#0).

'The table value of t at 5% level of significance for 27 degree of freedom is 2.05. The calculated value of t is .106. Since the calculated value of t is less than the table value of t, we accept H_0. Thus, it can be inferred that the co-relation between women entrepreneurship in SSI and female literacy in India is *statistically insignificant*.

PUSH AND PULL FACTORS CONTRIBUTING TO WOMEN ENTREPRENEURSHIP

The Business Development Bank (1999) found significant differences between men's and women's business goals: for men, financial gain is a primary objective. Although there are variations, many women emphasize that their primary goals in starting a business are not financial (Chaganti, 1986; Cromie, 1987; Holmquist and Sundin, 1988; Lavoie, 1992). So why would women give up income security, job status and stability for the high risk, hard work and often low income of business ownership? One dominant motive reported by women surveyed in past studies was to create greater flexibility for balancing work and family (Chaganti, 1986; Kaplan, 1988). In more recent studies women continue to emphasize flexibility as a primary motivator for business start-up, along with other personal reasons: need for more challenge, independence, passion for a particular idea, and desire for greater fulfilment and meaning in their work (Business Development Bank, 1999; NFWBO, 1999a). Women also represent the fastest-growing group of home-based business-owners, entering five times more than men. Reasons appear to include low start-up costs, a perceived significant increase in personal productivity working at home, and the fact that personal skills that may not be marketable to an outside company can be used to start a business from home (Soldressen, Fiorito, and He, 1998).

Self-actualization is the most important reason given by women in a survey of 223 business owners (Lee and Rogoff, 1997), including goals of maximizing personal skills/abilities, contributing to society, and gaining respect and recognition. Interestingly, this study also found that women who have lost their jobs through 'restructuring' tend more than men to turn to self-employment instead of pounding the pavement in search of another job. In Gay's (1997) interview study, women business owners stated frequently their desire to prove "I can do it". Fasci and Valdez (1998) found business ownership attracts women accountants as a viable avenue to achieve career success, gain control of their destiny and the respect of their peers, create their own work environments, and ensure their advancement is truly based on merit—all dimensions that women perceive to be less available to them when employed in someone else's enterprise.

PROBLEMS FACED BY WOMEN ENTREPRENEURS

The main problems faced by the women entrepreneurs may be analysed as follows:

1. *Shortage of Finance*. Women and small entrepreneurs always suffer from inadequate financial resources and working capital. They are lacking access to external funds due to absence of tangible security and credit in the market. Women do not generally have property to their names. Owing to the lack of confidence in women's ability, male members in the family do not like to risk their capital in ventures run by women. The complicated procedure of bank loans, the inordinate delay in obtaining the loans and the running about involved deters many women from venturing. Women entrepreneurs also face the problem of obtaining working capital for financing day-to-day operations of their enterprises. Banks discourage women borrowers believing that they will leave their business and become housewives again. Women entrepreneurs rely often on personal savings and loans from family friends. Most of the women enterprises fail due to lack of financing.
2. *Inefficient Arrangements for Marketing and Sale*. For marketing their products, women entrepreneurs are often at the mercy of the middlemen who pocket large chunk of profit. Although the middlemen exploit the women entrepreneurs, the elimination of middlemen is difficult because it involves a lot of running about. Further, women entrepreneurs find it difficult to capture the market and make their products popular. This problem is all the more serious in the case of food production and processing ventures.
3. *Low Mobility*. One of the biggest handicaps for women entrepreneurs is mobility or travelling from

place. Women on their own find it difficult to get accommodation in smaller town's. A single woman asking for a room is still looked upon with suspicion, some of the women entrepreneurs complain that government clerks and private dealers harass them as women are believed to be less able to go through complicated court proceedings.

4. *Family Responsibilities*. In India, it is mainly a women's duty to look after the children and other members of the family. Her involvement in family leaves little energy and time for business. Married women entrepreneurs have to make a fine balance between business and home. Their success in this regard also depends upon supporting husband and family. Without the support and approval of husband, the female entrepreneurs cannot succeed. There arises a role conflict in many women entrepreneurs. Such conflict prevents them from taking prompt decisions in business. Despite modernization, tradition and family responsibilities slow down the movement of women. Occupational backgrounds of families and education level of husbands have a direct impact on the development of women entrepreneurship. The development of Kindergartens, day nurseries and crèches and family planning have to some extent helped women entrepreneurs to carry on business without affecting the social prestige of their husbands.
5. *Social Attitudes*. The biggest problem of a woman entrepreneur is the social attitude and the constraints in which she has to live and work. Despite constitutional equality, there is discrimination against women. In a tradition bound society, women suffer from male reservations about a woman's role and capacity.
6. *Low Ability to Bear Risk*. Women have comparative a low ability to bear economic and other risks because they have led a protected life. Sometimes they face discrimination in the selection for entrepreneurial development training. Some of them lack

entrepreneurial initiative or specialized training. Inferiority complex, unplanned growth, lack of infrastructure, late start, etc. are other problems of women entrepreneurs in India.

7. *Lack of Education*. In India literacy among women is very low. Due to lack of education, majority of women are unaware of technological developments, marketing knowledge, etc. Lack of information and experience creates further problems in the setting up and running of business enterprises.
8. *Low Need for Achievement*. Need for achievement, independence and autonomy are the prerequisites for success in entrepreneurship. But women are proud to bask in the glory of their parents, husbands, sons, etc. Their preconceived notions about their role in life inhibit achievement and independence. In the absence of the required urge to achieve, few women succeed as entrepreneurs.

GOVERNMENT SCHEMES FOR WOMEN EMPOWERMENT

The government programme for women development began as early as 1954 in India but the actual participation began only in 1974. At present, the Government of India has over 27 schemes for women operated by different departments and Ministries. Some of these are:

- Integrated Rural Development Programme (IRDP)
- Training of Rural Youth for Self-Employment (TRYSEM)
- Prime Minister's Rojgar Yojana (PMRY)
- Women's Development Corporation Scheme (WDCS)
- Working Women's Forum
- Indira Mahila Yojana
- Indira Mahila Kendra
- Mahila Samiti Yojana
- Rashtriya Mahila Kosh
- Khadi and Village Industries Commission
- Indira Priyadarshini Yojana

- SIDBI's Mahila Udyam Nidhi Mahila Vikas Nidhi
- SBI's Sree Shaki Scheme
- NGO's Credit Schemes
- National Banks for Agriculture and Rural Development's Schemes

SUGGESTIONS TO DEVELOP WOMEN ENTREPRENEURS

Right efforts on from all areas are required in the development of women entrepreneurs and their greater participation in the entrepreneurial activities. Following efforts can be taken into account for effective development of women entrepreneurs :

- Consider women as specific target group for all developmental programmes.
- Better educational facilities and schemes should be extended to women folk from government part.
- Vocational training to be extended to women community that enables them to understand the production process and production management.
- Counseling through the aid of committed NGOs, psychologists, managerial experts and technical personnel should be provided to existing and emerging women entrepreneurs.
- Making provision of marketing and sales assistance from government part.
- To encourage more passive women entrepreneurs the Women training programme should be organised that taught to recognize her own psychological needs and express them.
- State finance corporations and financing institutions should permit by statute to extend purely trade-related finance to women entrepreneurs.
- Making provision of micro-credit system and enterprise credit system to the women entrepreneurs at local level.
- Repeated gender sensitisation programmes should be held to train financiers to treat women with dignity and respect as persons in their own right.

- Industrial estates could also provide marketing outlets for the display and sale of products made by women.
- Women Entrepreneur's Guidance Cell set-up to handle the various problems of women entrepreneurs all over the state.
- District Industries Centres and Single Window Agencies should make use of assisting women in their trade and business guidance.
- Programmes for encouraging entrepreneurship among women are to be extended at local level.
- More governmental schemes to motivate women entrepreneurs to engage in small scale and large-scale business ventures.
- Involvement of Non-Governmental Organisations in women entrepreneurial training programmes and counseling.

CONCLUSION

The success of women entrepreneurs differs from State to State. In Kerala and Maharashtra women entrepreneurs have been most successful. Entrepreneurial movement among women started late and is still in its infancy. The movement requires pre and post-follow-up support to utilize women power in the country's economic development. A coordinated role of Government and voluntary agencies with an integrated approach will help to develop women entrepreneurship. Re-orientation of educational system for women, curriculum change, career guidance, reservations, scholarships, and timely assistance are required. Satisfactory progress can be made only by honest, sincere and dedicated efforts by all. Only the joint efforts of both men and women entrepreneurs can change an under-developed India into a fully developed country.

References

Jose, P., Ajith Kumar and Paul, T.M., (1994) Entrepreneurship Development, Himalaya Publishing.

Medha Dubhashi Vinze (1987), Women Entrepreneurs in India: A Socio-Economic Study of Delhi, 1975-76, Mittal Publications, New Delhi.

Renuka, V. (2001), Opportunities and challenges for women in business, India Together, Online Report, Civil Society Information Exchange Pvt. Ltd.

http:// www.smallindustryindia.com.ssiindia/census.htm.

Census of India, 2001.

www.india invites.com

Foucault, M. (1980), *Power/knowledge: Selected interviews and other writings by Michel Foucault, 1972-77* (C. Gordon, ed.). New York: Pantheon.

Gay, K. (1997), *In the company of women.* Toronto: HarperCollins.

Godfrey, J. (1992), *Our wildest dreams: Women business owners making money, having fun, doing good.* New York: HarperCollins.

Gougeon, T. and Hutton, S. (1993), Communication in the workplace: Effects of culture and sex on principal-teacher communication in schools. *Human Resource Development Quarterly,* 4(3), 277-90.

Gould, S. and Parzen, J. (Eds.) (1990), *Enterprising women.* Paris: Organization for Economic Cooperation and Development.

Index